Tax and Financial Planning
for Family Businesses

Tax and Financial Planning for Family Businesses

Noel J Ince FCA, AT11
of Thomson McLintock & Co/KMG
Chartered Accountants

George J R Bell MA, ACA, AT11
of Thomson McLintock & Co/KMG
Chartered Accountants

London
Butterworths
1984

England	Butterworth & Co (Publishers) Ltd, 88 Kingsway, LONDON WC2B 6AB
Australia	Butterworth Pty Ltd, SYDNEY, MELBOURNE, BRISBANE, ADELAIDE, PERTH, CANBERRA and HOBART
Canada	Butterworth & Co (Canada) Ltd, TORONTO and VANCOUVER
New Zealand	Butterworths of New Zealand Ltd, WELLINGTON and AUCKLAND
Singapore	Butterworths & Co (Asia) Pte Ltd, SINGAPORE
South Africa	Butterworth Publishers (Pty) Ltd, DURBAN and PRETORIA
USA	Butterworth Legal Publishers, ST PAUL, Minnesota, SEATTLE, Washington, BOSTON, Massachusetts, AUSTIN, Texas and D & S Publishers, CLEARWATER, Florida

© Butterworth & Co (Publishers) Ltd 1984

All rights reserved. No part of this publication may be reproduced or transmitted in any form or by any means, including photocopying and recording, without the written permission of the copyright holder, application for which should be addressed to the publisher. Such written permission must also be obtained before any part of this publication is stored in a retrieval system of any nature.

This book is sold subject to the Standard Conditions of Sale of Net Books and may not be re-sold in the UK below the net price fixed by Butterworths for the book in our current catalogue.

Ince, Noel J.
 Tax and financial planning for family businesses.
 1. Small business—Great Britain—Finance
 I. Title II. Bell, George J. R.
 658.1′592′0941   HG4027.7

ISBN 0 406 55730 6

Typeset by Polyglot

Printed and bound in Great Britain by
Biddles Ltd, Guildford and King's Lynn

Preface

The family business has always played an important part in the economic life of the UK. In this book we have set out to explain a number of ways in which the tax liabilities of such businesses may be reduced to a minimum through effective planning. We make no apology for offering a book on this subject: in times of economic difficulty the impact of taxation on the resources of a business can make the difference between survival and failure. That apart, the entrepreneur who is prepared to undergo the risks involved in financing and running his own business will be less inclined to do so if he can see taxation taking an unacceptably large proportion of the profits he earns or making it impossible to hand on the business to his heirs as a going concern.

This book is not intended as a general textbook on business taxation. We have assumed a knowledge of the basic provisions of the Taxes Acts and have resisted the temptation to rewrite the legislation except where a detailed knowledge of a section or Schedule is required to appreciate a planning point. In short, we have tried to write a book on *tax planning* and not a book on tax.

Our partners and colleagues in Norwich have had to suffer the inconveniences of our obsession with this book over several weeks. That they have done so willingly has made our task easier and we are very grateful to them all. We would also like to thank our colleagues elsewhere in the firm for giving us the opportunity to write this book and for the helpful suggestions they have made.

Special thanks are due to our secretaries, Sheila Mackay and Jennifer Pykett, who converted our frequently amended manuscript into impeccable typescript with admirable calmness, speed and efficiency.

N J Ince
G J R Bell
Norwich

May 1984

Contents

Preface v
Table of Statutes XIII
Table of Cases XIX

PART I FUNDAMENTALS

1 **Introduction** 3
1.1 What is a family business? 3
1.2 What is tax planning? 4
1.3 The implications of Ramsay etc 4

2 **Business Structures** 10
2.1 Factors in the choice of a business structure 10
2.2 Unincorporated businesses 10
2.3 Companies 13
2.4 Planning conclusions 16

PART II THE BUSINESS

GENERAL

3 **Need to Forecast Results** 23

4 **Capital Expenditure** 25
4.1 Capital allowances and the timing of expenditure 25
4.2 Financing the expenditure 28
4.3 Claiming the best relief 34
4.4 Disclaimer of capital allowances 36

5 Stock Relief 39

6 Pre-Trading Expenditure 41
6.1 Revenue expenditure 41
6.2 Capital expenditure 42
6.3 Value added tax 42

7 Value Added Tax 44
7.1 Registration 44
7.2 Dividing a business 47
7.3 Transferring a business 48
7.4 Taking over another's VAT number 49
7.5 Time of supply 50
7.6 Credit notes 51
7.7 Partial exemption 52
7.8 Retail schemes 54
7.9 Second-hand schemes 55
7.10 Selling on commission 56

INCOME TAX

8 Choice of Accounting Date 57
8.1 General tax factors 57
8.2 Commencement of trading 58
8.3 Cessation 61
8.4 Change of accounting date 63
8.5 Non-tax factors 64

9 Partnership Changes 65
9.1 General rules 65
9.2 Continuation basis election 65
9.3 Planning opportunities 66

10 Conventional or Earnings Basis and Post-Cessation Receipts 69
10.1 General principles 69
10.2 Post-cessation receipts 70

11 Partnership Service Companies 73
11.1 Introduction 73
11.2 Setting up the company 73
11.3 Profit uplift 74
11.4 Holding the service company shares 75
11.5 Cessation and liquidation 76

12	**Sharing Profits with the Proprietor's Family** 78	
12.1	Why share profits? 78	
12.2	Payment of wages 79	
12.3	Partnership 80	

13	**Loss Relief** 84	
13.1	Statutory provisions 84	
13.2	Strategy 86	

CORPORATION TAX

14	**Incorporation** 90	
14.1	Timing of incorporation 90	
14.2	Transfer of business to a company 91	

15	**Basic Strategy for the Proprietary Company** 96	

16	**Small Companies Rate Relief** 97	
16.1	Background 97	
16.2	Reducing taxable profits 98	
16.3	Associated companies 100	

17	**Remuneration of Proprietors** 102	
17.1	General principles 102	
17.2	Paying the proprietor's family 104	
17.3	Commercial constraints 106	
17.4	Waiver of remuneration 107	
17.5	Accounts basis 108	
17.6	Benefits in kind 108	

18	**Distributions** 114	
18.1	General principles and definitions 114	
18.2	Dividend waiver 118	
18.3	Timing of dividend payments 119	
18.4	Apportionment 120	
18.5	Loans to participators 123	

19	**Financing the Family Company** 125	
19.1	Shares or loans? 125	
19.2	Who should hold the shares? 128	
19.3	Relief for interest paid 128	
19.4	Business expansion scheme 131	
19.5	Purchase by a company of its own shares 133	

20 Interest and Charges 142
20.1 Interest—trading expense or charge on profits? 142
20.2 Timing of payment of charges 144

21 Company Chargeable Gains 146
21.1 General principles 146
21.2 Use of capital losses 147
21.3 Relief for trading losses 147

22 Company Losses 148
22.1 Statutory provisions 148
22.2 Strategy 149
22.3 Change of accounting date 152

23 Receivership and Liquidation 155
23.1 Receivership 155
23.2 Liquidation 156

24 Groups of Companies—Income and Distributions 157
24.1 General principles 157
24.2 Group relief for losses 157
24.3 Group dividends and interest 159
24.4 Surrender of ACT 159
24.5 Reconstructions 160
24.6 Payment of tax 162

25 Groups of Companies—Chargeable Gains 164
25.1 Intra-group transfers of assets 164
25.2 Roll-over relief 165

CAPITAL GAINS TAX

26 Roll-Over Relief 167
26.1 General principles 167
26.2 Strategy 169
26.3 Deemed disposals and deemed consideration 171

27 Partnership Capital Gains 172
27.1 Partnership assets 172
27.2 Transactions between partners 173

28 Development Land Tax 178

PART III THE OWNERS OF THE BUSINESS

29   Retirement Relief   187

30   Gifts   195
30.1   General relief for gifts   195
30.2   Gifts of business assets   198

31   Providing for Retirement   200
31.1   Retirement annuities   200
31.2   Company pension schemes   205
31.3   Small self-administered pension schemes   212

32   The Use of Trusts   218
32.1   How trusts can help   218
32.2   How to ensure that income is alienated   218
32.3   Fixed interest trusts   219
32.4   Discretionary trusts   220
32.5   Accumulation and maintenance trusts   223
32.6   Trading trusts   225
32.7   Employees' trusts   225
32.8   Dealing with income in accumulation trusts   226

33   Sheltering Income   229
33.1   Deeds of covenant   229
33.2   Industrial buildings   232
33.3   Business expansion scheme   234

34   Handing on the Business   238
34.1   Sole trader   238
34.2   Partnerships   240
34.3   Family companies   246
34.4   Agricultural relief   253

35   Selling the Family Company   256
35.1   Business or shares   256
35.2   Payments to 'family' directors   257
35.3   Stamp duty saving   259
35.4   TA 1970 ss 460–468   262

PART IV OTHER PLANNING POINTS

36   Farming   267
36.1   Averaging of profits   267

xii Contents

36.2 Herd basis election 268
36.3 Losses 269

37 Pitfalls to Avoid 271
37.1 Capital sums paid to settlor (TA 1970 s 451) 271
37.2 Transactions in securities (TA 1970 ss 460–468) 273
37.3 Transfer of assets abroad (TA 1970 s 478 and FA 1981 s 45) 273
37.4 Company migration (TA 1970 s 482) 273
37.5 Change in ownership of company: losses (TA 1970 s 483) 274
37.6 Sale of income from personal activities (TA 1970 s 487) 275
37.7 Artificial transactions in land (TA 1970 s 488) 275
37.8 Value shifting (CGTA 1979 ss 25 and 26) 276
37.9 Transactions between connected persons (CGTA 1979 s 62) 278

Index 281

Table of statutes

	PAGE
Partnership Act 1890	
s 1	11, 80
2 (3)	82
5	12
9	11
10	12
Law of Property Act 1925	
s 136	241
Trustee Act 1925	
s 69 (2)	224
Finance Act 1927	
s 55	261
Finance Act 1930	
s 42	261
Companies Act 1948	
s 66, 67	114
Sch 1	
Table A	
art 114, 115	119
Income Tax Act 1952	
s 228	228
Variation of Trusts Act 1958	224
Perpetuities and Accumulations Act 1964	
s 13	224
Capital Allowances Act 1968	
s 1 (1)	26
5 (1)	233
7	233
71 (1)	232
72	61
79	67
Sch 7	
para 4	67
Finance Act 1970	206
s 19, 20	208
21 (1)	208
23	208

	PAGE
Finance Act 1970—*contd*	
s 23 (2)	208
24 (1)	208
Sch 16	
para 13	77
Income and Corporation Taxes Act 1970	218
s 24 (7)	156
26	81
27	228
52 (2)	142
81	245
99, 100	228
108	69
110 (2)	270
115	57, 59, 90
(2) (G)	59, 63, 88
(3)	63
116	57, 59, 75
117	57, 59, 61, 67, 88
118	20, 57, 61, 62, 67, 76, 90, 267
(1) (b)	89, 90, 91
130	29, 41
(a)	75, 104
137	70, 71, 93, 94
(1) (a)	93
138	70, 71
(3)	71
139	268
143	70, 71, 72
144	68, 70, 71, 72
145	70, 72
(1)	71
146	70, 71
147	70
(2)	71
148	70

xiii

xiv Table of statutes

Income and Corporation Taxes Act 1970—contd

Section	Page
s 149	70, 72
150	70
151	70
(2), (3)	69
154	62, 66
(1)	58, 62, 63, 65, 66, 67, 70, 71, 75
(2)	60, 62, 65, 66, 67, 70, 224
(3) (b)	67
(7)	66
155 (3) (b)	66
159	228
168	17, 41, 84, 86, 87, 89, 125, 269
(2)	269
(3)	87
169	84, 86
170	86, 269
171	84, 85, 86, 87
172	85, 90
174	85
177	274
(1)	143, 147, 148, 152
(2)	15, 16, 37, 120, 121, 147, 148, 149, 150, 152, 153, 158, 163
(3)	37
(3A)	15, 16, 147, 148, 149, 150, 151, 152, 153, 158
(8)	143, 144, 148
(10)	150
178	148
180	86
(1), (3), (8)	269
181	108
183 (1)	108
187	257, 258
188	257
226 (1), (2)	200
(9)	204
226A	200, 201, 205
227 (1)	201
(1A)	87
(1BB)	201
(5)	88
227A (1)–(3)	203
(4), (5)	204
233	114, 115, 133, 134

Income and Corporation Taxes Act 1970—contd

Section	Page
s 233 (2)	106
(3)	106, 115
234	115, 261
237 (1)	114
238	13
(1)	146
(4)	146
(a)	147
243 (4)	162
244	163
245 (2), (3)	156
247	153
(3) (c)	155
248	142
(1)	143, 144
(2)	142
(3)	30, 142, 144
251 (2)	142, 144
(3)	142
252	155, 161, 162
(1) (7)	160, 161
254	148, 151, 152
(1), (2)	151
(3)	152
(5)	151
256	155, 156, 159
(1)	159
257	159
258	148, 155, 156, 157
259	148, 155, 156, 157
(1)	148, 152
(6)	153, 157
260	148, 155, 156, 157
261	148, 155, 156, 157
(2)	152
262	148, 153, 155, 156, 157, 158
263	148, 155, 156, 157
(2)	152
265 (1)	147
(2)	146
272	164
273	155, 156, 164, 165, 166
276	155, 165
278	164
(1)	165
280	278
282	96, 130
284	115
(2)	106

Table of statutes xv

Income and Corporation Taxes Act 1970—contd	PAGE
s 285	124, 129
286	123, 124
(2)	123
(3)	124
287	124
303	136
(3) (a)	76
434	231, 232
(1A)	231
437	219, 229
439	219
441 (2)	83
444 (2)	83
445–448	219
451	219, 239, 245, 271, 272, 273
(1), (8)	271
451 (3A)	271
(3B)	272
(9)	272
451A	219
(1)–(3), (6)	272
454	141
(3)	83, 141
457 (1A)	231
460	134, 139, 215, 253, 260, 261, 262
461	261
461D	261, 262
461E	262
462, 463	261
464	139, 261, 263
465–468	261
478	273
(5)	273
482	273
483 (1), (3)	274
484	274
487	275
488	165, 275, 276
(2)	275
(3), (7)	276
(8)	275
(10)–(12)	276
526	14, 276
527 (3)	119
531	112
532	164
Sch 6	268
Sch 8	257

Income and Corporation Taxes Act 1970—contd	PAGE
Sch 14	
para 1	228
Taxes Management Act 1970	
s 43 (1)	85, 195
50, 54	107
Finance Act 1971	206
s 41	26
(3)	36, 37
42 (1)	26
44	61
(2)	36
45	27, 28
(1)	26, 30
(b)	27, 30
Sch 8	
para 7	42
10, 12	33
13	62, 67
Town and Country Planning Act 1971	179
Finance Act 1972	
s 75	129, 204
85	155
(3)	150, 159
92	155, 159
(3), (3A)	159
(4)	156, 160
93	146
(2)	147
95	97, 100, 101
(3)	100, 101
(7)	100
Sch 9	129
para 10, 12	29
17	151
Sch 16	76, 120, 156
para 1	120, 191
8	120, 121
9	122
10	120
12A	121
13	122
18	123
Sch 20	145
Finance Act 1973	206, 212
s 14	207
17	227
29	158
Sch 19	
para 10	261

xvi Table of statutes

	PAGE
Finance Act 1974	
s 16	243
17	34
Sch 1	
para 4	130
7	131
9	129, 237
10	129
12	130
13	129
14	130
Finance Act 1975	220
s 14, 15	34
20 (4)	241, 250
(7)	243, 252
39 (5)	252
44	197, 251
(2)	254
Sch 4	
para 13	246
Sch 5	
para 1	222
16	207
17	226
Sch 6	
para 19, 20, 23	249
Sch 10	
para 2	249, 255
4	246
5	241, 242, 243
9	244
Finance (No 2) Act 1975	
s 34	261
48	149
Companies Act 1976	
s 3 (1), (5), (6)	153
Development Land Tax Act 1976	
s 1	178
12	180
(3)	180
(4)	166, 180
(5)	94, 166, 180
(9)	181
18	181
(3)	132
19, 19A	182, 183
45 (2) (a)	181
Sch 1	
para 2	179
Sch 4	
Pt II	179
para 7 Class E	182

	PAGE
Development Land Tax Act 1976— *contd*	
Sch 8	
para 52	93
Finance Act 1976	115, 238
s 41	86
61	109
(1) (a)	109
(2)	109
63 (A)	112
64	110
64A	111
(3)	111
(6)	111
(a)	111
66	113
75 (5) (e)	110
86, 87	196
90	226
91	107, 253
92	119, 253
Sch 7	110
para 2, 3, 5	110
Sch 10	
para 2	239, 246
3	76, 239, 240, 244, 246
4	240, 246
5, 8, 10–12	240
13	246
Finance Act 1977	
s 33	112, 113, 115
(1)	111
(2), (4), (5)	112
33A	113
Finance Act 1978	
s 28	88, 267
(2), (3)	267
(5)	267
(a)	88
(6), (8)	267
30	17, 41, 85, 86, 87, 88, 270
(7)	87
36 (2)	121
37	31
38	232
67	226
Sch 5	121
Sch 11	226
Capital Gains Tax Act 1979	
s 22	147
(2)	126

Table of statutes xvii

Capital Gains Tax Act 1979—
contd
s 25 .... 140, 141, 246, 251, 252
 25 (2) 276
  (3)–(5) 277
 26 .... 245, 251, 252, 277
  (1) 198, 277
   (b) 277
  (2), (4), (5) 277
  (6), (7) 278
 27 146
 29A (1) 174, 278
 43 (4) 196
 44 166
 60 .... 172, 173
 62 174
  (2) 278
  (3) 197, 278
  (4)–(6) 279
 63 .... 74, 180
  (4) 174
 75 116
 77 251
 85 190
 101 .... 190, 196
 104 220
 115 .... 166, 167, 170, 171, 192
  (1) 166, 170, 171, 192
  (3) 169
  (5)–(7) 168
  (8) 171
 116 .... 166, 167
 117 .... 167, 168
  (3)–(5) 170
 118 .... 166, 167
 119 167
  (2) (b) 74
 120 167
 121 .... 167, 169
 123 .... 93, 94, 95
  (1) 91, 92
 124 .... 18, 187, 192
  (1) 187, 188
   (b) 18, 257
  (2) 187, 189
  (3) 187
  (4), (5) 190
  (8) 188, 189, 190, 198
 126 ..... 74, 94, 95, 171, 192, 198
  (6) 94
  (7) 198
 134 (1) 191

Capital Gains Tax Act 1979—
contd
s 136 126
 141 226
 Sch 4
  para 5 198
Companies Act 1980
s 49–53 124
Finance Act 1980 200
s 31 87
 37 125
 38 126
 39 .... 59, 85
 44 76
  (1), (3) 121
 70 86
 72 (3) 86
 74 232
 79 .... 8, 171, 177, 192, 198,
      238, 252, 255
  (1) 195
  (3) 195, 196, 197
  (4) 198
  (5) 195
 116 (2) 166, 180
 Sch 9 76
 Sch 13 232
Companies Act 1981 133
s 29 82
Finance Act 1981
s 21 113
 45 273
 53–67 234
 78 .... 195, 197, 238
  (3) 198
 79 198
 131 181
 Sch 9
  para 17 .... 38, 150
   18, 19 39
   22 40
   23 39
   24 40
 Sch 12 234
 Sch 14
  para 2 254
   3 255
   14 255
Finance Act 1982 .... 133, 220
s 52 (1) 140
 53 134
  (1) 134, 137, 138, 140

xviii Table of statutes

	PAGE
Finance Act 1982—*contd*	
s 53 (2)	134, 138
56	134
60	115
73	232
82	195, 238
(1)	195
(2)	198
107, 108	224
113	225
114	223
(4)	224
Sch 9	134, 135
para 1–4	136
5, 7	137
8	140
10–12	139
14	136
15	138
Industrial Development Act 1982	
s 7, 8	25
Finance Act 1983	
s 26	234
Sch 5	234
para 19	236
Finance (No 2) Act 1983	
s 5	234

	PAGE
Finance (No 2) Act 1983—*contd*	
s 26	131
Sch 1	234
Sch 5	131
Value Added Tax Act 1983	
s 4	50
15	52
Sch 1	
para 1	44, 47
2	46, 47
7	47
8	46
9	47
Finance Act 1984	10, 11, 26, 39, 60, 117, 126, 150, 187, 222, 232, 257, 267
s 18	97, 156, 239
20	97, 156
48	39, 268
(6)	40
58	13, 25, 42, 248, 256
118	180
119	183
Sch 12	13, 25, 42
para 5–8	98

Table of cases

PAGE
Aluminium Industrie Vaassen BV v Romalpa Aluminium Ltd [1976] 2 All ER 552,
 [1976] 1 WLR 676, CA 26, 30
Anderton v Lamb [1981] STC 43, [1980] TR 393 167
Atherton v British Insulated and Helsby Cables. See British Insulated and Helsby
 Cables Ltd v Atherton
A-G v Boden [1912] 1 KB 539, 81 LJKB 704, 105 LT 247 241
Bagel v Miller [1903] 2 KB 212, 72 LJKB 495, 88 LT 769, DC 11
Belmont Garage (Edinburgh) Ltd v Customs and Excise Comrs [1981] VATTR 228
 51
Birmingham and District Cattle By-Products Co Ltd v IRC [1919] 12 TC 92 .. 58, 59
Booth (EV) (Holdings) Ltd v Buckwell [1980] STC 578, [1980] TR 249 168
Bredon Motor Co Ltd v Customs and Excise Comrs LON/82/204 51
British Insulated and Helsby Cables Ltd v Atherton [1926] AC 205, 10 TC 155, 95
 LJKB 336, HL 225
British United Shoe Machinery Co Ltd v Customs and Excise Comrs [1977] VATTR
 187 52
Brodie's Will Trustees v IRC (1933) 17 TC 432 227
Bullock (Alexander) & Co v IRC [1976] STC 514, 51 TC 563, [1976] TR 201, L (TC)
 216 82
Bulmer v IRC [1967] Ch 145, [1966] 3 All ER 801, 44 TCI, [1966] TR 257 .. 83, 141
Burman v Hedges and Butler Ltd [1979] STC 136, [1979] 1 WLR 160, [1981] TC
 501, [1978] TR 409 165
Butt v Haxby [1983] STC 239 86
Callaghan v Customs and Excise Comrs MAN/77/187 56
Carins v MacDiarmid [1983] STC 178, CA 6, 9
Chilcott v IRC [1982] STC 1, [1981] TR 357 276
Clark v Customs and Excise Comrs LON/82/338 .... 47, 48
Clark v IRC [1978] STC 614, [1979] 1 All ER 385, [1979] 1 WLR 416, [1981] TC
 482, HL 262
Cleary v IRC [1968] AC 766, [1967] 2 All ER 48, 44 TC 399, [1967] TR 57, HL 262
Cohan's Executors v IRC (1924) 12 TC 602, 131 LT 377, CA 62
Cole Bros Ltd v Phillips [1982] STC 307, [1982] 2 All ER 247, [1982] 1 WLR 1450,
 HL 35, 36
Congreve v IRC [1948] 1 All ER 948, 30 TC 163, 41 R & IT 319, 27 ATC 102, HL
 273
Cooke v Beach Station Caravans Ltd [1974] 3 All ER 159, [1974] 1 WLR 1398, [1974]
 STC 402, 49 TC 514 35

xix

xx *Table of cases*

PAGE
Copeman v William Flood & Sons Ltd [1941] 1 KB 202, 24 TC 53, 110 LJKB 215
    79, 102, 104
Corbitt (JH) (Numismatists) Ltd v Customs and Excise Comrs [1980] STC 231 .. 56
Cripwell (Peter) & Associates v Customs and Excise Comrs CAR/78/131 52
Cunard's Trustees v IRC [1946] 1 All ER 159, 27 TC 122, 174 LT 133, CA 227
Customs and Excise Comrs v Woolfold Motor Co Ltd [1983] STC 715 51
Dale v de Soissons [1950] 2 All ER 460, 32 TC 118, [1950] TR 221, 43 R & IT 886,
    CA 258
Davenport v Hasslacher [1977] STC 254, [1977] 3 All ER 396, [1977] 1 WLR 869, 51
    TC 497 188
De Vigier v IRC [1964] 2 All ER 907, [1964] 1 WLR 1073, [1964] TR 239, 43 ATC
    223 271
Dickenson v Gross (1927) 11 TC 614, 137 LT 351 .... 80, 81
Dickson Motors (Glasgow) Ltd v Customs and Excise Comrs EDN/80/42 51
Dollar v Lyon [1981] STC 333 104
Dracup v Radcliffe (1946) 27 TC 88, 25 ATC 455 108
Dracup (Samuel) & Sons Ltd v Dakin (1957) 37 TC 377, [1957] TR 169, 50 R & IT
    594, 36 ATC 250 104
Duff v Barlow (1941) 23 TC 633 258
Eilbeck v Rawling [1981] STC 174,]1982] AC 300, [1981] 1 All ER 865, [1981] 2
    WLR 449, HL 277
Floor v Davis [1979] STC 379, [1980] AC 695, [1979] 2 WLR 830, HL 277
Furniss v Dawson [1984] STC 153, [1984] 1 All ER 530, [1984] 2 WLR 226, HL
    5, 6, 7, 8
Garforth v Newsmith Stainless Ltd [1979] STC 129, [1979] 2 All ER 73, [1979] 1
    WLR 409, [1978] TR 477 107
Gartside v IRC [1968] AC 553, [1968] 1 All ER 121, [1967] TR 309, 46 ATC 323, HL
    220
Greenberg v IRC [1972] AC 109, [1971] 3 All ER 136, 47 TC 240, [1971] TR 233, HL
    261
Gulbenkian's Settlement Trusts (No 2), Re, Stephens v Maun [1970] Ch 408, [1969] 2
    All ER 1173, [1969] 3 WLR 450 220
Hampton v Fortes Autogrill Ltd [1980] STC 80, [1979] TR 377, L(TC) 2756 35
Heather v P-E Consulting Group Ltd [1973] Ch 189, [1973] 1 All ER 8, 48 TC 293,
    [1972] TR 237, CA 59, 69, 225
Heaton v Bell [1970] AC 728, [1969] 2 All ER 70, 46 TC 211, [1969] TR 77, HL 109
Henry v Foster (1932) 16 TC 605, [1932] All ER Rep 753, HL 258
Hepworth v William Smith Group [1981] STC 354 188
Hillerns and Fowler v Murray (1932) 17 TC 77, [1932] All ER Rep 814, 146 LT 474,
    48 TLR 213, CA 62
Humphries (George) & Co v Cook (1934) 19 TC 121 66
Hunter v Dewhurst (1932) 16 TC 605, [1932] All ER Rep 753, HL 258
Hurll v IRC (1922) 8 TC 292 .... 119, 120
IT Special Comrs v Pemsel [1891] AC 531, [1891-4] All ER Rep 28, 3 TC 53, 61
    LJQB 265, HL 169
Inglewood (Lord) v IRC [1981] STC 318 223
Ingram (JG) & Son Ltd v Callaghan [1969] 1 All ER 433, [1969] 1 WLR 456, 45 TC
    151, [1968] TR 363, CA 62
IRC v Barclay Curle Co Ltd [1969] 1 All ER 732, [1969] 9 WLR 675, 45 TC 221,
    [1969] TR 21, HL 35
IRC v Blackwell Minor's Trustees [1926] 1 KB 389, 10 TC 235, 95 LJKB 465, 134
    LT 372, CA 226

Table of cases xxi

	PAGE
IRC v Burmah Oil Co Ltd [1982] STC 30, [1982] TR 535, HL	4, 5, 7
IRC v Cleary. *See* Cleary v IRC	
IRC v Countess of Longford [1928] AC 252, 13 TC 573, 97 LJKB 438, 139 LT 121, HL	226
IRC v D Devine & Sons Ltd (1963) 41 TC 210, [1963] TR 381, 42 ATC 358, CA	189
IRC v De Vigier. *See* De Vigier v IRC	
IRC v Joiner [1975] STC 657, [1975] 3 All ER 1050, [1975] 1 WLR 1701, [1975] TR 257, HL	261
IRC v Morrison (1932) 17 TC 325, 1932 SC 638, 1932 SLT 441	70, 72
IRC v Scott Adamson (1932) 17 TC 679, 11 ATC 481, 1933 SC 23, 1933 SLT 33	88
IRC v Scottish and Newcastle Breweries Ltd [1982] STC 296, [1982] 2 All ER 230, [1982] 1 WLR 322, HL	35
IRC v Thompson Bros (London) Ltd [1974] STC 16, 49 TC 110, 52 ATC 312, L (TC) 2497	121
IRC v White Bros Ltd (1956) 36 TC 587, [1956] TR 167, 47 R & IT 432, 35 ATC 196	122
IRC v Williamson (1928) 14 TC 335	80
Jackson's Trustees v IRC (1942) 25 TC 13, 1942 SC 579	227
Jarrold v John Good & Sons Ltd [1963] 1 All ER 141, [1963] 1 WLR 214, 40 TC 681, [1962] TR 371, CA	35
Kirk and Randall Ltd v Dunn (1924) 8 TC 663, 131 LT 288	61
Law Shipping Co Ltd v IRC (1923) 12 TC 621, 1924 SC 74	59, 60
Leedale v Lewis [1982] STC 835, [1982] 3 All ER 808, [1982] 1 WLR 1319, HL	220
Lindus and Hortin v IRC (1933) 17 TC 442	227
McCash and Hunter v IRC [1955] TR 117, 36 TC 170, L (TC) 1728, 48 R & IT 366	69
McGregor v Adcock [1977] STC 206, [1977] 3 All ER 65, [1977] 1 WLR 864, 51 TC 692	188
McPheeters v IRC [1946] 1 All ER 159, 27 TC 122, 174 LT 133	227
MacTaggart Scott & Co Ltd v IRC [1973] STC 180, 48 TC 708, [1973] TR 81, 52 ATC 115	122
Malayalam Plantations Ltd v Clark (1935) 19 TC 314	66
Mannesmann Demag Hamilton Ltd v Customs and Excise Comrs LON/82/370	52
Marner v Customs and Excise Comrs MAN/77/140	47
Marshall Hus & Partners Ltd v Bolton [1981] STC 18, [1980] TR 371, L (TC) 2804	154
Marshall Richards Machine Co Ltd v Jewitt (1956) 36 TC 511, [1956] TR 135, 49 R & IT 414, 35 ATC 186	101
Marshall's Executors, Hood's Executors and Rogers v Joly [1936] 1 All ER 851, 20 TC 256	62
Mead v Customs and Excise Comrs CAR/77/344	56
Metravision (GB) Ltd v Customs and Excise Comrs [1977] VATTR 26	45
Newbarns Syndicate v Hay (1939) 22 TC 461, CA	62
Nixon v Customs and Excise Comrs [1980] VATTR 66	56
Odeon Associated Theatres Ltd v Jones [1973] Ch 288, [1972] 1 All ER 681, 48 TC 257, [1971] TR 373, CA	59, 60
O'Kane (J & R) & Co v IRC (1922) 12 TC 303, 126 LT 707, 66 Sol Jo 281, 56 ILT 25, HL	61
Oldham v Customs and Excise Comrs MAN/80/240	47
Owen, Re, Owen v IRC [1949] 1 All ER 901, [1949] TR 189	29
Paton v IRC [1938] AC 341, [1938] 1 All ER 786, 21 TC 626, HL	29

xxii Table of cases

	PAGE
Petrotim Securities Ltd v Ayres [1964] 1 All ER 269, [1964] 1 WLR 190, 41 TC 389, [1963] TR 397, CA	76
Pilkington Bros Ltd v IRC [1982] STC 103, [1982] 1 All ER 715, [1982] 1 WLR 136, HL	158
Potel v IRC [1971] 2 All ER 504, 46 TC 658, [1970] TR 325, 49 ATC 355	120
Pott's Executors v IRC [1951] AC 443, [1951] 1 All ER 76, 32 TC 211, [1950] TR 379, HL	272
Ramsay (WT) Ltd v IRC [1981] STC 174, [1982] AC 300, [1981] 1 All ER 865, 54 TC 101, HL	4, 5, 7, 9, 165, 193, 196, 277
Rankine v IRC (1952) 32 TC 520, [1952] TR 1, L (TC) 1575, 1952 SC 177	69
Reid's Trustees v IRC (1929) 14 TC 512, 1929 SC 439	226
Renton v Customs and Excise Comrs EDN/79/12	47
Robroyston Brickworks Ltd v IRC [1976] STC 329, [1976] TR 151	62
Rowntree & Co Ltd v Curtis [1925] 1 KB 328, 8 TC 678, 93 LJKB 570, 131 LT 41, CA	225
St John's School (Mountford and Knibbs) v Ward [1975] STC 7, 49 TC 524, [1974] TR 273, L (TC) 2531, CA	36
Sansom v Peay [1976] STC 494, [1976] 3 All ER 353, [1976] 1 WLR 1073, [1976] TR 205	220
Schofield v R & H Hall Ltd [1975] STC 353, 49 TC 538, CA	36
Sharkey v Wernher [1956] AC 58, [1955] 3 All ER 493, 36 TC 275, [1955] TR 277, HL	76
Shipstone (James) & Sons Ltd v Morris (1929) 14 TC 413	62, 161
Smethurst v Cowtan [1977] STC 60, 51 TC 577, [1976] TR 279	192
Smith (George J) & Co Ltd v Furlong [1969] 2 All ER 760, 45 TC 384, [1968] TR 437, 47 ATC 463	258, 259
Snook (James) & Co Ltd v Blasdale (1952) 33 TC 244, [1952] TR 233, 31 ATC 268, L (TC) 1598, CA	258
Stanley v IRC [1944] KB 255, [1944] 1 All ER 230, 26 TC 12, 113 LJKB 292, CA	226
Stekel v Ellice [1973] 1 All ER 465, [1973] 1 WLR 191	82
Stephenson v Payne, Stone, Fraser & Co [1968] 1 All ER 524, [1968] 1 WLR 858, 44 TC 507, [1967] TR 335	75
Stokes v Costain Property Investments Ltd [1984] STC 204, CA	30
Temperley v Visibell Ltd [1974] STC 64, 49 TC 129, 52 ATC 308, L (TC) 2501	167, 190
Temple Gothard & Co v Customs and Excise Comrs LON/78/238	52
Tennant v Smith [1892] AC 150, 3 TC 158, 61 LJPC 11, 66 LT 327, HL	109
Thomson and Balfour v Le Page (1923) 8 TC 541, 1924 SC 27, 61 Sc LR 25	161, 162
Torrens v IRC (1933) 18 TC 262	29
Vestey v IRC [1980] STC 10, [1980] AC 1148, [1979] 3 All ER 976, [1979] 3 WLR 915, HL	273
Waddington v O'Callaghan (1931) 16 TC 187	81
Wadsworth Morton Ltd v Jenkinson [1966] 3 All ER 702, [1967] 1 WLR 79, 43 TC 479, [1966] TR 289	161
Watson Bros v Lothian (1902) 4 TC 441, sub nom. Watson Bros v Inland Revenue 4 F (Ct of Sess) 795, 39 Sc LR 604, 10 SLT 49	161
Westminster (Duke) v IRC (1935) 19 TC 490, [1936] AC 1, 104 LJKB 83, HL	4, 7
Wetton, Page & Co v Attwooll [1963] 1 All ER 166, [1963] 1 WLR 114, 40 TC 619, [1962] TR 301	69
Wilcock v Frigate Investments Ltd [1982] STC 198, [1981] TR 471	142, 143
Williams v Bullivant [1983] STC 107	147

	PAGE
Williams v Evans [1982] STC 498, [1982] 1 WLR 972	167
Williams v IRC [1980] STC 535, [1980] 3 All ER 321, [1980] TR 347, HL	262
Wilson and Garden Ltd v IRC [1982] STC 597, [1982] 3 All ER 219, [1982] 1 WLR 1069, 1982 SLT 541, HL	121
Winterton v Edwards [1980] STC 206, [1980] 2 All ER 56, [1981] TC 655, [1979] TR 475	276
Wiper v Customs and Excise Comrs LEE/74/57A	47
Woodward v Customs and Excise Comrs LON/77/247	56
Yarmouth v France (1887) 19 QBD 647, DC	35
Yuill v Wilson [1980] STC 460, [1980] 3 All ER 7, [1980] 1 WRL 910, [1981] TC 674, HL	275, 276

PART 1

Fundamentals

1. Introduction
2. Business structures

1 Introduction

1.1 WHAT IS A FAMILY BUSINESS?

The term 'family business' is used in this book to refer to a business which is largely owned by one or more families. It may be carried on by a sole trader. Often it will be carried on by a partnership, perhaps of husband and wife alone or with their grown-up children. Sometimes the partners will include the trustees of a discretionary settlement set up for the benefit of young children. Or it may be carried on by a family company the shares of which are owned by members of the family.

The family business can range in size from a 'one-man band' to a large group with widespread interests. In the case of a company, it will almost invariably be a close company. Whatever its size there are certain underlying common problems arising from the close identity of the family with the ownership and management of the company. Identifying the problems and suggesting solutions to them is one of the main objects of this book.

Very often the family or families which own the business will have younger members who, it is hoped, will carry on the business when the older members retire. The preservation of the business and the minimisation of capital taxes on handing it on are, therefore, matters of considerable importance which will be considered.

The importance of the family business in the national economy is being increasingly recognised as the large number of tax incentives for small businesses introduced over the last few years bear witness. The authors share this belief in the importance of the family business and feel no reluctance in suggesting ways in which the burden of taxation in all its varied forms can be mitigated.

1.2 WHAT IS TAX PLANNING?

Lord Tomlin's dictum in *Duke of Westminster v IRC* (1935) 19 TC 490, HL that 'Every man is entitled if he can to order his affairs so that the tax attaching under the appropriate Acts is less than it otherwise would be' remains, in the authors' view, the clearest and most straightforward answer to the question posed above.

In the recent case of *IRC v Burmah Oil Co Ltd* [1982] STC 30, HL Lord Diplock, commenting on Lord Tomlin's dictum, said that it 'tells us little or nothing as to what methods of ordering one's affairs will be recognised by the courts as effective to lessen the tax that would attach to them if business transactions were conducted in a straightforward way'. It cannot be denied that tax planning has often involved elaborate, artificially contrived schemes, totally divorced from commercial reality, but this book is not concerned with these; nor is it remotely concerned with tax evasion as that term has come to be commonly understood, ie the illegal evasion of tax.

Tax planning, for the purposes of this book at least, means the arrangement of business and personal affairs so as to make maximum use of the allowances, reliefs and exemptions which the law and Inland Revenue practice afford, and in particular of those tax shelters which have the government seal of approval, whilst having proper regard to the commercial objectives of the business and the personal feelings and aspirations of the owners. It will have regard to the fact that tax must be seen in a wider context. It is only one aspect in the life of a business and its owners, albeit an important one for the most part. Tax planning must therefore make financial and commercial sense, and must be acceptable to those involved in it.

Tax planning will also seek to protect the innocent taxpayer from the pitfalls which have been created as a result of tax avoidance legislation. It is an unfortunate fact that this legislation often leads to the innocent suffering with the guilty and perfectly innocent transactions can fall foul of it in a way that was never intended when the legislation was framed. The more important of these pitfalls are discussed briefly in the last chapter of this book.

Finally, tax planning must also have regard to the possibility of future changes, both in the circumstances of the business and its proprietors and in tax legislation. Tax planning arrangements should, therefore, be as flexible as possible.

1.3 THE IMPLICATIONS OF *RAMSAY* ETC

The decision of the House of Lords in *WT Ramsay Ltd v IRC* [1981] STC 174 introduced a completely new approach to tax-avoidance

1.3 The implications of Ramsay etc

schemes, an approach which was reaffirmed in *IRC v Burmah Oil Co Ltd* [1982] STC 30 and more recently, in *Furniss v Dawson* [1984] STC 153. In the *Burmah* case at 32 Lord Diplock gave the following warning:

'It would be disingenuous to suggest, and dangerous on the part of those who advise on elaborate tax-avoidance schemes to assume, that *Ramsay's* case did not mark a significant change in the approach adopted by this House in its judicial role to a pre-ordained series of transactions (whether or not they include the achievement of a legitimate commercial end) into which there are inserted steps that have no commercial purpose apart from the avoidance of a liability to tax which in the absence of those particular steps would have been payable'.

It must not be thought that this change in the judicial attitude to tax avoidance schemes is to be confined to very elaborate, artificially contrived schemes. The *Dawson* case illustrates that the new approach is of equal relevance to more general tax planning. The *Dawson* scheme was 'simple and honest' and its object was merely to postpone the payment of tax, not to avoid it completely. The scheme was based on a specific CGT provision to the effect that what would otherwise have been a disposal was not to be treated as such. Furthermore, the scheme produced 'enduring legal consequences' in that, at the time when the case was being considered, the parties to it were in a different position from what they were in before the scheme started, and from what they would have been in if they had carried out the substance of the transaction without using the scheme.

Prior to the *Dawson* case it was thought that the new approach was to be directed only at 'self-cancelling' schemes, ie schemes which bring about no real change in the financial and legal positions of the parties involved. It is clear that this view is no longer tenable, for in *Dawson* it was accepted that the scheme was not self-cancelling and yet it was still defeated. The courts may look at the positions of the parties before and after the transactions and tax them according to the substance of what has happened, setting aside the formalities by which the parties' positions were changed.

However, there are limits to this approach. First, there must be a pre-ordained series of transactions which are carried through from beginning to end (whether or not there was any contractual obligation to do so) according to a pre-arranged timetable. The transactions involved, while real (not sham) transactions, must have no significance except as steps in the whole scheme, so that they can, in effect, be looked at as one single composite transaction. Secondly, some of the steps in the series of transactions must have no purpose other than the avoidance of tax. On this last point, whilst the House of Lords referred to there being no commercial purpose, it is thought that what is meant is that tax avoidance should be the only purpose. For example, a gift to provide for one's family, although not serving a business purpose, would not be caught as it would not be made purely for tax avoidance.

It is emphasised, as stated earlier, that a scheme does not have to be a very complex or sophisticated one in order to be caught. Any scheme designed to reduce or defer tax is potentially vulnerable, subject to the limitations mentioned above. That it may be part of a wider commercial transaction will not exempt it.

The essential feature, emphasised in all three cases, is that the transactions must be pre-planned in the sense that there is some arrangement under which they are carried through, although the arrangement need not be a contractual one. Whether there is such a pre-planned series of transactions is a question of fact for the commissioners to determine. This means that the appeal hearing before the commissioners will be extremely important and it will be necessary to convince them on the evidence either that there was no series of transactions or, if there was, that it was not pre-planned. The necessity for there to be a pre-planned series of transactions suggests that the effect of a single transaction cannot be ignored by the new approach. So, eg a deed of covenant by a parent in favour of his student child should still be effective.

In order that some of the steps in the series of transactions can be disregarded, they must have no purpose other than the avoidance of tax, but, as Lord Brightman made clear in *Dawson's* case, this does not mean that they must have no legal or commercial effect.

Where the new approach is applied to a CGT scheme it is not at all clear at what stage the disposal takes effect. In a *Dawson* type situation it could be the time of the first transaction, ie the disposal of the shares by the shareholders, since the effect of the new approach is to deny the application of the CGT relieving provision. On the other hand, the tax liability is computed by reference to the consideration paid by the ultimate purchaser. Further, until the series of transactions is completed there can be no certainty that the new approach will apply. In the *Dawson* case, the transactions took place over a very short time span, so the timing of the disposal didn't matter, but the point could be important where a scheme is started in one accounting period and completed in another. It is thought that a scheme may be regarded as pre-ordained even though the parties to it are independent persons as, for example, in *Cairns v MacDiarmid* [1983] STC 178, CA. Even so, the existence of a single directing mind will be a strong factor pointing to pre-ordination. To

1.3 The implications of Ramsay etc

quote Lord Diplock again in the *Burmah* case [1982] STC 30 at 32:

'The *Duke of Westminster's* case was about a simple transaction entered into between two real persons each with a mind of his own, the Duke and his gardener, even though in the 1930s and at a time of high unemployment there might be reason to expect that the mind of the gardener would manifest some degree of subservience to that of the Duke. The kinds of tax-avoidance schemes that have occupied the attention of the courts in recent years, however, involve interconnected transactions between artificial persons, limited companies, without minds of their own but directed by a single master-mind. In *Ramsay* the mastermind was the deviser and vendor of the tax-avoidance scheme; in the instant case it was *Burmah*, the parent company of the wholly-owned subsidiary companies between which the pre-ordained series of transactions took place.'

Whilst the new approach enables the tax consequences to be determined by the substance of the transaction rather than its form, this does not mean that the Inland Revenue can recategorise the transaction as something entirely different. To put it another way, if an agreement or transaction is found to have a particular legal nature, the Inland Revenue cannot ignore the form of that agreement or transaction and treat it as something else. Thus, in *Duke of Westminster v IRC* (1935) 19 TC 490 the Duke used a deed of covenant instead of paying wages to put money into his employees' hands. Accepting that the deed of covenant was genuine, the Inland Revenue could not argue that the payments under it were wages because they achieved the same result. It has been suggested that the *Duke of Westminster's* case might be decided differently if it was heard today, but it is significant that, despite being invited to do so, the Law Lords in *Dawson's* case declined to overrule it explicitly.

It is, therefore, considered that, for example, genuine cross options (to buy and to sell) could not be treated as being, in substance, an unconditional contract of sale. Or a deferred share scheme for CTT purposes cannot, it is thought, be negated by contending that the shares could have been issued to the taxpayer and later given to the intended donees. Or again, if A grants a 999 year lease of land to B, the Inland Revenue cannot maintain that A has in substance sold his freehold interest in the land.

The ability of the Inland Revenue to disregard a statutory provision where a transaction is part of a pre-ordained series (as in *Dawson*) presumably extends to cases where the relief under the statutory provision has to be claimed. For example, suppose a claim

1 Introduction

for roll-over is made on a gift under FA 1980 s 79 and the donee subsequently sells the asset and utilises his annual CGT exemption to avoid tax. It seems that such a transaction might well be caught by the new approach if the steps in it are regarded as pre-ordained and some of them have only a tax-avoidance purpose.

The implications of disregarding a step in a series of transactions on other particular tax liabilities or consequences could be of considerable importance. Where the transaction gives rise to a tax liability which stands in its own right, eg stamp or capital duty or VAT, it is thought that the liability cannot be avoided. The position is less certain where the tax consequence is one which is inherent in the scheme itself. For example, in the case of an intra-group transfer of an asset to a capital loss company, could the Inland Revenue on the one hand apply the new approach to treat the transferor company as disposing of the asset and, on the other hand, reduce the transferee company's losses because it also disposed of the asset at a gain?

Whilst the answer to this question is not clear, it is thought that, once the new approach has been applied to a series of transactions to determine the end result, the individual steps in the series are ignored for the purposes of the particular tax provisions in question in relation to all taxpayers concerned and not merely in relation to that taxpayer whose tax liability the Inland Revenue are seeking to alter.

The future tax treatment of new assets, rights or liabilities acquired or undertaken by the parties to a scheme which is caught by the new approach is one of the most unsatisfactory features of the new approach. The principle seems to be that the end result proposed must not give rise to a double tax liability. Thus Lord Brightman in *Furniss v Dawson* [1984] STC 153 at 165:

'There could be no additional CGT in the steps by which that disposal was achieved ... because it is the Crown's case that the fiscal consequences of the introduction of (the intermediate company) are to be disregarded. The Crown cannot, and does not claim to, have it both ways'.

Just how the court may apply the new approach to negate the tax advantage and yet leave the parties concerned in a position which does not prejudice them for the future remains to be seen. In *Dawson's* case it was presumed that the taxpayers could extract their money from the intermediate investment company without tax penalty through liquidation or sale. However, if extracted by way of dividend it seems that there will be nothing to prevent its being taxed.

1.3 The implications of Ramsay etc

The new approach is not limited only to CGT schemes and could apply to most taxes. In *Cairns v MacDiarmid* [1983] STC 178, CA it was applied to an income tax saving scheme. However, it could probably not apply to stamp duty, which is a tax on documents and not upon transactions. It is also doubtful if it could apply to VAT if only because it is difficult to conceive of planning for VAT by means of a series of transactions.

If the Inland Revenue decide not to seek to apply the new approach it is difficult to see how the court could take the initiative and apply it anyway. The points will not have been an issue before the commissioners so there would presumably be no findings for the court to consider. Thus it seems that, for example, intra-group transfers to utilise group losses, if not challenged by the Inland Revenue under the *Ramsay* doctrine, will still be effective for tax purposes.

In conclusion, it should be remembered that, *Ramsay* etc notwithstanding, tax avoidance is still lawful, still possible, and can still be profitable. However, it has become all the more important to plan one's tax affairs well in advance so that gains and losses arise in the most tax-efficient way and exemptions and reliefs are available to the right persons at the right time. A series of transactions over a short period of time, which may be vulnerable to attack, should be avoided.

2 Business structures

2.1 FACTORS IN THE CHOICE OF A BUSINESS STRUCTURE

In choosing the form in which to carry on a family business, the proprietor or proprietors will normally wish to achieve some or all of the following objectives:

(1) to minimise the tax liabilities arising from the profits earned by the business. In achieving this objective the proprietors should bear in mind their relative requirement for:

    (a) cash drawings for personal expenditure; and
    (b) accumulating funds within the business to finance capital expenditure and working capital.

Both these requirements are likely to increase over the years as a result of inflation, even if the volume of business done remains static. Where a business is growing, the need to finance working capital can be crucial;

(2) to facilitate long-term planning to hand on the business to the next generation of the family without the viability of the business being threatened by capital taxation liabilities;

(3) to achieve non-tax objectives such as limited liability or the status in the business world which comes from adopting a particular business form.

These objectives may sometimes conflict. In the remainder of the chapter there follows a discussion of the advantages and disadvantages of the business forms generally available.

2.2 UNINCORPORATED BUSINESSES

The fundamental decision facing the proprietors of a family business is whether or not that business should be incorporated. The changes in the business tax regime introduced in FA 1984 relating to progressive reductions in the rate of corporation tax and the immediate reduction in the small companies rate of 30% (see **16.1**); the abolition of the investment income surcharge (see **18.1**); and the reductions in the rate of first year and initial capital allowances (see **14.1**) have changed significantly the parameters of this decision. These changes have been taken into account in the discussion which follows.

Sole trader

Except where profits are very modest or where the proprietor of a business has no members of his family with whom he wishes to share the income generated by the business (see Chapter 12 and **17.2**), the sole trader business form has little to commend it from a tax planning point of view. Most of the tax factors relevant to the affairs of a sole trader apply equally to partnerships and are discussed in the following part of this chapter.

Partnership

A partnership is a very flexible and tax-effective business form. Before the FA 1984 changes, the authors' experience was that a partnership was almost invariably the structure to be recommended for a family business unless the level of profits per proprietor were very high indeed.

Non-tax factors

'Partnership is the relation which subsists between persons carrying on a business with a view of profit' (Partnership Act 1890 s 1). The extent of the evidence necessary to establish that such a relationship exists is discussed at **12.3** below; where the proprietors of a family business are actively engaged in the management of the business there will usually be no difficulty in establishing that they are partners. Indeed, it would probably be difficult to prove that they were not partners, should the need arise.

The fundamental non-tax disadvantage of partnership (and indeed to sole trading) is that each partner is jointly liable with the other partners up to the full extent of his personal assets in respect of all debts and obligations of the firm entered into whilst he is a partner and that after his death his estate has several as well as joint liability, but only for debts incurred before his death (Partnership Act 1890 s 9 and *Bagel v Miller* [1903] 2 KB 212). Similarly, each partner is liable for the tort of a partner if he authorised the act which gave rise to the tort or the partner who did the tortious act did so in the ordinary

2 Business structures

course of the business of the firm (Partnership Act 1890 s 10). Each partner is an agent of the firm and of the other partners (Partnership Act 1890 s 5), and to the extent that he has apparent authority for acts he does on behalf of the firm, the effects of those actions are binding on the other partners. The joint effect of these provisions is that any partner may make ordinary business contracts on behalf of the firm, and once he does so all the partners are liable for the consequences up to the full extent of their assets. Anyone contemplating entering into a partnership should be very certain that he is prepared to trust his partners to that extent.

Partnership is by its nature a relationship of extreme good faith (*uberrimae fide*). Where a partner breaches good faith or acts outside his actual authority as a partner his co-partners may have an action against him, but any claim between partners does not affect the rights of an outsider to pursue a claim against all the partners.

The business of a partnership may be conducted with a minimum of formality. A unanimous decision is, however, usually required for all major decisions affecting the partnership business; this can afford some protection to a partner with a minority interest in the partnership. The drawing up of a partnership agreement is desirable but not a legal requirement, and partnerships do not at present have to comply with any statutory rules for the filing of accounts.

Tax advantages

As stated above, the fundamental choice of a business form lies between an unincorporated structure and a company. In the paragraphs which follow there are set out the relative advantages and disadvantages of a partnership as compared with a company:

(1) For reasons set out at **12.3** below, a partnership represents the most flexible way of spreading income among the members of a family where those concerned can be shown to be carrying on a business in common. Once the existence of a partnership is established, the Inland Revenue have no power to interfere with the allocation of profits in accordance with the partnership deed.

(2) Partners will pay lower levels of National Insurance contribution than would directors of a company making the same net drawings from the business; however, they will also enjoy lower levels of benefit.

(3) Partnership profits are assessed on the preceding year basis; this offers scope for tax mitigation by exploiting the rules establishing the basis periods for assessment in the early years of trading (see **8.2** and **9.3**).

(4) Losses arising in the business can be relieved against the total income of the partners (see Chapter 13).

Tax disadvantages

(1) Partnership profits are liable to progressive rates of income tax, up to a top rate of 60%.
(2) Tax is charged on profits as they arise, whether they are drawn by the partners for personal expenditure or retained in the business to finance working capital or capital expenditure. Following the reductions in capital allowances in FA 1984 s 58 and Sch 12, profitable partnerships will find it increasingly difficult to finance capital requirements out of taxed income.
(3) The tax-effective level of retirement provision open to partners is in general limited to the benefits provided by contributions restricted to 17½% of net relevant earnings (see **31.1**).
(4) A partnership is not a legal person for tax purposes (except in Scotland). Changes in the members of a firm may involve a deemed cessation of the trade with consequent application of the cessation assessment provisions and balancing charges (see **8.3** and **9.2**).
(5) The transfer of interests in a partnership or in assets used by a partnership for capital taxes planning purposes may be administratively more complicated than a transfer of shares in a company.

2.3 COMPANIES

Non-tax factors

Shareholders in a limited company by definition enjoy limited liability. In the case of a family company, however, this limitation of liability will often be significantly restricted by the demands of the company's bankers for personal guarantees from the proprietors. (Paradoxically, the larger the scale of the company's operations and the finance become, the less likely it is that onerous personal commitments will be required.) It is likely, therefore, that limitation of liability will be effective only against ordinary trade creditors.

The price of limited liability is compliance with statutory provisions as to the form, audit and filing of accounts and the attendant fees and professional costs. Where the proprietors of a family business wish to bring the business within the corporation tax regime but do not consider that limited liability is a material advantage, consideration should be given to the use of an unlimited company. TA 1970 s 238 charges corporation tax 'on profits of companies'; 'company' is defined in TA 1970 s 526 as including 'any body corporate', a term which clearly includes an unlimited company. Such a company is exempt from the Companies Act requirements as to filing of accounts etc.

The limited liability company enjoys the availability of sources of finance not available to the unincorporated trader. The use of a 'floating charge' over assets is exclusive to companies. At present business expansion scheme funds can offer equity investment in companies on very advantageous terms (see **19.4**)—this opportunity is denied to unincorporated businesses.

Minority shareholders in a company have few rights. They need not be consulted on the management of the company's business and cannot procure the payment of dividends or remuneration. The value of a minority shareholding is likely to be small compared with an equivalent percentage of the value of the company as a whole.

Tax advantages

(1) Company profits are taxed at relatively low rates: 30% in the case of a company making profits of £100,000 or less (see **16.1**). This makes it possible for a company to accumulate post-tax profits to fund working capital and capital expenditure.
(2) The proprietors of a company can allow value to accumulate in the company and extract it at a later date via a sale or liquidation of the company; any gains arising will be liable only to CGT.
(3) Generous pension provision can be made for active directors (see **31.2** and **31.3**).
(4) The legal distinction between the company as employer and the director/shareholder as employee makes possible the use of tax-efficient benefits in kind (see **17.6**) and terminal payments (see **35.2**).
(5) Trading losses of a company may be offset against capital gains (see **21.3**).
(6) A company is a legal person separate from its shareholders. Accordingly, the death of a shareholder or the sale of the business do not cause a cessation of the trade.
(7) It is administratively easy to transfer shares in small parcels, eg to make use of CTT annual exemptions.

Tax disadvantages

(1) The major disadvantage inherent in a corporate structure is the potential double charge on the disposal of assets. If a company owns

an asset which has appreciated in value and the shareholders wish to sell the asset and pass the proceeds into their own hands,
  (a) the company will pay corporation tax on the chargeable gain arising during its ownership of the asset; and
  (b) the shareholders can receive only the net disposal proceeds as remuneration, dividends or as distributions in the course of a winding up. Each of these alternatives will result in tax being payable by the recipent.
(2) The proprietors of a family company bear the burden of both the employer's and employee's national insurance contributions, currently about 20% in aggregate.
(3) Where the level of profits is low, amounts drawn by the directors or employees will incur liability to tax under Schedule E/PAYE whilst creating losses in the company which may not lead to any immediate repayment of corporation tax, so increasing the overall tax burden.
(4) Company losses cannot be relieved against the personal income of shareholders or directors. In cases where there are no profits in earlier periods against which the losses can be carried back, relief for the losses may be deferred for several years.
(5) Levels of wages paid to family employees of the business may be challenged by the Inland Revenue (see **17.2**).

Groups of companies

The grouping of companies under a holding company is a structure commonly adopted where several corporate trades or other activities are carried on under the same ownership. Except where it is necessary to preserve full limited liability in relation to a particular activity (eg where the risks involved in that activity are so great that a claim might prejudice the viability of the other trades carried on), the authors can see no advantage in the adoption of a group structure for family trading companies. The grouping provisions in the Taxes Acts do not fully achieve the effect of causing all the companies in a group to be treated as though they were one company for tax purposes, and the extent to which that effect is not achieved can lead to the restriction of certain reliefs:

(1) Group relieved losses (see **24.3**) cannot be carried back under TA 1970 s 177(2) or (3A); and losses brought forward cannot be group relieved.
(2) Similarly, surrendered advance corporation tax (ACT) (see **24.4**) cannot be carried back.

(3) Capital losses cannot be surrendered within a group and it is necessary to contrive intra-group transfers of assets to ensure matching of gains and losses (see **25.1**).

In general, carrying on several trades in one company rather than a group of companies will maximise relief for expenditure incurred. This is particularly true when a new activity is started, as within the single company it may be possible to present the new activity as a mere extension of the existing trade rather than a new trade, so setting-off expenses of the new activity against income from the existing trade (to the extent that those expenses exceed the income from the new activity) if necessary by way of a carry back of losses under TA 1970 s 177(2) or (3A) or by carrying forward the losses against the aggregated profits of future periods.

Where, despite the disadvantages described above, it is decided to carry on business through a number of companies, those companies should normally be established in a group relationship under a holding company (see **24.1** and **25.1**) to take advantage of the group reliefs available (see Chapters 24 and 25). In a family company context it will usually be preferable to group the companies under a trading parent company rather than a non-trading holding company. Both retirement relief (see Chapter 29) and hold-over relief for gifts of business assets (see **30.2**) depend on the company in respect of the shares of which relief is claimed being a family company and carrying on a trade. The definition of family company is by reference to direct shareholding; indirect shareholding in a trading company through a (non-trading) holding company does not qualify.

Where, exceptionally, the proprietors of a family business intend from the start that a new activity is to be built up with a view to selling it as a going concern, it may be advantageous if the activity is started in a separate company the shares in which are held directly by the proprietors rather than through a group holding company. On a sale of the shares the proceeds will be received by the proprietors personally rather than by the company, so avoiding the double charge to tax referred to above.

2.4 PLANNING CONCLUSIONS

It is relatively easy to incorporate a business without tax penalties (see Chapter 14) but difficult and expensive in tax to disincorporate. Accordingly, a family business should not generally be carried on by a company until it has reached a stage where the advantages of incorporation are incontrovertible and the circumstances leading to that conclusion are likely to continue into the foreseeable future.

2.4 Planning conclusions

Reviewing the objectives set out at **2.1** above in the light of the comments at **2.2** and **2.3** on the advantages and disadvantages of unincorporated and company business structures leads to the conclusions set out below:

(1) When losses or low levels of profits are expected in the early years of trading, the business should be commenced as a partnership. This will make it possible to take advantage of:
   (a) the fact that up to three years assessments will be based on the profits of the first year of trading (see **8.2**);
   (b) loss relief against general income under TA 1970 s 168 and FA 1978 s 30 (see Chapter 13);
   (c) the generally lower levels of taxation on unincorporated businesses when only modest profits are being earned (see below);
   (d) the flexibility inherent in a family partnership for spreading income round the family (see **12.3**).

(2) The business should be incorporated only when the levels of profits being earned and likely to be earned in the foreseeable future justify that step. The point at which incorporation becomes tax efficient will to a large degree depend on the extent to which the proprietors are prepared to leave profits in the company to fund working capital etc, or simply to increase the value of the shares. It is obvious that if the proprietors of a family company intend to draw all the company's profits to meet their private expenditure, no tax saving will result from the interposition of the company between the proprietors and the trade. *Table A* illustrates the relative overall tax and National Insurance contribution liabilities suffered by a sole trader and a company earning various levels of profit where the proprietor needs net drawings or net remuneration of £12,000 pa to meet his personal requirements. The table shows that profits in excess of £25,000 are required before incorporation becomes beneficial. *Table B* makes the rather more realistic assumption that income from the business is shared between a husband and wife who elect for separate taxation of wife's earnings. In both illustrations the use of a company would lead to further savings (employer's and employee's National Insurance contribution) if dividends were to be paid rather than remuneration. However, for reasons set out at **18.1** below that course will not always be desirable. In making the decision to incorporate it is necessary to bear in mind that whilst the allocation of a share of profits to a family member who is a genuine partner in the business cannot generally be challenged (see **12.3**), the payment of remuneration to a family director or employee may have to be justified by reference to the value of the work done (see **17.2**).

Table A

Assumptions: single proprietor entitled to higher personal allowance only
1984–85 and FY 1984 tax rates
1984–85 National Insurance contribution rates
£12,000 net cash drawn by proprietors

Trading profits before salary £	Total tax and National Insurance contribution payable Sole trader £	Company £
0	—	6,384
5,000	858	6,384
10,000	2,674	6,384
15,000	4,363	6,384
20,000	6,007	6,869
25,000	8,190	8,369
30,000	10,627	9,869
40,000	15,939	12,869
50,000	21,876	15,869
60,000	27,876	18,869
80,000	39,876	24,869
100,000	51,876	30,869

(3) It will usually be advisable to keep appreciating assets out of the company to avoid the double charge to tax on their disposal. Where assets are retained outside the company but used for the purposes of the company's trade, it will usually be desirable that no rent should be charged to the company for the use of the assets; if necessary remuneration may be increased to compensate. Reitrement relief under CGTA 1979 s 124 (see Chapter 29) is not available under the statutory rules, but Extra-Statutory Concession D11 allows retirement relief where a full-time working director of a company disposes of an asset which he owns and:

(a) it has throughout his period of ownership been used *rent-free* for the purposes of a trade carried on by the company;

(b) throughout his period of ownership he has been a full-time working director of the company and the company has been his family trading company; and

(c) the disposal is associated with a disposal by him of shares in that company which qualifies for relief under s 124(1)(b) or which would have so qualified had it given rise to a gain.

Table B

Assumptions: husband and wife are joint proprietors, sharing profits equally and electing for separate taxation of wife's earnings when appropriate
1984–85 and FY 1984 tax rates
1984–85 National Insurance contribution rates
£20,000 net cash drawn by proprietors

Trading profits before salary £	Total tax and National Insurance contribution payable	
	Partnership £	Company £
0	—	12,208
10,000	2,063	12,208
20,000	5,567	12,208
30,000	9,416	12,208
40,000	12,935	14,546
50,000	17,414	17,546
60,000	22,404	20,546
80,000	33,143	26,546
100,000	45,133	32,546
120,000	57,133	38,546
150,000	75,133	50,882
200,000	105,133	75,257

Where the company pays rent for the use of the asset, then relief is given only to the extent that the rent is clearly less than a market rent.

Note that keeping assets outside the company is not always advantageous: a controlling shareholding attracts CTT business property relief at 50%, but property owned by a controlling shareholder personally and used in the business attracts relief at only 30%. Where the shareholder does not have a controlling interest, the choice is between relief at 30% or no relief at all.

(4) After incorporation, use should be made of tax-efficient benefits in kind (see **17.6**) and of the generous provisions relating to pension arrangements for working directors of trading companies (see **31.2** and **31.3**).

(5) Where a business is started in an unincorporated form and substantial profits are expected in the future which will justify incorporation, it may be worthwhile to use two parallel structures from the beginning. A partnership and a company may be run side

by side. In the early days the partnership will undertake most of the trading and incur the capital expenditure; any losses can be relieved against personal income. As the business grows new contracts can be directed to the company. Care should be taken to ensure that it is new business and not the existing business of the partnership which goes to the company, to avoid the possible application of the cessation provisions of TA 1970 s 118. After a period the partnership business can be gradually wound down.

PART II

The business

GENERAL

3 Need to forecast results
4 Capital expenditure
5 Stock relief
6 Pre-trading expenditure
7 Value added tax

INCOME TAX

8 Choice of accounting date
9 Partnership changes
10 Conventional or earnings basis and post-cessation receipts
11 Partnership service companies
12 Sharing profits with the proprietor's family
13 Loss relief

CORPORATION TAX

14 Incorporation
15 Basic Strategy for the proprietory company
16 Small companies rate relief
17 Remuneration of proprietors
18 Distributions
19 Financing the family company
20 Interest and charges
21 Company chargeable gains
22 Company losses
23 Receivership and liquidation
24 Groups of companies—income and distributions
25 Groups of companies—chargeable gains

CAPITAL GAINS TAX

26 Roll-over relief
27 Partnership capital gains
28 Development land tax

GENERAL

3 Need to forecast results

In many cases effective tax planning requires that action should be taken during an accounting period; once a period has ended scope for affecting the tax liabilities determined by the results of the period is severely limited. Any business expecting to make significant profits requires a system which will, at the very least, allow the results of an accounting period to be predicted some time before the end of the period. Many of the planning opportunities described below will not be available unless such a system is in existence.

In today's economic climate it is more than ever the case that traders are conscious of the level of professional fees; many will react with horror to the suggestion that they should increase these fees still further by paying for interim or management accounts. In the authors' view such a reaction is almost invariably shortsighted. Quite apart from tax planning possibilities the preparation of regular management accounts, preferably linked with budgets, can prove fundamental to the success or even survival of a family business. Ironically, it is when times are most difficult and the pressure on costs greatest that the availability of up-to-date management information is likely to be most valuable.

Whatever the advantages of management accounts, no businessman will be willing to have them prepared unless he can see that the cost is reasonable in relation to the benefit he perceives. The more of the work that the trader himself can do, the smaller will be the costs of professional advisers. Cost-effective solutions to the problem include the following:

(1) Many professional accountants use small computers for the preparation of client accounts. The main cost involved is the inputting of data from the client's records. If the client can be persuaded to format the data properly, it makes relatively little difference whether the data is input in monthly batches or in one large batch at the year end. The preparation of accounts from the

input data is largely automatic, with the result that the cost of monthly accounts should be to a significant extent offset against the cost of producing the annual accounts.

(2) If a businessman has the necessary inclination and aptitude he can extract his own monthly figures if the book-keeping system is set up to facilitate this. Probably the most satisfactory procedure involves the setting up of analysed sales and purchases daybooks, receipts and payments cash books and a petty cash book kept on an imprest system. If these records are kept up to date and a little thought is applied to whether any major invoices are yet to be issued or received in respect of transactions during a particular period, any trader capable of preparing a bank reconciliation should be able to extract figures which can be slotted into a pro-forma to produce a set of management accounts.

(3) Many businesses base their records on an analysed cash book. If such a book is used in conjunction with open invoice files in which invoices which have not been settled are filed separately from those which have, it is again relatively simple to extract figures for insertion into an accounts pro-forma.

4 Capital expenditure

4.1 CAPITAL ALLOWANCES AND THE TIMING OF EXPENDITURE

FA 1984 s 58 and Sch 12 made fundamental changes to the capital allowances system which had been in operation since 26 October 1970. The 100% first year allowance for machinery and plant was reduced to 75% for expenditure incurred after 13 March 1984, and to 50% from 1 April 1985. From 1 April 1986 no first year allowance will be given, but the existing 25% writing-down allowance will continue to be available (on a reducing balance basis). These changes apply automatically to certain other expenditure (such as fire safety and thermal insulation costs) which is treated by the legislation in the same way as expenditure on plant.

Where expenditure is incurred before 1 April 1987 under a binding contract entered into before 14 March 1984, the 100% first year allowance will continue to be given. It will also apply to expenditure after 13 March 1984 on certain projects in development or special development areas in respect of which an offer of selective assistance under the Industrial Development Act 1982 s 7 or 8 (or equivalent Northern Irish legislation) has been made between 1 April 1980 and 13 March 1984.

The 75% initial allowance on industrial buildings and houses let on assured tenancies was reduced to 50% in respect of expenditure incurred after 13 March 1984 and to 25% for expenditure incurred from 1 April 1985 to 31 March 1986. Thereafter it is to be abolished. The rate of annual writing-down allowance remains at 4%, on a 'straight line' basis. Transitional provisions will apply to give the full 75% allowance for expenditure before 1 April 1987 under existing contracts, and for projects in development and special development areas as described above.

Under the pre-1984 capital allowance legislation, traders could often obtain significant tax advantages by bringing forward the legal

4 Capital expenditure

acquisition of industrial buildings and plant and machinery without necessarily bringing forward payments to the builder or supplier. The Capital Allowances Act 1968 s 1(1) gave an initial allowance 'where a person *incurs* capital expenditure' on an industrial building; FA 1971 s 41 gave a 100% first year allowance where:

'(a) a person carrying on a trade *incurs* capital expenditure on the provision of machinery or plant for the purposes of the trade; and (b) in consequence of his incurring the expenditure the machinery or plant belongs to him at some time during the chargeable period related to the incurring of the expenditure.'

The legislation did and still does not require that the machinery or plant acquired is brought into use during the accounting period in which the expenditure is incurred (although if the asset is never brought into use in the trade any allowance given is withdrawn). As a matter of general law, expenditure is 'incurred' when it is contracted for; no payment need pass at the time of the contract. FA 1971 s 42(1) is authority for claiming an allowance in respect of the whole of the expenditure contracted for irrespective of the amount actually paid during the accounting period in which the contract is made. It is, however, essential that property in the plant or machinery does actually pass to the purchaser, with the result that where there is a hire purchase agreement or retention of title by the vendor under a *Romalpa* clause, the first year allowance is restricted to amounts actually paid for the plant etc until the plant is brought into use in the trade (FA 1971 s 45(1)).

Under the 1971 legislation, if plant and machinery could be acquired on deferred terms, a cash flow advantage could be obtained from the purchase of plant where the immediate reduction in tax liability exceeded the instalments of purchase consideration. The successive reductions in rates of first year and initial allowances included in FA 1984 mean that traders would, but for anti-avoidance provisions, have an even greater incentive to accelerate the date on which capital expenditure should be incurred in order to obtain the allowance at a higher rate. This was foreseen in the legislation, which provides that where a person incurs capital expenditure under a contract:

(a) which is entered into after 13 March 1984 and on or before 31 March 1986; and
(b) which either specifies no date on or by which the contractual obligations must be fully performed or specifies such a date which is after 31 March 1985; and

4.1 Capital allowances and the timing of expenditure

(c) in the case of plant or machinery, the contract provides that the person making the contract shall or may become the owner of the plant or machinery on the performance of the contract,
the expenditure is spread over the period between the date of the contract and the date by which the contract must be fully performed. The spreading is achieved by defining the maximum allowable expenditure for each of the financial years commencing 1 April 1984 and 1 April 1985 as a fraction of the total expenditure. The fraction for the financial year 1984 is arrived at by taking the number of complete months in that year falling after the date of the contract and dividing that by the total number of complete months in the whole period from the date of the contract to the date set in the contract by which the contract must be fully performed (or 31 March 1987 if no date is set in the contract). For the financial year 1985 the denominator of the fraction is again the number of complete months in the contract period; the numerator is 12 unless the contract was made during that year when the numerator will be the number of complete months in the financial year falling after the contract date. The result of applying this fraction is that the amount of expenditure qualifying for first year allowance in a financial year may be less than the amount actually paid in that year.

EXAMPLE

G Ltd, which makes up accounts to 31 March each year, contracts on 1 January 1985 to purchase plant for delivery on 31 March 1986 at a cost of £100,000 of which 25% is payable as a deposit when the contract is signed and the balance on delivery.

Under the 1971 rules, the whole of the £100,000 would have qualified for first year allowances in the year to 31 March 1985. The 1984 legislation means that the expenditure which will qualify for first year allowances at 75% is

$$\frac{3}{15} \times £100,000 = £20,000$$

which is less than the money actually laid out in the accounting period to 31 March 1985. The balance of the expenditure, £80,000, will qualify for initial allowances at the 50% rate in the accounting period to 31 March 1986.

The anti-avoidance provisions do not apply to hire purchase contracts in respect of plant or machinery acquired on hire purchase to which FA 1971 s 45(1)(b) applies. Section 45 provides that where a person acquires plant or machinery under a contract providing that

4 Capital expenditure

he shall or may become the owner of the machinery or plant on the performance of the contract:

(a) the asset is treated as belonging to him at the time when he is entitled to the benefit of the contract; and
(b) all capital expenditure to be incurred by him under the contract after the time when the machinery or plant is brought into use in the trade is treated as having been incurred at that time.

The combined effect of FA 1971 s 45 and the 1984 legislation is that:

(1) In the unusual case where payments are made under a hire purchase agreement before plant or machinery is brought into use, the spreading provisions will apply to the amounts paid before the plant is brought into use, but at the time the plant is first used the balance of the capital expenditure due under the agreement qualifies for a first year allowance.
(2) In the more usual case where the plant is brought into use as soon as the hire purchase contract is made, the whole of the capital expenditure under the contract qualifies for first year allowance at once.

It appears, therefore, that in cases where assets are to be acquired on deferred terms and can be brought into use in the trade immediately, the use of a hire purchase contract rather than outright purchase on deferred payment terms may be the route to maximise allowances. Alternatively, where a supplier is prepared to offer deferred terms, it may be possible to avoid the application of the spreading provisions by having one contract for the supply of the asset and a separate contract for a loan equal to the price of the asset.

4.2 FINANCING THE EXPENDITURE

A trader requiring assets for use in a business can finance the acquisition of those assets in a number of alternative ways, ie:
— outright purchase for cash;
— purchase from the supplier on deferred payment terms;
— hire purchase;
— leasing.
Each of the options is considered below in turn.

Purchase for cash

A person purchasing assets for cash clearly incurs the expenditure, becomes the owner of the asset and is entitled to the capital allowances as soon as he completes the purchase contract. Such a purchase may be made by using available cash resources or by borrowing—which of these courses is adopted will generally be decided on commercial grounds rather than by tax considerations.

Interest paid on borrowings by a trader to acquire assets for use in the trade can always be structured to obtain tax relief for the interest paid:

(1) Under TA 1970 s 130 (general rules governing the deductibility of expenditure), interest paid on a loan or overdraft used by an unincorporated trader to acquire a business or business assets will be deductible as a business expense provided that the money is used wholly and exclusively for business purposes.
(2) A company which borrows money to acquire trading assets will obtain relief for the interest it pays either as a trading deduction or as a charge on its income. For a discussion of the distinction between these reliefs, see **20.1** below.
(3) Where a partner borrows money to buy machinery or plant (eg a motor car) which he uses for the purposes of the firm's business and for which the firm can claim capital allowances, he is entitled to relief on the loan interest payable during the three tax years after the end of the year of assessment in which the loan was obtained (FA 1972 Sch 9 para 10).
(4) Similar relief is available to an employee who borrows money to buy a car or other item of machinery or plant for use in carrying out his duties (FA 1972 Sch 9 para 12).

There may be circumstances in which it would be beneficial to accelerate or defer the payment of interest so that relief is available in an earlier or a later year, eg where there is insufficient income to absorb the interest or to avoid the loss of personal allowances. To be allowable, interest must be paid. When interest can be said to have been paid can sometimes be a difficult question. On a practical level, most people would probably consider a payment as having been made when they had drawn a cheque and sent it to the lender. However, it was decided in *Re Owen, Owen v IRC* [1949] 1 All ER 901 that a gift of money by cheque is not complete until the cheque is cleared and the money credited to the transferee's account.

The position is more difficult when interest is debited to the borrower's account with the lender. If the account is in credit there is probably no great problem, but where the account is in debit the position is not so clear. In *Paton v IRC* (1938) 21 TC 626, HL it was held that there had been no payment of interest on advances by a bank debited to the borrower's account in a year in which he had made no payments into the account in reduction of either the amount advanced or the accruing interest. See also *Torrens v IRC* (1933) 18 TC 262.

For companies paying bank interest the question is resolved by the statutory provision that the interest is paid when it is debited to the company in the bank's books (TA 1970 s 248(3)). For further discussion of this point see **20.1** below.

Purchase on deferred terms and hire purchase

Notwithstanding the fact that as a matter of general law an asset acquired on hire purchase does not become the property of the hirer until he exercises his option to buy (usually for a nominal sum) at the end of the hire period, for capital allowances purposes the hirer is treated as the owner of the asset as soon as he brings it into use in the business. A purchaser on deferred terms will normally acquire legal ownership of the asset as soon as the purchase contract is made; for a discussion of the timing of capital allowances on a purchase on deferred payment terms, see **4.1** above.

It is not uncommon for suppliers selling assets on deferred payment terms to retain the legal title to the assets until payment is made in full. The leading case on reservation of title is *Aluminium Industrie Vaassen BV v Romalpa Alluminium Ltd* [1976] 2 All ER 552, CA; a discussion of what is necessary to achieve effective reservation of title is outside the scope of this book. It appears that the inclusion in a sale contract of a reservation of title clause will bring the contract within the definition of a hire purchase contract at FA 1971 s 45(1) (discussed at **4.1** above). The recent case of *Stokes v Costain Property Investments Ltd* [1984] STC 204, CA establishes that it is a prerequisite for the grant of capital allowances under the general rules of FA 1971 45(1)(b) (set out at **4.1** above) that the asset on which the allowance is claimed should 'belong' to the claimant. Assets sold on terms reserving title to the vendor until payment is made in full cannot 'belong' to the purchaser until he has made those payments; accordingly, any claim for allowances must be based on the fact that the asset will or may become the property of the purchaser, bringing the purchase contract within the definition of a hire purchase contract at FA 1971 s 45(1). It may, however, be possible to argue for the treatment of a purchase subject to reservation of title as being an outright purchase at the time the purchase contract is concluded by relying on SP 9/76. In that statement of practice the Inland Revenue accepted that 'if the circumstances indicate that the reservation of title is regarded by the parties as having no practical relevance except in the event of the insolvency of the buyer, the goods should, notwithstanding the strict legal position, normally be treated as purchases in the account of the buyer and sales in the accounts of the supplier' where both parties to the contract follow that treatment. Although the statement was concerned with stock relief, it does refer to the treatment described above as being 'accepted for tax purposes', and should therefore be applicable to capital purchases as well as purchases on trading account.

Leasing

A trader who takes a lease of a qualifying industrial building will be entitled to industrial buildings allowances on expenditure which he incurs in his capacity as lessee (his 'relevant interest' in the building). The allowances due to the lessee on expenditure which he has incurred are unaffected by any transactions affecting the relevant interest of the landlord (eg a sale of the building subject to the lease). The creation of a subsidiary interest in the property, such as the grant of a lease out of a freehold, does not of itself transfer the relevant interest of the owner of the principal interest (the freeold). FA 1978 s 37, however, provides that where a long lease is granted out of a relevant interest the lessor and lessee may jointly elect for the industrial buildings allowances to be transferred to the lessee. The grant of the lease is treated as a sale to the lessee of the relevant interest at a price equal to any capital sum paid for the grant of the lease. Such an election may be useful if the lessor has losses or other allowances with which to cover any balancing charge; the lessee will then be entitled to a writing-down allowance calculated by dividing the residue of expenditure by the number of years remaining in the twenty-five years period since the construction of the buildings, and may be prepared to pay a higher rent to reflect that fact.

Where the leasing of plant or machinery is concerned, it is necessary to draw a distinction between operating leases and finance leases. An operating lease is a short-term hire of equipment from a lessor who usually supplies equipment for different periods to a number of successive lessees with the rent being determined by the hirer's use of the asset. A finance lease, on the other hand, 'transfers substantially all the risks and rewards of ownership of an asset to the lessee'. It is, as the name suggests, a financial arrangement under which the lessor provides the funds and the lessee enjoys the use of the asset but not the legal ownership. This is particularly the case where the lessee specifies or even orders the asset from the supplier, with the lessor's role being purely to provide the finance. Other features of a finance lease include the following:

(1) The lease often provides for a primary lease period during which the lessor recovers his capital outlay and makes his profit, and a

secondary period during which the lessee enjoys the use of the asset for a nominal rent.

(2) Finance leases are usually non-cancellable during the primary period, to protect the lessor from the effects of the heavy initial depreciation suffered by most items of plant etc, especially motor cars. If the lessee were able to cancel the agreement the lessor might find that the rentals received and the sale proceeds after cancellation did not cover his initial outlay.

(3) The lessor is often prepared to structure payments to suit the lessee's circumstances. In the case of agricultural machinery, for instance, it is common for lease payments to be made only during the months of October to April when the farmer has received the money from the sale of the year's harvest.

Commercial considerations aside, leasing of plant etc is likely to prove an attractive option to traders in the following circumstances:

(1) If the trader cannot use the full capital allowances he would obtain on an outright purchase because he has insufficient taxable income, he will often be able to negotiate advantageous terms with a finance house on the basis that the finance house enjoys the benefit of the capital allowances and reflects that fact in reduced charges to the lessee.

(2) The results of the first year of trading of an unincorporated trader will form the basis for up to three years' tax assessments. Accordingly, leasing charges paid in the first year will be relieved up to three times over. Even with 100% first year allowances this could make leasing very attractive; as the rates of first year allowances fall away up to 1 April 1986 leasing will become even more tax efficient in this situation.

When first year allowances are abolished after 1 April 1986, leasing may well offer a faster rate of tax relief on capital expenditure than outright purchase. After 1 April 1986 capital allowances on plant etc will be restricted to writing-down allowances at 25% on a reducing balance basis. Leasing, on the other hand, will normally cover the cost of the asset (and the finance charge) in equal annual instalments, ie on a straight line basis. Assuming that the finance charge will be approximately the same whether the asset is leased or purchased with borrowed money, leasing will offer a faster rate of tax relief if the lease period is reasonably short.

EXAMPLE

In May 1986 V Ltd needs plant costing £8,000 for use in a manufacturing process. After five years the plant will be valueless and will be

4.2 Financing the expenditure

scrapped. V Ltd intends to pay for the asset out of earnings over four years. A leasing company will charge V Ltd the same effective rate of interest as the bank would charge on a loan over the same period; the interest element can, therefore, be ignored when comparing leasing and outright purchase.

The capital cost of the asset will qualify for tax relief as follows:

		Leasing		Purchase	
			Cumulative relief		Cumulative relief
Cost		£8,000		£8,000	
Year 1:	lease payment	2,000	2,000		
	WDA 25%			2,000	2,000
		6,000		6,000	
Year 2:	lease payment	2,000	2,000		
	WDA 25%			1,500	1,500
		4,000	4,000	4,500	3,500
Year 3:	lease payment	2,000	2,000		
	WDA 25%			1,125	1,125
		2,000	6,000	3,375	4,625
Year 4:	lease payment	2,000	2,000		
	WDA 25%			844	844
		—	8,000	2,531	5,469
Year 5:	balancing allowance			2,531	2,531
				—	8,000

One area of activity where leasing is particularly popular is the provision of motor cars. Specialist vehicle leasing organisations will often provide a package deal under which the lease payments cover servicing and repairs as well as the actual provision of the vehicle. Such a deal can be very attractive to a busy entrepreneur as it takes out of his hands the administration of the business motor vehicles. However, any person leasing motor vehicles should be aware that there is a tax penalty when a motor car costing more than £8,000 is leased rather than purchased. Where such a car is purchased, FA 1971 Sch 8 para 10 restricts the annual writing-down allowance to a maximum of £2,000. Over the period of ownership of the vehicle, however, the owner will obtain full relief for the net cost to him of the vehicle by means of writing-down and balancing allowances. Where a car costing more than £8,000 is leased, on the other hand, FA 1971 Sch 8 para 12 restricts the amount deductible in computing profits to the leasing payments made multiplied by the fraction

$$\frac{£8{,}000 + \dfrac{\text{new retail price of car} - 8{,}000)}{2}}{\text{new retail price of car}}$$

Any excess over this fraction of the total payments is not deductible in computing profits; the amount disallowed is not carried forward but is lost forever, with the result that if over the lease period the whole of the capital cost of the car is paid to the lessor, part of that cost will not have qualified for any tax allowance.

4.3 CLAIMING THE BEST RELIEF

Some types of expenditure may qualify for capital allowances under more than one heading—for instance an item of plant may also be part of a building.

The capital allowances legislation includes provisions designed to prevent allowances being given twice for the same expenditure; the effect of these provisions is that a trader may claim the allowance which will relieve the expenditure at the highest rate. At the time of writing allowances should normally be claimed in the following order:

(a) scientific research allowance, business buildings in enterprise zones and 'very small workshops' allowances all of which continue to qualify for 100% allowances;
(b) machinery and plant allowances;
(c) industrial buildings allowance;
(d) agricultural buildings allowance.

It should not be overlooked that the legislation provides that certain expenditure on buildings is to be treated as though it were on plant, notably:

(a) fire safety expenditure (FA 1974 s 17, FA 1975 s 15);
(b) thermal insulation expenditure (FA 1975 s 14).

Most expenditure, if it qualifies for capital allowances at all, will fall clearly into one of the categories of asset for which allowances are available. The type of expenditure for which it is likely to be most difficult to decide which allowance is due is expenditure on items within a building which may be regarded either as parts of the building or as items of plant in their own right. A review of the decided cases on the definition of plant is outside the scope of this

4.3 Claiming the best relief

book. It is, however, possible to lay down some guidelines in this area.

Case law concerning the definition of plant is founded on the words of Lindley LJ in *Yarmouth v France* [1887] 19 QBD 647 at 658:

'In its ordinary sense, it includes whatever apparatus is *used by a businessman for carrying on his business*—not his stock-in-trade which he buys or makes for sale; but all goods and chattels, fixed or moveable, live or dead, which he keeps for permanent employment in his business.'

The emphasis has been added by the authors to show that plant is identified by applying a 'functional' test—how is the plant used in the trade? This involves a number of steps:

(1) The trade being carried on must be identified. What is important is the particular taxpayer's trade, not merely the type of trade (*Jarrold v John Good & Sons Ltd* (1962) 40 TC 681, CA). It is not necessary to reduce the trade to its bare essentials: in *IRC v Scottish and Newcastle Breweries Ltd* [1982] STC 296, HL the court recognised that the trade of a hotelier extends beyond the mere selling of food, drinks and accommodation and includes the creation of atmosphere or ambiance, with the result that the furnishings, fittings and decorations may form part of the hotelier's plant.

(2) It is then necessary to identify what constitutes the plant. That statement is not quite the truism it appears at first sight. In *IRC v Barclay, Curle & Co Ltd* (1969) 45 TC 221, HL the Crown was prepared to concede that the pumps and valves associated with a drydock were plant, but the taxpayers succeeded in their contention that the drydock as a whole, including the concrete lined excavation, was a single item of plant. A similar contention was upheld in *Cooke v Beach Station Caravans Ltd* [1974] STC 402 in respect of a swimming pool. In *Cole Bros Ltd v Phillips* [1982] STC 307 the House of Lords accepted in principle that an electrical system in a building can be a single item of plant; the decision in that case rested on the particular facts found by the commissioners.

(3) Having identified the trade and the putative item of plant, it is necessary to decide what function the plant in question plays in relation to the trade—is it part of the apparatus with which the taxpayer carries on his trade? The fact that an item may be commercially desirable for the taxpayer's trade does not make it plant (*Hampton v Fortes Autogrill Ltd* [1980] STC 80); the item must perform some function in the trade. The function may be performed passively as well as actively, as was the case with the office partitions

in *Jarrold v John Good & Sons Ltd*; the fact that the item is not subject to wear and tear does not prevent it being plant, nor does the fact that the item performs more than one function, one of which is not characteristic of plant (*Schofield v R & H Hall Ltd* [1975] STC 353, CA.

Where does all this leave the taxpayer anxious to claim the maximum allowances for plant in a building? The first point to be made is that detailed records should be kept, distinguishing expenditure on plant from expenditure on the structure itself. In *St John's School (Mountford and Knibbs) v Ward* [1975] STC 7, CA a school claimed plant allowances on the prefabricated structures of a laboratory and a gymnasium as well as the equipment they contained. The claim on the structures failed; the school had kept no record of the cost of the equipment and the court refused to apportion any part of the overall expenditure as plant in the absence of such records.

It is the practice of the Inland Revenue to accept as plant equipment used to provide electric light or power, hot water, central heating, ventilation or air conditioning, alarm and sprinkler systems. Hot water pipes, baths, wash basins etc, also qualify as plant but the provision of mains services such as electrical wiring, cold water piping and gas piping are regarded as part of the cost of the building and not as plant. This is an area where tax law is developing. At present, most difficulty is likely to be encountered with the treatment of electrical installations. Following *Cole Bros Ltd v Phillips* an installation of the type generally found in buildings is unlikely to qualify as plant. Where, however, the system has some particular feature tailored to the particular trade, there may be good grounds for claiming that the system as a whole meets the functional test in relation to the trade in question, and so is a single item of plant.

4.4 DISCLAIMER OF CAPITAL ALLOWANCES

Sole traders and partnerships

FA 1971 s 41(3) allows an unincorporated trader to specify when making a claim for first year allowances what expenditure, if any, is to be the subject of the claim. FA 1971 s 44(2) allows claims for writing-down allowance to be restricted similarly. These provisions will normally be used when a trader has insufficient total income to absorb his personal allowances and charges without the inclusion in that total income of some income from his trade, and there would be

4.4 Disclaimer of capital allowances

insufficient taxable trading income if full capital allowances were to be claimed. Unused personal allowances and non-trade charges cannot, of course, be carried forward. In such a case it is possible to claim only sufficient capital alowances to leave in charge to tax sufficient profits to absorb the personal allowances and charges. Where less than the full first year allowance is claimed, the balance of the expenditure qualifies for a writing-down allowance in future years, with the result that the tax relief for the expenditure is not lost.

Companies

FA 1971 s 41(3) allows a company to disclaim first year allowances, or to claim a reduced allowance. This right is rarely exercised, but should be considered when the following circumstances obtain:

(1) Current losses exceed current investment income, and substantial investment income is expected in future. On disclaimer the writing-down allowances in future years are increased and can be used to augment a loss to set against the investment income instead of being carried forward as excess first year allowances included in trading losses available only against future trading profits.

(2) First year allowances create a loss such that relief against other income of the period or preceding periods displaces non-trade charges on income which are accordingly unrelieved. A claim to offset losses against other income is not, of course, mandatory, but in the absence of such a claim losses can only be carried forward against future profits from the same trade. If the company has income from other sources, the principle set out at (1) above may make disclaimer the best policy.

(3) The company receives income subject to foreign tax, and after first year allowances has no UK tax liability. Double tax relief cannot be carried forward, and so might otherwise be lost. However, the alternatives of treating the foreign tax as an expense, or of converting foreign income into UK income through management charges, interest or royalties, should be considered where applicable.

(4) If there is in a group a company making losses with no prospect of profits in the immediate future, the only relief for those losses (once the possibilities of TA 1970 s 177(2), (3) and (3A) have been exhausted) is through group relief. If no other company in the group has taxable profits after capital allowances etc, it may be worthwhile for a profitable company to disclaim sufficient first year allowances to leave profits in charge to tax to use the available losses.

4 Capital expenditure

(5) The carry forward of the stock relief element of trading losses is limited by FA 1981 Sch 9 para 17(1) to six years from the end of the period for which the relief was claimed. If a company would otherwise be unable to use carried forward stock relief within the six-year period, it should consider disclaiming first year allowances to increase the profits against which the stock relief can be offset.

5 Stock relief

FA 1984 s 48 provides that no stock relief is to be given and no relief is to be clawed back in respect of any period of account beginning after 12 March 1984. Where a period straddles 12 March, stock relief will continue to be given and received up to that date—the stock relief provisions (but not any other tax provision) will be applied as though the period of account had ended on 12 March 1984.

Notwithstanding the abolition of relief from 13 March 1984, stock relief remains relevant to business tax planning in a number of areas:

(1) An opportunity for some planning exists on the commencement of a trade before 13 March 1984. The rules for determining stock relief for the first period of account are contained in FA 1981 Sch 9 para 19 now amended by FA 1984. Stock relief for the first period is calculated using a notional figure of stocks deemed to have existed at the end of a previous notional period, using the formula:

$$\text{actual closing stock} \times \frac{\text{all stocks index of the month containing the last day before the end of the first period}}{\text{all stocks index for March 1984}}$$

The £2,000 restriction and the increase in the all stocks index are applied to the resulting figure. It follows from the method used to calculate the notional opening stock that as long an initial period of account as is possible, up to a maximum of 18 months, should be taken to allow a high level of stocks to be built up as a basis for the determination of notional opening stock. However, the benefit of this measure is reduced the nearer the commencement of trading is to March 1984. The eighteen months maximum duration for the period of account is suggested to avoid the need to split the period for stock relief purposes under the provisions of FA 1981 Sch 9 paras 19(5) and 23 and to determine the stock at the end of the first twelve months of the period on the 'reasonable and just' basis prescribed by FA 1981 Sch 9 para 24(2). Attention is drawn to the provisions of FA 1981 Sch 9 para 22. If a long initial period is followed by a change of accounting date, para 22(2)(c) may operate to allow the inspector to negate the additional stock relief obtained. It does not, however, appear that the choice of a long initial period alone (not associated with a change of accounting date) is open to counteraction under para 22.

(2) Unused stock relief and company trading losses to the extent that they comprise stock relief can only be carried forward for six years (see **22.2** below). It may be necessary to disclaim first year or initial capital allowances to ensure that the benefit of unused relief is not lost (see **4.4** above).

(3) FA 1984 s 48(6) extends the time limit for herd basis election by farmers (see **36.2** below).

6 Pre-trading expenditure

6.1 REVENUE EXPENSES

The date on which a trade commences for tax purposes is considered in detail at **8.2** below. Once the trade has commenced, expenditure incurred wholly and exclusively for the purposes of the trade is relieved under the general expenses rules at TA 1970 s 130.

Where, after 1 April 1980, expenditure is incurred for the purposes of a trade during the three years before the person incurring that expenditure begins to carry on the trade then:

(a) if the person incurring the expenditure is a company, the expenditure is treated as being incurred on the day on which the company first begins to trade, with the result that the expenditure is relieved against the income of the first accounting period; and
(b) if the expenditure is incurred by a sole trader or a partnership it is treated as a trading loss incurred in the year of assessment in which the trade is set up and commenced. The loss is available for relief under TA 1970 s 168 or FA 1978 s 30.

The obvious planning point arising from this legislation is that trading should normally start within three years of any significant expenditure being incurred. For a discussion of when a trade is commenced, see **8.2** below. In the case of a company, the main benefit of the relief is that there is no need to contrive the commencement of trading to ensure that expenditure is relieved. Where the unincorporated trader is concerned, and there is scope for timing expenditure before or after commencement of trading, it is necessary to balance the immediate repayment available under TA 1970 s 168 and FA 1978 s 30 (together with repayment supplement which may be significant in the case of a s 30 claim) against the fact that expenditure incurred in the first twelve months of trading will be relieved up to three times over. Incurring expenditure during the first period of account rather than before the commencement of

41

trading will generally result in the maximum tax relief overall, but the prospect of an immediate cash injection may prove more attractive than future reductions in liability. This may be particularly the case where a previously high rate taxpayer gives up employment to start a business which may take some years to yield high levels of profit.

6.2 CAPITAL EXPENDITURE

FA 1971 s 50(4) provides that 'any expenditure incurred for the purposes of a trade by a person about to carry it on shall be treated as if it had been incurred by him on the first day on which he does carry it on'. The effect of this is that the trader obtains capital allowances in the first period in which the trade is carried on; there is no immediate loss relief like that available for revenue expenditure. The falling rates of capital allowances provided in FA 1984 s 58 and Sch 12 suggest that a trader intending to begin business before 1 April 1986 should start trading as soon as possible after he incurs significant capital expenditure to ensure that he obtains allowances at the highest possible rate.

A person starting a trade will sometimes use in the trade assets which he has owned before he started trading. In such circumstances FA 1971 Sch 8 para 7(1)(a) provides that the trader is to be deemed to have incurred capital expenditure equal to the open market value of the asset at the time it is brought into use in the business. There is clearly scope for negotiation with the inspector about what value should be attributed to assets introduced.

6.3 VALUE ADDED TAX

VAT General Regulations 1980, SI 1980/1536, reg 29 provides relief for input tax suffered by an intending trader on:

(a) goods on hand at the time of registration; and
(b) services supplied in the six months prior to registration.

The rules differ slightly in the case of companies and unincorporated traders. In both cases the trader must draw up and retain:

(a) in respect of goods, a stock account showing separately quantities purchased, quantities used in the making of other goods, date of purchase and date and manner of subsequent disposals of both such quantities; and

(b) in respect of services, a list showing their description, date of purchase and date of disposal, if any.

Companies

A company may recover input tax on supplies of the type described above where the input tax was tax on the supply or importation of goods acquired for the company before its incorporation, or on the supply of services before that time for its benefit or in connection with its incorporation, provided that the person to whom the supply was made or who paid tax on the importation:

(a) became a member, officer or employee of the body and was reimbursed, or has received an undertaking to be reimbursed, by the body for the whole amount of the price paid for the goods or services; and
(b) was not at the time of the supply or importation a taxable person; and
(c) acquired the goods or services for the purpose of a business to be carried on by the body and has not used them for any purpose other than such business.

Unincorporated traders

In the case of unincorporated traders, the only requirements are that goods supplied should be on hand at the time of registration and that services should have been supplied within the previous six months.

7 Value Added Tax

7.1 REGISTRATION

Where a person (and this includes partnerships, companies and sole traders) makes supplies of goods or services above certain limits he must register for VAT. If he doesn't do so he will find himself in a very difficult position because, whilst his supplies will still be taxable, he will not be able to recover the input tax he has suffered on his purchases and expenses. Furthermore, he will be unable to give a valid tax invoice to his customers who, in turn, will be unable to obtain relief for any tax he may have charged them. It is, therefore, of vital importance that an application for registration is made as soon as it is known that the limits have been or will be exceeded.

Under VATA 1983 Sch 1 para 1 a person is required to register if:

(a) taxable supplies for a quarter exceed £6,200, unless the Customs and Excise are satisfied that the taxable supplies for that quarter and the next three-quarters will not exceed £18,700;

(b) taxable supplies for the four quarters then ending exceed £18,700;

(c) there are reasonable grounds for believing that taxable supplies will exceed £18,700 in the period of 12 months beginning at that or any later time.

These limits apply with effect from 14 March 1984. Where the limits are exceeded, the trader must notify the Customs and Excise within ten days of the end of the quarter concerned in the case of (a) or (b), and immediately in the case (c).

It will be seen, therefore, that a trader must not only keep a close watch on his quarterly turnover but also consider his future turnover to see if he should register.

Three other points are worth noting:

(1) Where a trader intends to make taxable supplies which will

exceed the limits but has not yet done so, it would be to his advantage to apply for immediate registration so that he can begin to reclaim input tax on his purchases and expenses.

(2) Where a trader is making only zero-rated supplies and suffers very little input tax he could have all the bother of VAT administration for little or no advantage. In these circumstances, he may apply to be exempt from registration.

(3) Where a trader is making taxable supplies below the limits for registration, he may apply for voluntary registration. This will enable him to recover his input tax.

Group registration

Groups of companies can elect for group registration. The main advantage of this is that VAT is not payable on inter-company supplies. This means an obvious saving in administrative time and effort. On the other hand, there may be cash flow advantages in having the companies registered separately with different VAT accounting periods.

However, where one of the companies in the group is making exempt supplies, it could be disadvantageous to include that company in the group registration because of the potential loss of input tax under the special rules for partially exempt traders dealt with at 7.7 below. Where such a company is left out of the group care must be taken to ensure that an additional tax liability is not accidentally created. This could happen, for instance, where management charges are made to the exempt company by a management company in the group. The management company will have to account for the tax charged but the exempt company will not be able to reclaim it (see *Metravision (GB) Ltd v Customs and Excise Comrs* [1977] VATTR 26).

If there is no group registration and one of the companies in the group is partially exempt it would make sense for that company to undertake the management services for all the companies in the group. This will enable all the output tax charged to the fully taxable companies to be recovered and will increase the amount of input tax which the partially exempt company can recover. If it is not practicable to do that an alternative way to achieve the same result is to group the management services company with the partially exempt company.

Divisional registration

Very large companies which operate by means of separate self-accounting autonomous divisions may apply to have each of their divisions registered separately, just as if they were separate companies in a group. However, supplies between the divisions are not treated as taxable supplies. The company still remains liable for the tax and the divisions must all have the same accounting period. The advantage of divisional registration is the saving in accounting and administration time which would be involved if all the divisions had to be registered as one unit.

Partnerships

Although in English law (but not Scottish) a partnership is not a separate legal person, it is treated as one for VAT registration purposes and must register in the firm name (if there is one) or in the names of the partners. Where the partners carry on different businesses, each with their own firm name, they must all come within one registration. However, provided the partners are not completely common to both firms, each firm will have its own separate registration.

There can be a trap here for the unwary. Suppose two partnerships have partners A and B and A, B and C respectively, and C dies. The two businesses are now no longer separate for VAT purposes and, if the joint turnover is above the registration limit, a single VAT registration will be required.

These rules can provide an opportunity for tax planning. For example, a man might carry on a small business as a sole trader with a turnover below the registration limits. He could start up a second business in partnership with his wife. He would not have to register either business until the turnover of either business exceeds the limits. Similarly, he could carry on one business making taxable supplies and another in partnership with his wife making exempt supplies. In this way he could avoid a partial exemption situation in his first business with the consequent loss of input tax.

Deregistration

A registered trader can deregister if he has been registered for the last two years and his taxable supplies in each of those two years have been less than £18,700, unless there are reasonable grounds for believing that taxable supplies for the next year will exceed £18,700. In these circumstances, if the trader wishes to deregister he should notify the Customs and Excise in writing and they will cancel his registration as from the end of fourteen days after receiving the notification, or such other date as is mutually agreed (VATA 1983 Sch 1 paras 2, 8).

He can also deregister at any time if the Customs and Excise are satisfied that the annual turnover from that date will be less than £17,700. If he wishes to deregister he should notify the Customs and Excise in writing and the registration will be cancelled as soon as they are satisfied (VATA 1983 Sch 1 paras 2, 9). These limits apply from 1 June 1984.

In addition to the above, a trader must give written notice to the Customs and Excise within 10 days if he ceases to make taxable supplies (VATA 1983 Sch 1 para 7).

Failure to notify the Customs and Excise can be very expensive indeed. In *Renton v Customs and Excise Comrs* EDN/79/12 a coal merchant inherited a boarding house on his wife's death. He gave the coal merchant's business to his daughter but failed to deregister as a coal merchant. The Customs and Excise accepted that he had given the business to his daughter but, because he had not deregistered, he remained liable to charge VAT on all taxable supplies made in the boarding house even though the turnover was below the registration limit.

A dairy roundsman fell into a similar trap when he changed his trade and became a ladies hairdresser (*Wiper v Customs and Excise Comrs* LEE/74/57A).

7.2 DIVIDING A BUSINESS

Splitting a business into two or more separate parts carried on by separate persons to avoid a single registration can save VAT in a number of ways, eg:

(1) The turnover of one or more of the separate business may be below the registration limit or within the level for deregistration.

(2) Exempt activities can be hived off to reduce or eliminate the restriction of input tax recovery by the partial exemption rules.

One of the commonest examples of this is where a married couple run a pub and the wife is responsible for the bar catering. Where the catering is below the registration limit, there will be a VAT saving if this is carried on by the wife as a separate business, assuming the same prices are charged after the split (see *Marner v Customs and Excise Comrs* MAN/77/140; *Oldham v Customs and Excise Comrs* MAN/80/240; *Clark v Customs and Excise Comrs* LON/82/338).

In a Press Release no 762 dated 20 September 1982, the Customs and Excise laid down the criteria which they consider should be met if a single business is to be divided into independent parts for VAT

7 Value added tax

registration purposes. The main points are:

(1) Appropriate premises and equipment should be owned or rented by the person carrying on each business.
(2) Separate records and accounts should be maintained and purchase and sale invoices should be in the name of each person.
(3) Any staff should be separately employed by each person.
(4) Each business should be separately assessed for income tax.
(5) The bank accounts should be in the name of each person, each of whom should be the sole drawer.

The Customs and Excise stated that failure to meet all these criteria might affect a person's liability to VAT. However, in *Clark v Customs and Excise Comrs* LON/82/338, the tribunal rejected this view and held that a publican's wife carried on a separate business despite the facts that she did not own or rent separate premises or equipment, employ separate staff or maintain a separate bank account.

This case illustrates the obvious truth that what is a separate business must depend on the facts of the case. Clearly, if the above criteria are met there should not be any difficulty in establishing that a separate business is being carried on, but failure to meet all of them will not necessarily be fatal.

Obviously there are practical limitations on the extent to which business activities can be separated, but in appropriate circumstances the VAT saving may well make it worthwhile. Any proposals along those lines should be agreed with the local VAT office, if possible, right at the start to avoid running into a dispute with them later.

7.3 TRANSFERRING A BUSINESS

Where a business, or part of a business, is transferred as a going concern no VAT will be chargeable provided the conditions imposed by the VAT (Special Provisions) Order 1981, SI 1981/1741, art 12 are satisfied. The following points should be noted:

(1) The business or part of the business must be transferred as a going concern. If only assets are transferred VAT will probably be chargeable.
(2) Where only part of a business is transferred, it must be capable of separate operation.
(3) There is no longer any requirement that all of the assets be transferred.
(4) The transferee must carry on the same kind of business as the transferor. Since it is the transferor who will be liable for the tax if

the conditions are not met, and since he will have no control over the transferee after the transfer, it is advisable for him to obtain a warranty from the transferee that he will use the assets in carrying on the same kind of business.
(5) Where the transferor is a taxable person, the transferee must also be one, or become one as a result of carrying on the business. Obviously, if the transferor is not a taxable person, no question of VAT will arise.

It is important to ensure that the above conditions are satisfied and that, if they are, the purchaser does not pay any VAT on the assets of the business. If he does, the VAT paid may not be deductible as input tax. His only recourse will be against the transferor, who may have gone into liquidation.

Retaining the seller's VAT number

The rules which enable a purchaser to take over the vendor's VAT number are discussed in the next section.

7.4 TAKING OVER ANOTHER'S VAT NUMBER

It is possible for a person to take over another person's VAT number. The rules are contained in the VAT (General) Regulations 1980, SI 1980/1536, reg 4. They are really intended for use in situations such as a sole trader taking in a partner or incorporating his business, or the transfer of a business between members of the same family. Although they can be used for arm's length transactions they will not usually be appropriate. Form VAT 68 must be signed by both parties and the purchaser accepts responsibility for any outstanding VAT liabilities and returns for periods prior to the transfer.

Acquisition of company

When a company is bought, the purchaser takes over the existing VAT registration also. Care must be taken to ensure that the company's VAT returns are up to date and that there are no undisclosed VAT liabilities. It is usual to include VAT in the matters on which letters of representation are required from the vendors. They would be expected to confirm that all VAT has been correctly accounted for, that no input tax has been incorrectly recovered, and that there are no contentious matters outstanding with the Customs and Excise or any other matters which might give rise to a VAT liability.

7.5 TIME OF SUPPLY

VAT returns must generally be made quarterly and the tax accounted for by the end of the month following the end of the quarter. The return covers all transactions during the quarter, and the factor which determines in what quarter a transaction falls is the tax point or point of supply.

It is, therefore, of considerable importance to know when a supply of goods or services is made. The basic rules are to be found in VATA 1983, s 4, but Customs and Excise are given power to determine the time of supply in certain special cases. The current regulations are the VAT (General) Regulations 1980 SI 1980/1536.

Supply of goods

The basic time of supply of goods is the earlier of the time when:
(a) the goods are removed; or
(b) the goods are made available to the customer; or
(c) a tax invoice in respect of the supply is issued; or
(d) a payment is received for the supply.

In the case of (c) and (d), the supply will be treated as being made only to the extent that it is covered by the invoice or payment.

In the case of (a) and (b), the time of supply will be delayed (unless the trader elects otherwise) by the issue of a tax invoice within fourteen days (or a longer period if the Customs and Excise agree). The supply will then be treated as being made on the date of issue of the invoice.

The above rules are modified in the case of certain types of supply, such as sale or return, retention of property, power, land, self-supplies and disposal of business assets.

Supply of services

The basic time of supply of services is the time of their performance or, if earlier, the date of issue of an invoice or receipt of payment. As in the case of goods, the issue of a tax invoice within 14 days of the time of performance of the services will delay the time of supply.

There are special rules for certain particular kinds of services. Of special importance is the rule relating to a continuous supply of services. Where the consideration for a supply is determined or payable periodically (eg lease rentals or professional services), the supply is treated as supplied successively at the earlier of each payment or the date of the tax invoice.

Issue of an invoice

It will have been seen above that the time of supply or tax point can be fixed by the issue of an invoice. The meaning of 'issue' in this context has been considered in four cases and interested readers may like to refer to them. They are *Customs and Excise Comrs v Woolfold Motor Co Ltd* [1983] STC 715; *Dickson Motors (Glasgow) Ltd v Customs and Excise Comrs* EDN/80/42; *Belmont Garage (Edinburgh) Ltd v Customs and Excise Comrs* [1981] VATTR 228 and *Bredon Motor Co Ltd v Customs and Excise Comrs* LON/82/204. On a practical level, the trader will not go far wrong if he interprets the word in accordance with its normal primary meaning, ie act of sending out (*Chambers Twentieth Century Dictionary*).

Planning

Since the tax point determines whether and when VAT is chargeable there may be occasions when it is expedient to advance or delay it. For example, a trader who has not yet registered may wish to delay the tax point until he has registered or, perhaps, the supply can be ignored altogether following a group registration. Or it may simply be a matter of cash flow. Delaying the issue of an invoice from towards the end of one quarter to the beginning of the next postpones the payment of tax to Customs and Excise by three months. A trader who is about to make a large purchase may wish to get a tax invoice towards the end of a quarter rather than at the beginning of the next one so as to accelerate the recovery of input tax.

As mentioned above, if the supply of services is continuous it is not practicable to make the tax point the date of performing the services. Instead, the tax point is the earlier of the issue of a tax invoice or receipt of payment. If, therefore, the supplier issues a request for payment and not a tax invoice, the tax point is delayed until the payment is received.

Many professional firms, such as accountants and, possibly, solicitors, who are rendering services on a continuous basis throughout the year could take advantage of this.

It is important that the document requesting payment should clearly state that it is not a tax invoice. It should not carry a VAT number and preferably should not show any VAT amount.

7.6 CREDIT NOTES

The issue of credit notes is not specifically provided for in the VAT legislation but it was clearly established in *British United Shoe*

Machinery Co Ltd v Customs and Excise Comrs [1977] VATTR 187, that, as long as a credit note is issued bona fide in order to correct a genuine mistake or overcharge, or to give a proper credit, it is valid.

However, the issue of a credit note cannot be used as a way of getting relief on a bad debt. In *Peter Cripwell & Associates v Customs and Excise Comrs* CAR/78/131, a firm of architects issued a tax invoice to a client for fees of £4,168 including VAT of £373. Before the account was paid the client went into liquidation. The firm, realising that it was not going to be paid, issued a credit note and deducted the VAT of £373 from the tax due in its next return. It was held that the credit note was not bona fide and the credit was not allowed.

Similarly, in *Temple Gothard & Co v Customs and Excise Comrs* LON/78/238, a firm of chartered accountants issued credit notes in respect of unpaid fees to six companies in the same group after a receiver had been appointed. The argument that the credit notes were bona fide because they would preserve goodwill was rejected.

In *Mannesmann Demag Hamilton Ltd v Customs and Excise Comrs* LON/82/370, a credit note was issued purporting to cancel the original transaction altogether after the customer went into receivership. A fresh invoice was issued showing considerably less VAT than was shown in the first invoice. It was held that the credit note was ineffective.

These cases illustrate the need for care when issuing credit notes. A credit note issued incorrectly will mean more tax to pay later when it is discovered.

7.7 PARTIAL EXEMPTION

The recovery of input tax will be restricted where a trader makes exempt supplies as well as taxable supplies (VATA 1983 s 15). The rules are set out in the VAT (General) Regulations 1980, SI 1980/1536 to which significant changes were made by SI 1984/155 with effect from 1 April 1984.

De minimis rules

Regulation 27 contains certain *de minimis* rules which enable a partially exempt trader whose exempt supplies fall below certain limits to recover all his input tax. The rules, as amended by SI 1984/155 with effect from 1 April 1984, are as follows.

Outputs rules

Where in any prescribed accounting period the value of a trader's exempt supplies amounts to less than:

7.7 Partial exemption

(a) £200 per month on average; or
(b) 1% of all his supplies; or
(c) both 25% of all his supplies and £16,000 per month on average; or
(d) both 50% of all his supplies and £8,000 per month on average,

then all supplies in that period are treated as taxable supplies.

Inputs rules

Where in any prescribed accounting period the amount of trader's input tax attributable to exempt supplies is less than both 5% of the whole of his input tax and £200 per month on average, then all his supplies in that period are treated as taxable if the Customs and Excise see fit. This rule applies only to traders using a special method of calculating deductible input tax, unless the Customs and Excise allow otherwise.

Exclusion of certain exempt supplies

The following supplies are excluded when considering the above limits (VAT (General) Regulations 1980, SI 1980/1536, reg 25):

(a) the grant, assignment or surrender of an interest in land habitually occupied in the course of carrying on a business;
(b) most dealings in securities, where the supply is incidental to one or more of the business activities;
(c) the assignment of a debt;
(d) most credit transactions, except where the business is wholly or mainly financial or insurance services.

If the exempt outputs of securities and interest ((b) and (d) above) are excluded, then any similar zero-rated outputs must also be excluded.

Apportionment

If the exempt supplies are above the *de minimis* limits it will be necessary to apportion the input tax between taxable and exempt supplies, and only the tax apportioned to taxable supplies can be recovered. Regulation 24 originally provided two basic methods for doing this, but under SI 1984/155, method 2 has been withdrawn as from 1 April 1984. Method 1, which provides a simple basis for the calculation of deductible input tax according to the ratio of taxable to total supplies, continues as the only method which can be used without prior approval of the Customs and Excise. Thus there is now one standard method and anything else is a special method.

A special method may be used provided the Customs and Excise are satisfied that it will produce a fair and reasonable apportionment.

Planning

It will be apparent from the above that very careful planning is required to avoid the loss of input tax. In certain circumstances it may be possible for a business to be carried on by a separate partnership, as mentioned earlier, or for a group of companies to fragment, to keep below the *de minimis* limits, but the changes to the rules made by SI 1984/155 will make it much more difficult for large groups of companies to shelter significant amounts of exempt income.

7.8 RETAIL SCHEMES

Under the VAT (Supplies by Retailers) Regulations 1972, SI 1972/1148 as amended, retailers are permitted to calculate their output tax by using one of nine special schemes which are set out in detail in Customs and Excise Notice No 727. Given such a wide choice of schemes one may well conclude that the main problem is choosing the right one, although helpful guidance on this is given in Notice No 727 para 22. The difficulty is not as great as it might at first appear. In practice, the choice is narrowed down since some schemes can be used only in certain circumstances.

Scheme A can be used only where all the goods and services are subject to the same rate of VAT. It is the simplest scheme in the sense that it uses daily gross cash takings as the basis for calculating the tax.

Scheme B is designed for a case where there are supplies of goods at two (and two only) different rates of tax (zero counting as a rate), and of services (if any) at the higher of those two rates. Although this scheme involves rather more bookkeeping it may well produce more accurate results.

Scheme C is a simple scheme for very small businesses with an annual turnover of not more than £50,000.

Scheme D is similar to scheme C but for rather bigger businesses with a turnover of up to £125,000, and it is not confined to particular trade classifications as scheme C is.

Scheme F is for use where both standard rated and zero-rated supplies are made.

Scheme G may be used where the turnover is more than £125,000 a year. The trouble with this scheme is that it can lead to an overpayment of tax if used in the wrong circumstances. This is because, to allow for the effect of ignoring the trader's different profit margins on different lines of goods, the output tax has to be increased by a further ⅛th. It is probably best to avoid the scheme if possible.

Schemes E, H and J are likely to be more suitable for larger businesses which have the accounting resources to deal with them.

Planning for retail schemes is mainly a question of choosing the right scheme in the first place, and then ensuring that the schemes are operated correctly. Scheme F in particular, should be monitored carefully because it is based on distinguishing at the point of sale between sales at positive and zero rates. In a crowded shop it is easy to make mistakes. It would be prudent to run checks from time to time by using a scheme D type calculation on the purchases. If there is a significant difference in results between the two methods the matter should be investigated further.

7.9 SECOND-HAND SCHEMES

Under the VAT (Special Provisions) Order 1981, SI 1981/1741 VAT is payable only on the supplier's margin and not on the full sale price in the case of the following types of goods:

(a) works of art, antiques and collector's pieces;
(b) used motor cycles;
(c) used caravans;
(d) used boats and outboard motors;
(e) used electric organs;
(f) used aircrafts;
(g) used firearms.

The VAT (Cars) Order 1980, SI 1980/442 extends similar treatment to used motor cars.

In order to use these schemes the trader must keep records in the form laid down by the Customs and Excise in the relevant Notices or obtain approval from the Customs and Excise to use a system of his own. This is in addition to the usual VAT records. The general requirement is that a stock book is kept containing detailed particulars of purchases and sales. It is up to the dealer to show that he qualifies to use a margin scheme and most of the cases on the subject have been concerned with the question as to whether the dealer's records meet the requirements of the Customs and Excise. In particular, the question may frequently arise as to whether a dealer who has not kept proper records at the time of the transactions can reconstruct the records later to comply with the requirements of the scheme. It is outside the scope of this book to discuss these cases in detail but interested readers may like to refer to *Woodward v Customs and Excise Comrs* LON/77/247; *Callaghan v Customs and Excise Comrs* MAN/77/187; *Mead v Customs and Excise Comrs* CAR/77/344; *Nixon v Customs and Excise Comrs* [1980] VATTR 66; *JH Corbitt (Numismatists) Ltd v Customs and Excise Comrs* [1980] STC 231, HL.

7.10 SELLING ON COMMISSION

A trader who sells goods which he buys from non-registered persons might consider selling the goods on commission instead. VAT will be chargeable on the commission, of course, but there will be no VAT on the selling price.

For example, if the retail price is £115 and the trader takes a commission of £30 plus VAT of £4.50, the supplier receives £80.50. On a purchase and resale basis, the trader pays VAT of £15 on the sale price and to make a profit of £30 he must pay the supplier £70, which is £10.50 less than he would have got by selling on commission.

To achieve these benefits the sale must be on an agency basis and it would be advisable to record this in writing.

INCOME TAX

8 Choice of accounting date

8.1 GENERAL TAX FACTORS

The basis of assessment of trading and professional profits is set out in TA 1970 s 115, and is not repeated here. The effect of the preceding year of assessment set out in s 115 is that it will generally be beneficial to adopt an annual accounting date falling just after 6 April rather than just before that date; 30 April is a date commonly chosen. This is because:

(1) A 30 April year end gives the maximum period between the end of the accounting year and the date on which the tax based on that year is due. This is important for two reasons: in times of inflation the cash flow advantage is significant, but just as important is the fact that more time is allowed to complete the accounts and calculate the liabilities based on them, with the result that the payment of estimated (and possibly excessive) amounts of tax can be avoided. The first instalment of tax based on an accounting period ending on 30 April will be due 20 months after the end of an accounting period, with the assessment being issued within the preceding three or four months. In the case of a 31 March year end the interval is only nine months.

(2) The rules for the opening and closing years of a business at TA 1970, ss 116–118 mean that in the early years one period will form the basis for more than one year of assessment, and in the closing years a period will not fall into the basis period for any year of assessment. If the first trading year of a business runs to 30 April, the first twelve months results will form the basis of thirty-five months assessments; in the case of a 31 March year end only twenty-four months assessment would be based on the first twelve months. Assuming no changes in accounting date, if the business were to be permanently discontinued (either as a result of an actual cessation of trade or a deemed discontinuance under TA 1970

s 154(1)), with the 30 April accounting date twenty-three months profits drop out of the computation, whereas with the 31 March year end only twelve months profits escape assessment. On the not unreasonable assumption that the profits of the business are likely to increase over the years, the 30 April year end is clearly preferable, as it increases the number of years of assessment based on the low profits of the early years, and minimises the assessments based on the higher profits of later years.

(3) In any event, if the trend of profits is rising, the adoption of an account date shortly after 5 April results in a valuable deferment of liability.

EXAMPLE

An unincorporated trader who has been trading for several years is making profits of £1,500 per month at 1 April 1982 and expects profits to grow by 25% over each of the next two years.
The profits assessable for 1984–85 would be:
(1) based on year ended 30 April 1983
£1,500 × 125% = £1,875 × 12   = £22,500

(2) based on year ended 31 March 1984
£1,875 × 125% = £2,344 × 12   = £28,128

8.2 COMMENCEMENT OF TRADING

Whether a trade has commenced and the date of its commencement is a matter of fact, dependent on factors such as when the assets of the trade are first worked, and when the trader first holds himself out as offering goods or services to the customers with whom he intends to trade. The leading case on this point is *Birmingham and District Cattle By-Products Co Ltd v IRC* (1919) 12 TC 92, in which a company was incorporated in June 1913 to carry on a business making use of some of the by-products of the butchers trade. Premises were erected in July and a works manager engaged in August, but the processing of meat products did not commence until October. The commissioner's finding that trading did not commence until October was upheld by Rowlatt J. An interesting feature of the case is that Rowlatt J did not regard any entry in the company's minute book to the effect that business should commence on 6 October as being material to the decision, saying that he wished to 'look at the substance of the matter'.

8.2 Commencement of trading

The point at issue in the *Birmingham and District Cattle By-products* case was not, in fact, relief for pre-trading expenditure, but prior to the enactment of FA 1980 s 39, which is effective from 1 April 1980, such expenditure could not be relieved against profits earned after the commencement of trading. Section 39 is considered in detail at **6.2** above; at this point it is sufficient to draw attention to the fact that s 39 affords a person setting up a trade the opportunity to arrange the date of commencement of trading without regard to any requirement to maximise relief for the expenditure he incurs by beginning to trade at the earliest possible date.

The rules determining the basis periods for the years of assessment in which a trade is first carried on are set out in TA 1970 ss 115 and 116 and are not repeated here. Attention is drawn to s 115(2)(b) which allows the Inland Revenue the choice of basis period for the third year of assessment where the first accounting period is longer than twelve months. In practice inspectors normally choose the twelve months ending on the accounting date which the business intends to adopt in future, but they are not bound to do so. Readers will also be familiar with the right of election set out in s 117 to have the profits of the second and third years of assessment computed by reference to the actual profits of those years and not on the basis prescribed by s 116. The time limit for an election under s 117 is seven years from the end of the second year of assessment (not seven years from the end of the second year of trading).

The principal planning point to be borne in mind on the commencement of a business is that as the results of the first twelve months will form the basis for up to three years of assessment, steps should be taken to keep the profits of the first year as low as possible. Measures useful for achieving this aim include:

(1) Taking the obvious step to ensure that all relevant expenses are included in the first accounts. These include an appropriate part of home expenses where any business is done at home and bad debt provisions where these can be justified (even if the debt is recovered in the next period, the original deduction will have been relieved at least twice).

(2) Where expenditure is incurred on repairs to assets acquired in a dilapidated state for use in the trade, expenditure that can be reasonably regarded as repairs on normal accounting principles should be charged to revenue and not capitalised. The *Law Shipping* case principle (1923) 12 TC 621 has been overtaken by the decision in *Odeon Associated Theatres Ltd v Jones* (1971) 48 TC 257, CA, although *Heather v P-E Consulting Group Ltd* (1972) 48 TC 293, CA has restricted the weight to be given to accounting practice where statute or case law contradict it. The principle to be extracted from

the *Law Shipping* and *Odeon* cases is that where the asset acquired was in a fit state to be used in the business on acquisition, without significant repair work being necessary, subsequent repair expenditure is a deductible expense even if the dilapidation being repaired arose in part before acquisition. Reasonable expenditure on redecoration of newly acquired premises is unlikely to be challenged in any event.

(3) Where a partnership is intending to trade from premises owned by one of the partners which is not partnership property, a rent may be paid up to a limit of what is commercially justifiable. Although the rent will be taxed in the hands of the recipient it will be relieved up to three times in the business; the abolition of the investment income surcharge in FA 1984 makes this course particularly attractive.

(4) Where it is intended to bring family members into the business, it will usually be beneficial to employ them during the first year, rather than taking them into partnership immediately on commencement. If desired they can be brought into partnership at the start of the second accounting period, and the advantage of the up to treble deduction of their wage for the first period preserved by making a continuation election under TA 1970 s 154(2). If this route is followed, the liability to pay Class I National Insurance contributions on employees' wages should not be overlooked, but significant overall tax savings can be achieved.

(5) The financing structure of the business should be considered. Interest paid in the first period will be relieved at least twice over, which may make borrowing more attractive and release the proprietor's own funds for other things. Leasing of plant or vehicles may also help the cash flow of the business as well as the tax position, particularly if a modest degree of front-loading of the finance element can be arranged.

(6) The use of a service company is considered in Chapter 11.

The factors within the control of the trader are:
(a) the date of commencement of trading;
(b) the length of the first accounting period; and
(c) the date of which accounts are to be drawn up in the future.

The determination of each of these factors in practice is a matter for detailed calculation based on the figures applicable to the case under consideration. If profits are expected to show a rising trend, a short initial accounting period ending on a date shortly after the 5 April after commencement, followed by annual accounts to the same date, is likely to lead to the greatest possible deferral of the assessment of profits.

The timing of capital expenditure will affect the year of assessment in which first year allowances arise. The rules in the Capital Allowances Act 1968 s 72 dealing with overlapping basis periods are as follows:

(a) the general rule is that the 'basis period for any year of assessment is the period on the profits or gains of which income tax for that year falls to be finally computed under Case I of Schedule D'; but
(b) where basis periods overlap, expenditure in the common period is treated as incurred in the earlier period; and
(c) expenditure in an interval between two basis periods is treated as incurred in the later period unless that later period is the period of permanent discontinuance of the trade, in which case the expenditure is treated as incurred in the earlier period.

In many cases it will be inevitable that most of the expenditure will have to be incurred early in the first accounting period, and will be relieved only in the first year of assessment against the profits from the date of commencement to the following 5 April. Where commercially possible, it may be beneficial to postpone some expenditure until after the first 5 April following commencement, so that first year allowances are given in the second year of assessment.

The possibility of an election under TA 1970 s 117 should be considered even where such an election is prima facie disadvantageous when trading profits alone are considered. The effect of a s 117 election is generally to bring forward capital allowances into an earlier year at the expense of later years; whether this is to the claimant's benefit depends on the facts of the individual case.

8.3 CESSATION

As with commencement, the date of cessation is a matter of fact. The provisions of TA 1970 s 118 and FA 1971 s 44 (balancing charges and allowances) mean that it is essential that the date of cessation is timed with care. As with commencement the date of cessation is a question of fact. Factors relevant to determining when a trade has ceased include the following:

(1) Where the ordinary pattern of dealing with customers continues, a reduction in the level of activity, even a substantial reduction, does not of itself amount to a cessation: *J & R O'Kane & Co v IRC* (1922) 12 TC 303, HL; *Kirk & Randall Ltd v Dunn* (1924) 8 TC 663.
(2) The formal dissolution of a partnership on a given date does not mean that its trade will be regarded as ceasing on that date if activities associated with winding up the business such as realising

stock or work-in-progress take place subsequently and amount to continued trading: *Hillerns and Fowler v Murray* (1932) 17 TC 77, CA.
(3) A trade may be suspended without being discontinued and revived at a later date without having ceased and recommenced: *JG Ingram & Son Ltd v Callaghan* (1968) 45 TC 151, CA.
(4) The running down of a business to help moving to a new location where the same business will be carried on may not amount to cessation of one trade and the commencement of another: *Robroyston Brickworks Ltd v IRC* [1976] STC 329.
(5) The sale of major trade assets does not necessarily imply cessation of the trade if the business is continued with other assets: *James Shipstone & Sons Ltd v Morris* (1929) 14 TC 413.
(6) On the death of a trader his executors may continue the trade (subject to TA 1970 s 154–see below): *Cohan's Executors v IRC* (1924) 12 TC 602, CA and *Newbarns Syndicate v Hay* (1939) 22 TC 461, CA, but see also *Marshall's Executors, Hood's Executors and Rogers v Joly* (1936) 20 TC 256.

TA 1970 s 154(1) provides that on a change in the persons carrying on a trade, the trade is to be treated as permanently discontinued on the date of change, and a new trade set up. Section 154(2) allows all the persons carrying on the trade before and after the change to elect that the trade should be treated as continuing throughout provided that one person at least carrying on the trade before the change continues to do so after it. The use of this election is discussed at **9.2** below.

It is difficult to extract general principles governing the planning of the timing of cessation, and it will always be necessary to carry out detailed calculations to assess the effect of alternative dates in terms of tax. The following points may be helpful:

(1) Where profits are falling cessation should be arranged just prior to 6 April; where they are arising a cessation early in the next fiscal year may be beneficial.
(2) Where possible a gradual run down of the business over several years will mitigate the effects of TA 1970 s 118.
(3) If the cessation will result under TA 1970 s 154(1) from a sale of the trade, it is possible first to transfer the trade to a company in exchange for shares, and to avoid balancing charges by making an election under FA 1971 Sch 8 para 13. The shares can then be sold to the intending purchaser, converting the income tax liability on balancing charges into a chargeable gain. The purchaser is likely to require some discount on the purchase price to reflect the tax liabilities he is inheriting, but as these liabilities are unlikely to

crystallise if the trade continues the amount of the discount should be modest.

(4) Extra statutory concession A7 provides that TA 1970 s 154(1) is not to be applied where a surviving spouse continues a business carried on by his or her deceased spouse, either alone or in partnership with the surviving spouse.

(5) Under extra statutory concession A20, where a trader reduces the scale of his business to qualify for a National Insurance retirement pension, his assessments will, if it is to his advantage, be computed as if at the time of the reduction in scale his trade had been discontinued and a new one set up.

8.4 CHANGE OF ACCOUNTING DATE

Significant tax savings can be achieved through changes of accounting date, particularly where a change from a date late in the fiscal year to a date early in the year is involved. In some cases a change giving rise to tax benefits may also have commercial advantages; many businesses adopt and retain as an accounting date the anniversary of the commencement of the business, without giving any thought to whether a better date could be chosen.

A change of accounting date disrupts the normal preceding year basis of assessment, and brings into effect TA 1970 s 115(2)(b) and (3) which allows the Board of Inland Revenue to determine what period of twelve months will form the basis period for the year of assessment following the year in which the new accounting date falls and to adjust the preceding year's assessment to correspond with the altered accounting date. The Board have published the practice they adopt on a change of accounting date in leaflet IR 26.

It is impossible to give general rules to determine whether a change of accounting date will be tax effective, and it is necessary to prepare detailed calculations in every case. This will require both up to date accounts and accurate forecasts of profits and capital expenditure.

The following points should be borne in mind:

(1) Extending the accounting period may be beneficial if profits are expected to rise; however it will not usually be beneficial to extend an accounting period from a date early in the fiscal year to a date later in the year.

(2) Shortening the period may be beneficial if profits are falling, particularly where the original accounting date was late in the fiscal year and the new date is earlier in the year.

(3) The practice set out in IR 26 contains *de minimis* limits below which no adjustment to certain years is required. These can have a significant effect on the overall liability.

(4) A change of accounting date may affect the periods in which relief is given for capital allowances, which may in turn affect the rates at which tax is suffered in each fiscal year. It is therefore necessary to carry through the trial computations to consider the total tax bill of the trader; it is not sufficient to consider only the effect on assessable profits.

8.5 NON-TAX FACTORS

The choice of an accounting date cannot always be determined purely by tax considerations. Many traders choose an accounting date at a time of year when stocks are low, to minimise the trouble and expense of stock taking. Where a trade is seasonal and relies on outside finance, it may be desirable to prepare accounts at a time of year when stocks have been converted into cash. In some trades, a particular year end is traditional.

In some cases these factors may dictate an accounting date late in the fiscal year. However, the advantages of preparing accounts to a date early in the tax year can be significant, and in such cases professional advisers should make very sure that it is not mere mental inertia that is preventing a change of accounting date.

9 Partnership changes

9.1 GENERAL RULE

The nature of partnership and the conditions to be satisfied if the existence of a partnership is to be established are touched on at **2.2** above and discussed in some detail at **12.3** below. The purpose of this chapter is to consider the tax consequences of changes of the persons carrying on an established partnership.

TA 1970 s 154(1) provides that where there is a change in the persons carrying on a trade, profession or vocation, assessments to income tax are to be made as if the trade etc had been permanently discontinued at the time of the change and a new trade etc set up and commenced.

9.2 CONTINUATION BASIS ELECTION

The effect of TA 1970 s 154(1) may, however, be nullified by an election under s 154(2) which allows all the persons carrying on the trade etc before and after the change to elect that the trade should not be treated as discontinued and recommenced at the date of the change. Particular attention is drawn to the two year time limit for making an election under s 154(2), which is applied by the Inland Revenue with total inflexibility. The two year time limit is by reference to the date of change, and not the end of the year of assessment in which the change occurs. In a Press Release on 17 January 1973, the Inland Revenue indicated that provisional elections under s 154(2) may be submitted, and withdrawn at any time within the two year time limit by a notice of withdrawal signed by all the partners. In adopting this procedure, due regard should be paid to the interests of individual partners: any one partner can block a s 154(2) election by refusing to sign the original election, but once he has signed he will require the consent of all the partners to withdraw.

9.3 PLANNING OPPORTUNITIES

Planning opportunities arise in connection with TA 1970 s 154 under two main headings:

(a) if a change of partners is inevitable, should a s 154(2) election be made and
(b) should a cessation be engineered using s 154(1) and the introduction or retirement of a partner?

In considering these points it is necessary to have regard to the partnership changes in the event of which a s 154(2) election is not possible, and deemed cessation under s 151(1) is mandatory, and to changes excluded from s 154. These include:

(1) A merger of two different trades into a combined new trade cannot be the subject of a s 154(2) election: *George Humphries & Co v Cook* (1934) 19 TC 121. For the general characteristics of a succession to a trade, see *Malayalam Plantations Ltd v Clark* (1935) 19 TC 314.
(2) Similarly, a split of a partnership into two separate trades precludes a s 154(2) election.
(3) Under s 154(7) a change in the personal representatives or trustees carrying on a trade is not a change for the purposes of s 154(1). The death itself, or the personal representatives or trustees as a body becoming or ceasing to be a partner, do however, trigger s 154(1).
(4) Where a member of a partnership is a company, s 155(3)(b) provides that the entry or departure of a corporate partner does not bring s 154 into effect, presumably to prevent contrived cessation by incorporating 'shell' companies.
(5) Extra statutory concession A7 has been referred to at **8.3** above. Where on the death of one spouse the trade passes to the surviving spouse, the discontinuance provisions will not be applied unless claimed; no s 154(2) election is required. The share of losses or unused capital allowances of the deceased spouse cannot, however, be carried forward.

Should a s 154(2) election be made?

It is impossible to provide a general answer to the question whether a s 154(2) election should be made when a partner retires or a new partner is admitted for commercial and not pure tax planning reasons. As with all elections concerned with basis periods, the answer will depend on the outcome of detailed calculations. Where profits are rising, an election will normally be beneficial. When

carrying out the calculations, the following points should be noted:
(1) The two year time limit for a s 154(2) election will normally allow time for profits for the period of account following the change to be estimated with reasonable accuracy.
(2) The possibility of future partnership changes should be considered.
(3) Where a partnership change takes place part of the way through the firm's normal annual period of account, the possible benefits of a change of accounting date should be considered.
(4) Where there has been a partnership change in respect of which a s 154(2) election has been made, and between that change and the end of the second year of assessment following the fiscal year in which the change occurred there is either a permanent discontinuance of the trade or a further change treated as such under s 154(1), s 154(3)(b) provides that TA 1970 s 118 applies to the discontinuance as though the earlier change had not occurred. This may have the effect of increasing the assessable profits of a partner who retired at the date of the first change when he might have assumed that all the tax consequences of his membership of the firm had been laid to rest.
(5) Whatever basis is adopted, capital expenditure will qualify for allowance once and only once. However, the year in which a particular allowance is due may have a material effect on the rates at which tax is payable. A s 154(2) election is not effective for capital allowances purposes, and the Capital Allowances Act 1968 s 79 provides that where trade assets are transferred by a discontinuing trader to a successor without being sold, the transfer is deemed to take place at market value, but the successor is not entitled to first year allowances. The effect of s 79, which triggers balancing charges without giving a compensating first year allowance, can be avoided if those carrying on the trade before and after the change elect under FA 1971 Sch 8 para 13 (in the case of plant or machinery; the Capital Allowances Act 1968 Sch 7 para 4 applies to other capital allowances) to have the new trade take over the assets at their written down value for capital allowances purposes.

Should a partnership change be engineered?

The purpose of engineering a partnership change would be to use s 154(1) to trigger off the cessation provisions of TA 1970 s 118. Because of the change from the preceding year basis to the actual basis in the year of assessment in which the cessation occurs (and in the penultimate and pre-penultimate years in some cases), the profits of a period of varying length do not form the basis period of any assessment.

9 Partnership changes

In businesses where profits fluctuate materially, the possibility of engineering a cessation by introducing a new partner should be considered at least as the end of each period of account approaches. As with other planning techniques depending on basis periods for assessment, the decision will depend on the outcome of detailed calculations. A pattern of successive years of low, high, high and low profits is likely to provide an opportunity for tax saving if the cessation provisions are applied.

Mergers

Where a partnership change involves the merger to two or more firms, it will be necessary to choose a common accounting date. Factors to be considered in making this choice are considered at **8.1** above and are not repeated here. The optimum accounting date will normally be early in the fiscal year. The question of whether the new date is achieved by the adoption of a short period of account covering the period from the current accounting date to the new date, or by extending an accounting period for more than twelve months will, as usual, depend on the outcome of detailed calculations.

Where one or more of the merged firms has prepared accounts on the cash basis or some other conventional basis, the fact that the Inland Revenue will insist that the accounts of the combined firms should be prepared on the earnings basis will result in the concentration into one year of income earned over a longer period by the firm previously on the cash basis. Cash received after the merger in respect of work done before the merger will be assessed as post cessation receipts under TA 1970 s 144 in the same year as the merged firm is assessed on income actually earned in the year. Extra Statutory Concession A18 provides a measure of relief in this situation by restricting the additional liability due on the post cessation receipts to six times what it would have been if only one sixth of amounts in question had been liable to tax (or to a proportionately higher fraction if the firm has been trading for less than six years) but this is of little help where partners are already paying tax at the top rate. It may be feasible to avoid the assessment of two years' income in one year by merging all the partners except one, and maintaining two firms trading under the same name. The partner who is not a partner in both firms would receive an increased share of profits of the firm of which he is a member; there is scope for achieving equity between the two firms by management or other similar changes.

10 Conventional or earnings basis and post-cessation receipts

10.1 GENERAL PRINCIPLES

TA 1970 s 108 imposes liability to tax under Schedule D on 'profits or gains'. 'Profits' are not defined in the Tax Acts, and have been treated by the courts in the case of trades or professions as being profits determined on the principles of normal commercial accounting, subject to any specific exceptions in statute or case law (*Heather v P-E Consulting Group Ltd* (1972) 48 TC 293, CA). Normal accounting principles indicate that the accruals or earnings basis is the accepted way of determining profits. TA 1970 s 151(2) defines the 'earnings basis' of computing profits as taking account of all credits and liabilities *accruing* during a period. However, in many professions 'conventional' bases of computing profits are found (the term is used in s 151(3) to describe bases other than the earnings basis). The most common alternatives to the earnings basis involve:

(a) considering only cash paid in or out; or
(b) preparing accounts on the earnings basis including debtors but excluding work-in-progress; or
(c) excluding both debtors and work-in-progress.

Significant advantages can arise from the adoption of one or other of these conventional bases where the income of a business is rising either as a result of inflation or through an increase in volume. It is likely that basis (c) above will prove to give the greatest advantage as expenses will be measured on an accruals basis, and so relieved at an early date, whereas income will be assessed only when the cash is actually received.

The conventional bases described above have received judicial approval, notably by the Lord President in *Rankine v IRC* (1952) 32 TC 520 at 527 and in *Wetton, Page & Co v Attwooll* (1962) 40 TC 619 and *McCash and Hunter v IRC* (1955) 36 TC 170.

Nonetheless, except in the case of barristers (who cannot sue for their fees) the Inland Revenue are reluctant to admit claims to change to a conventional basis, and will normally only do so if pressed hard by the claimant. In a press statement issued on 11 November 1969 by the Allied Accountancy Bodies, the Revenue's policy was set out. Those contemplating a change to a conventional basis should read the full statement; the key points are as follows:

(1) The profits of the first three years in which a business is carried on (*not* the first three years of assessment) must be computed on the earnings basis. This requirement applies to the first three years of trading following a deemed commencement under s 154(1) which is not subject to a continuation election under s 154(2) as well as to an actual commencement of trading.
(2) A change to a conventional basis will be accepted 'if the new basis seems likely to provide a reasonable measure of taxpayers' profit'.
(3) Receipts from debtors or work-in-progress already taxed on the earnings basis will be taxed again when the cash is received in the first period assessed on the conventional basis. This principle was established in *IRC v Morrison* (1932) 17 TC 325.
(4) The taxpayer is required to give a written undertaking that he will issue bills for work done at regular and frequent intervals, at least quarterly.
(5) A later change back to the earnings basis will be allowed, but a subsequent claim to revert to a conventional basis will be resisted.

In the authors' experience the main stumbling block in the way of persuading inspectors to accept a change to a conventional basis lies in establishing that the new basis is likely to provide a reasonable measure of the taxpayer's profit. It is in cases where the advantage of a conventional basis are most marked that the greatest difficulty is likely to be encountered. In practice it is only in the case of professional partnerships that the Revenue are likely to accept the use of a conventional basis.

10.2 POST-CESSATION RECEIPTS

A detailed examination of the post-cessation receipts legislation at TA 1970 ss 143–151 is outside the scope of the book. The intention of this section is to draw attention to the liabilities imposed by the post cessation receipts legislation, to the relationship of the legislation with the provision of TA 1970 ss 137 and 138 and to make tax planning suggestions.

10.2 Post-cessation receipts

TA 1970 s 137 (trading stock) and s 138 (professional work-in-progress) provide that when a trade or profession is discontinued (either on an actual cessation or a deemed discontinuance under s 154(1)), if the stock or work-in-progress is sold to a person who carries on or intends to carry on a trade and who is entitled to deduct the cost in computing his profits the value of the stock etc in the final accounts of the discontinuing trader shall be the amount he receives for it from the purchaser. In any other case the value to be included in the final accounts is the amount which would have been realised on an arm's length open market sale, except that in the case of professional work-in-progress the taxpayer may elect under s 138(3) that any excess of the value of the work-in-progress over its cost shall not be brought into the final accounts but shall be assessed under s 143 as a post-cessation receipt.

TA 1970 s 143 deals with receipts arising after the permanent discontinuance of a business whose profits have been computed on an earnings basis which have not been taken into account prior to the discontinuance, and with receipts of a business whose profits have been computed on a conventional basis which do not fall due until after the discontinuance. Section 144 is restricted to trades or professions the profits of which are computed on a conventional basis, and taxes amounts not otherwise chargeable to tax which are not brought into account in computing profits:

(a) on a discontinuance of the trade or profession; or
(b) on a charge of basis from earnings to a conventional basis, or a change of conventional bases, which has resulted in receipts dropping out of computation.

Section 146 provides that ss 143 and 144 apply to a deemed discontinuance under s 154(1) resulting from a change in the persons carrying on a trade as well as to an actual discontinuance. However, where the discontinuance is only as a result of the application of s 154(1), s 147(2) provides that if the successor partnership has the right to receive any amounts chargeable under ss 143 or 144, those amounts are charged to tax in the hands of the successor partnership when they are received and are not treated as post-cessation receipts.

In computing amounts chargeable under ss 143 and 144, s 145(1) provides that the taxpayer may deduct:

(a) any expenses which could have been deducted if the trade had continued; and
(b) any capital allowances to which he was entitled immediately before the discontinuance and which have not been otherwise relieved.

10 Conventional or earnings basis and post-cessation receipts

Section 149 allows a taxpayer to elect to have a post-cessation receipt included in the final accounts to the date of discontinuance rather than being assessed as a post-cessation receipt.

Particular attention is drawn to the following:

(1) In the case of a deemed discontinuance caused by a change in the persons carrying on a partnership, it will often be tax effective to arrange that the successor firm is not entitled to post-cessation receipts of the old firm, which are then assessable under ss 143 or 144. In that way the successor firm will not include the receipts in its accounts for its first year of trading, which will form the basis of assessment for its first three years.

(2) Many professional partnership assessed on an earnings basis value work-in-progress at a figure considerably below what will ultimately be received when the work is completed, often restricting the valuation to direct staff time at cost. The vendors of such a practice could, instead of transferring work-in-progress to the purchasers, arrange for the purchasers to complete the work for a fair proportion of the total fee calculated on the basis of work done before and after the sale of the practice. In this way the vendors will receive substantial sums representing the fees attributable to work done before the sale. It can be argued that provided the work-in-progress is brought in to the final accounts at its (low) market value the excess sums received are not caught by s 143 as that section refers to sums insofar as their *value* was not brought into account and the *value* of the work-in-progress *was* brought into account in the final accounts.

(3) Where there are unused losses at the date of discontinuance it will normally be desirable to make an election under s 149 to carry back post-cessation receipts and have them assessed as though they were received on the last day of trading. Note, however, that a s 149 election precludes relief under s 145 for subsequent losses.

(4) It appears that where the right to receive post-cessation payments is given away there can be no charge under ss 143 or 144 (although there would clearly be CTT consequences). Although ss 143 and 144 are silent on this point, s 147 would be redundant if ss 143 and 144 imposed a general liability on the transferor or transferee.

(5) The principle in *IRC v Morrison* (1932) 17 TC 325, mentioned above, which involves the double taxation of receipts from the realisation of work-in-progress and debtors on hand at the end of the last period the profits of which were calculated on the earnings basis implies that when a change to a conventional basis is contemplated, all possible steps should be taken to realise debtors and work-in-progress as cash before the end of the period of account.

11 Partnership service companies

11.1 INTRODUCTION

Many professional partnerships cannot incorporate their businesses because of the rules of the professional bodies of which they are members. In profitable practices partners will be liable to tax at a top rate of 60% whether their profits are withdrawn or reinvested in the business, and cannot take advantage of the relatively low rates of tax on company profits compared with a partnership earning a similar amount. In the authors' view the main benefit of a service company is to allow a firm to accumulate working capital: except in the opening years of a partnership (see below) the tax savings can only be achieved by leaving funds in the company with the result that the partners have to forgo spendable income. It is self-evident that if funds are withdrawn from the service company they will be taxed as income (directors' remuneration or dividends) which will defeat the tax saving objective. The alternative of liquidating the company and receiving funds taxed only at CGT rates does not commend itself as a solution capable of being repeated on a regular basis.

11.2 SETTING UP THE COMPANY

The service company will normally employ the staff, provide services such as telephones, mail handling and stationery and will usually but not necesssarily provide the accommodation used by the partnership. It may also be possible for the service company to factor debts invoiced by the partnership, charging a commercial interest rate and handling fee. In many cases a partnership will carry on activities which are not strictly of a professional nature, and these activities can also be transferred to the company.

The following points should be borne in mind when setting up a service company:

(1) The timing of commencement of trading by the company should be arranged to maximise the beneficial effect on the firm's tax assessment (see below).

(2) The partners and the company will be connected persons within the definition at CGTA 1979 s 63. The transfer of premises (freehold or leasehold) may involve the partners in CGT liability by reference to the market value of the premises at the time of transfer, although this liability can be deferred by making an election under CGTA 1979 s 126 (gifts of business assets).

(3) The transfer of chargeable assets to the company involves a potential double charge to CGT on the eventual disposal of the assets, as explained at **2.3** above. Even if the company intends to acquire further business premises, an immediate charge to tax will arise on any gain made by the company: CGTA 1979 s 119(2)(b) will generally preclude the granting of roll-over relief.

(4) Apart from the potential double charge to tax referred to above, there is a CTT advantage in leaving the partnership premises in the ownership of the partnership rather than the company. Partnership property attracts business property relief at 50%, whereas the minority holding each partner has in the service company will attract relief only at 30%.

(5) Staff will have to be transferred to the service company, and so will need new contracts of employment. Pension scheme arrangements may also need to be revised.

(6) The transfer of cars, fixtures and fittings will be at their written down values at the date of transfer.

(7) Where the partnership has an accounting date early in the tax year, payment of tax on the fee paid to the service company will be materially accelerated compared with the position if the fee had been retained in the firm. The nine month interval between the end of the company's accounting period and the due date for payment of corporation tax compares unfavourably with the interval likely to be available to the firm.

11.3 PROFIT UPLIFT

Apart from any income which the company may be able to generate on its own account through trading activities ancillary to the main partnership business, the service company will only have taxable profits if it makes a charge to the partnership for the services it provides in excess of the cost to it of providing those services. The advantage is compounded where the opening rules of assessment at

11.4 Holding the service company shares

TA 1970 s 116 apply following the actual commencement of trading or a deemed commencement following a cessation under s 154(1). In that case the benefit of the company's profit uplift is felt in the income tax computations for up to three years of assessment, but the corresponding amount is taxed only once in the hands of the company. In this context it should be noted that the case of *Stephenson v Payne Stone Fraser & Co* (1967) 44 TC 507 (discussed below) set a limit in principle on the amount of the profit uplift, but did not find the scheme as a whole to be ineffective.

If the profit uplift is excessive, the fee paid by the partnership cannot be said to be laid out wholly and exclusively for the purposes of the firm's trade within TA 1970 s 130(a), and the excess is liable to be disallowed in the firm's computation whilst being taxed on the company. *Stephenson v Payne, Stone, Fraser & Co* (1967) 44 TC 507 is often used by the Revenue to argue against anything more than a nominal uplift but it can be argued that the *Stephenson* case involved a blatant attempt to exploit the opening years of assessment rules and that there was no consistency in the principles applied in arriving at the amounts charged by the company in each of the two years with which the case was concerned. In the end the matter must be resolved by negotiation, in the course of which the criterion to be borne in mind is what the Appeal Commissioners are likely to consider reasonable and commercially justifiable for the work done, the risks taken and the capital employed. In the end the uplift is likely to fall in the range of between 5% and 15%. In some cases it may be possible to demonstrate a market price for the provision of similar services.

Where it may be intended to try to take advantage of the rules for assessment in the opening years of a business, perhaps following a deemed cessation under TA 1970 s 154(1) on a change of partners, it would probably help the success of the scheme if the service company were to be set up a year or two before the change so that a pattern of payments could be established. Once the principle of a reasonable uplift had been established Revenue would find it more difficult to argue that a consistently applied uplift had suddenly become excessive only because of a change in the persons carrying on the partnership business.

11.4 HOLDING THE SERVICE COMPANY SHARES

The question here is whether the shares should be held as partnership property or by the individual partners. If the shares are partnership property they will qualify for business property relief at

76 11 Partnership service companies

the 50% rate (FA 1976 Sch 10 para 3(1)(a)) whereas the minority holding which each partner would own directly would qualify only at the 30% rate (para 3(1)(bb)). On a change in the membership or profit sharing ratios of the firm, any resulting change in the partners' interest in service company shares held as a partnership asset would be covered by the Inland Revenue Press Statement of 17 January 1975 and would not normally give rise to an immediate CGT liability, whereas changing the relative shareholdings of partners who hold shares as individuals would inevitably lead to disposals for CGT.

Despite the tax benefits of holding the shares as partnership property, there will sometimes be sound non-fiscal reasons why shares should be held by individual partners. If, for instance, the company owns valuable property it may be desirable for an incoming partner to be able to defer acquiring shares in the company until some time after he has joined the partnership, so as to reduce the amount of capital he needs to raise on his joining the firm.

Because in practice the shares in the company will be held by partners who are 'associates' within TA 1970 s 303(3)(a), the service company will almost certainly be close and so subject to apportionment of income under FA 1972 Sch 16. If the company's only activity is the trade of providing services, it is likely that the exclusion of trading income of a trading company from liability to apportionment by FA 1980 s 44 and Sch 9 will eliminate any liability to apportionment. Where, however, significant amounts of rental or other investment income are received, it will be necessary to demonstrate that this income cannot be distributed without prejudice to the requirements of the company's business.

11.5 CESSATION AND LIQUIDATION

On a cessation of the partnership trade, the amount paid to the company for one period of account will not, as a result of the operation of TA 1970 s 118, give rise to a deduction in the firm's accounts although it will still be taxed in the hands of the company. It is of course inevitable that some expenses (and the corresponding income) of the firm will drop out of assessment: what is at issue is the element of uplift. If cessation is anticipated the service company fee can be reduced to the cost of providing the services, in which case the firm will be no worse off than if it had incurred the expenses itself. Notwithstanding cases such as *Sharkey v Wernher* (1955) 36 TC 275, HL and *Petrotim Securities Ltd v Ayres* (1963) 41 TC 389 which allow the Revenue to substitute market value in certain circumstances, it is unlikely that the Revenue could insist on the service company making a profit.

There is another reason why the service company should not make a profit during the period preceding its liquidation. When a close company ceases to trade or goes into liquidation, the whole of its distributable income for the accounting period in which the cessation or liquidation occurs and for any account period ending within 12 months of that event is liable to be apportioned (FA 1970 Sch 16 para 13). The distributable income of a trading company excludes its trading income, but the principle will apply where the service company has significant investment income.

If, on liquidation of the service company, assets are distributed in specie to the partners/shareholders, the distributions will be deemed to have taken place at the market value of the assets concerned. When considering the resulting CGT liabilities it is important not to overlook the existence of valuable assets which may not appear in the balance sheet of the company, for instance the benefit of a lease at a low rent.

12 Sharing Profits with the Proprietor's Family

12.1 WHY SHARE PROFITS?

The proprietor of a successful unincorporated business is likely to suffer income tax at high rates. The position has been made worse by the changes introduced in the 1984 Budget as a result of which first year allowances are to be phased out by 1 April 1986. There is a reduction in the rates of corporation tax intended to compensate for this reduction in capital allowances, but the unincorporated trader does not benefit from any reduction in the rates of tax which he pays. One way in which such a trader may be able to reduce the impact of high rates of tax on his income while retaining the benefit of the income within the family unit is to share profits with his family by paying wages or taking one or more of the family into partnership. If the recipient of the income is the proprietor's spouse, the existence of the wife's earned income relief will afford some benefit and the overall effective rate of tax can be reduced by an election for separate taxation of wife's earnings in appropriate cases. Other members of the family will have their individual personal allowances and progressive rates of tax.

The savings achieved by spreading income round the family can be very significant; taking that route is also much less liable to attack by the Inland Revenue than are some other tax saving schemes.

EXAMPLE

X, who is married with two teenaged children carries on an estate agency business; profits for the year to 31 March 1984 are expected to be £40,000. If X were to continue as a sole trader, he would pay on his 1984–85 assessment

Tax £19,254.75
Class 4 NIC 570.15
£19,824.90

an effective rate of tax of 49.56%. If, however, on 1 April 1983 he had
(1) taken his wife into partnership, sharing profits equally,
(2) begun to pay his children £30 per week each for part-time assistance such as delivering advertising material,
the position would have been:

	Self	Wife	Children
Trading income 1984–85	£18,500	£18,500	
Earnings 1983–84			£3,000
Personal allowances	1,785	1,785	3,570
Taxable income	£16,715	£16,715	Nil
Tax thereon	5,146.00	£ 5,146.00	
Class 4 NIC	570.15	570.15	
	£ 5,716.15	£ 5,716.15	
	£11,432.30		

an effective tax rate of 28.58% and an absolute saving of £8,392.60.

12.2 PAYMENT OF WAGES

This is the simplest way of transferring profits to members of the family, provided that the amount paid can be fairly related to the value to the business of the work done. The Revenue's right to challenge the payment of excessive remuneration is founded on *Copeman v William Flood & Sons Ltd* (1940) 24 TC 53; the implications of this case are discussed at **17.2** below under the heading 'Paying the proprietor's family'.

In determining tax-effective levels of remuneration, the liability to account for Class I National Insurance contributions should not be overlooked. The tax-effective level of wages for each period will have to be determined by calculation: the principle involved is that the tax saving to the payer should at least equal the tax and National Insurance contribution of the recipient and the employer's National Insurance contribution.

12.3 PARTNERSHIP

Taking into partnership a member of the family can be a tax-effective measure, but it is not a step to be undertaken without considering the non-tax consequences. The strengths (or weaknesses) of the underlying relationships should be borne in mind, and the partnership agreement drafted to ensure that matters such as entitlement to draw on the firm's bank account are framed appropriately. The rights and duties of partners both *inter se* and in relation to persons outside the partnership are considered at **2.2** above; it is sufficient at this point to draw attention to the fact that, in relation to acts done by partners in the ordinary course of business of the firm, each partner is effectively jointly and severally liable to the full extent of his assets for any resulting debts and obligations. The lack of actual authority on the part of any partner eg to make a contract is no defence against the claims of outsiders if the partner who made the contract apparently had the authority to do so. Anyone proposing to enter into a partnership purely for tax saving reasons should weigh the commercial risks against the tax they expect to save.

The general nature of partnership and its merits and shortcomings as a business structure are considered at **2.2** above. This section is concerned with the use of a partnership to spread income throughout a family group, often in circumstances where but for the tax savings no partnership arrangement would in fact be contemplated. In such cases it is particularly important to ensure that as many as possible of the indicia of partnership feature in the arrangement being set up.

The partnership agreement

The Inland Revenue can resist the allocation of a share of profits to a partner only if they can establish that the person receiving the profit share was not in fact a partner. Partnership is defined in the Partnership Act 1890 s 1 as 'the relation that subsists between persons carrying on a business in common with a view of profit'. Whether that relationship exists is a matter of fact, and cannot be affected by the existence or otherwise of a written agreement where the facts contradict the legal form: *Dickension v Gross* (1927) 11 TC 614; *IRC v Williamson* (1928) 14 TC 335. That is not to say that it is not important to have a written partnership agreement: apart from the non-fiscal advantage that a written agreement means that all the partners have a document setting out their rights and duties to which they can refer, such an agreement is an important piece of evidence that a partnership exists. What an agreement cannot do, however, is to override the facts. In *Dickenson v Gross* a partnership agreement between a father and his sons was properly drawn up but was never acted upon, in that the bank mandate was never varied to allow all the alleged partners to sign cheques (as they were entitled to do under the partnership agreement) and the father alone retained the power to draw on the bank account; no annual accounts had been prepared (another requirement of the partnership agreement); and there was no evidence of any distribution of profits. The commissioners' decision that no partnership existed in fact was upheld in the High Court. In *Waddington v O'Callaghan* (1931) 16 TC 187 a solicitor wished to take his son in partnership and made an oral declaration to his son on 31 December that he was to be a partner from 1 January. On 1 January another firm of solicitors were instructed to prepare a partnership agreement, which was finally executed on 11 May, purportedly with retrospective effect to 1 January. The son's share of profits was credited to him from 1 January, but letters were signed 'JC Waddington' until 11 May and 'Waddington and Sons' thereafter. It was clear from the correspondence that the terms on which the son entered into the partnership were not settled until they were set out in the agreement. The High court held that any partnership could only be in contemplation until the terms were agreed and acted upon, and refused to disturb the commissioners' finding that the partnership commenced on 11 May.

TA 1970 s 26 is the statutory basis for the assessment of partnership profits, and it contains no provision allowing the Revenue to allocate the assessable profits to partners in any way other than that provided in the partnership agreement. The agreement should be drafted to allow flexibility in determining tax effective sharing of profits; the allocation of profits in the accounts will then be conclusive. From a tax point of view, profits should be allocated so that available personal allowances for the period under consideration are fully utilised, and that the impact of higher rates of tax is minimised taking the firm as a whole. For commercial reason this may not, however, always be possible.

Other important factors

The central question to be answered when establishing if a partnership exists is whether the alleged partner is carrying on a business in common with the other persons involved. This implies participation in the essential decision making and management of the business rather than the mere carrying out of tasks on instructions from the proprietor. The amount of time devoted exclusively to the

12 Sharing profits with the proprietor's family

business of the firm is largely irrelevant. What does matter is the capacity of the alleged partner to take part in the running of the business: immaturity of an alleged partner is likely to be fatal to the taxpayer's argument: *Alexander Bullock & Co v IRC* [1976] STC 514. Accordingly, it will usually be easier to establish that one spouse has taken the other into partnership than to prove the existence of a partnership which includes children, particularly if those children are minors and so in a position to avoid the consequences of partnership. The most successful strategy for spreading income round the family unit is likely to involve the payment of wages where minor children are concerned, rather than bringing them into a family partnership. The time at which children are brought into the partnership should not precede the time at which they can be seen clearly to have the capacity to be involved in and contribute to the central decision making of the business.

The Revenue will normally seek to test the existence of a partnership by reference to the following criteria:

(1) How are profits shared, and who is responsible for losses? The Partnership Act 1890 s 2(3) provides that 'the receipt by a person of a share of profits is prima facie evidence that he is a partner in the business' (subject to certain exceptions). Evidence of liability to share in losses is particularly persuasive in establishing that a partnership exists.
(2) In whose name does the bank account stand, and who may draw on it?
(3) Whose names appear as the proprietors of the business under the provisions of the Companies Act 1981 s 29?
(4) Are creditors aware that a partnership exists?
(5) What is the title of each individual to the assets of the business?
(6) Who can dissolve the partnership (but note that the absence of this right is not conclusive against an alleged partner: *Stekel v Ellice* [1973] 1 All ER 465?
(7) What capital has each individual contributed?
(8) Has the alleged partner the right of access to the firm's books?
(9) Can he bind the firm or pledge its credit?

Apart from the question of profit sharing, none of these points is likely to be conclusive alone, but those seeking to establish family partnerships for reasons of tax mitigation (where the commercial pointers to partnership may be less strong than would be the case with a partnership formed only for business reasons) should ensure that as many as possible of the criteria are met.

Is a partnership a settlement?

TA 1970 ss 441(2) and 454(3) define 'settlement' as including 'any disposition, trust, covenant, agreement, arrangement or transfer of assets'. Prima facie a family partnership arrangement would fall within this definition, but case law (notably *Bulmer v IRC* (1966) 44 TC 1) has established that an arrangement will not amount to a settlement if it was entered into for bona fide commercial reasons and is without any element of bounty.

In the authors' view any partnership which in fact involves members of a family in carrying on a business in common, applying the indicia set out above, is likely to be a bona fide commercial arrangement under which the partners contribute to the running of the business in return for a share in the profits. Where, however, the Inland Revenue can establish on the facts that the persons involved are not carrying on a business in common, the fact that, for instance, a husband has given his wife or minor children an interest in income which was previously his alone would make it possible for the Revenue to treat him as a settlor (TA 1970 ss 444(2), 454(3)) and to tax all the income as his.

13 Loss relief

13.1 STATUTORY PROVISIONS

This section is concerned with planning how best to obtain relief for the trading losses of an unincorporated business, using the statutory provisions set out below with the time limits within which the claims for relief must be made.

TA 1970 s 168	Relief against general income of a year of assessment for any loss sustained in that year or the preceding year.	Two years from the end of the year of assessment in which the loss arises.
TA 1970 s 169	A loss for relief under s 168 may be augmented or created by capital allowances due for the year of assessment for which the year of loss is the basis year.	Included in s 168 claim.
TA 1970 s 171	Carry forward of losses not otherwise relieved.	(1) Amount of loss for future relief to be claimed within six years of the end of the year of assessment in which the loss arises. (2) Relief against the profits of a future year of assessment to be

13.1 Statutory provisions

TA 1970 s 171 (*continued*)		claimed within six years of the end of that later year. A formal claim is not normally required where the losses are shown in tax computations.
FA 1978 s 30	Relief for losses arising in the first four years of assessment in which a trade is carried on against income of the preceding three years of assessment. The losses may be augmented or created by the addition of capital allowances and stock relief.	Two years from the end of the year of assessment in which the loss arises.
TA 1970 s 174	Relief for losses sustained in the twelve months before the discontinuance of a trade against profits of the three years of assessment preceding that in which the discontinuance occurs.	Six years from the end of the year of assessment in which discontinuance occurs (TMA 1970 s 43(1)).
FA 1980 s 39	Pre-trading expenditure treated as a loss arising in the year in which the trade commences. See **6.2** above.	Six years from the end of the year of assessment in which the trade commences.
TA 1970 s 172	Losses of a trade transferred to a company offset against the income of the transferors from the company.	As for s 171 above.

13 Loss relief

Attention is also drawn to anti-avoidance legislation relating to losses:

TA 1970 s 170 — Denial of relief under s 168 for non-commercial losses.

TA 1970 s 180 — Denial of relief under s 168 for losses incurred in a trade of farming or market gardening if losses in the trade were also incurred in each of the five preceding years of assessment.

FA 1976 s 41 — Denial of relief under s 169 for first year allowances arising as a result of any scheme or arrangement the sole or main benefit of which was expected to be a tax saving.

FA 1980 ss 70, 72(3) — Denial of relief for capital allowances under s 169 where the allowances are in respect of machinery or plant used in a leasing trade carried on by an individual, unless the individual carries on the trade full-time.

The intention of this section is not to review the fundamentals of these provisions, but to draw attention to points of interest and to consider how the various reliefs may best be combined.

13.2 STRATEGY

The loss relief provisions should be used to obtain relief as soon as possible, within the overall constraint of maximising the total effective relief. Losses should generally be set off in the following order:

(a) against income already assessed, throwing back the losses as far as possible to maximise repayment supplement and to keep the options open for later years;
(b) to reduce income assessed for which the tax is not yet due;
(c) to reduce known income not yet assessed; and
(d) by way of carry forward against unquantified future income.

The order of reliefs set out above will generally mean that losses are first claimed under FA 1978 s 30, and then under TA 1970 ss 168 and 169, with any balance being carried forward under s 171. The recent case of *Butt v Haxby* [1983] STC 239 was concerned with the relationship between TA 1970 s 168 and FA 1978 s 30. It establishes that a taxpayer may choose between a claim under s 168 and a claim under s 30, but that once one relief or the other is claimed effect must be given to the claim up to the full extent of the claimant's income; it is not open to a claimant to split a loss and to claim part under s 168 and part under s 30. If, however, the loss available for relief exceeds an amount that can be relieved under either of the provisions alone, the claimant can specify which relief is to be given priority.

The order of set off above may also have to be varied to maximise the overall relief because the rate of tax at which relief is given (varying from 0% where income is covered by allowances to a maximum 60%) can have a material effect on the value of the relief in money terms.

The interaction of loss relief with a host of other reliefs creates many possible alternatives, each of which has to be evaluated. The expiry of time limits for claims and elections may pose practical problems.

Each situation has to be considered on its own facts. It is not possible to lay down useful general principles of income tax loss planning; the remainder of this section sets out hints relevant to particular circumstances.

Personal allowances

Relief for losses cannot be claimed in part: whether the relief is against total income under TA 1970 s 168 or FA 1978 s 30 or losses brought forward against trading income under TA 1970 s 171, losses must be offset up to the full extent of the income without regard to the fact that the income may be covered wholly or in part by personal allowances. Any loss set against income covered by allowances is effectively relieved at 0%, a situation to be avoided if possible.

In the case of relief against total income, loss of personal allowances can be mitigated by TA 1970 s 168(3) (extended to relief under FA 1978 s 30 by s 30(7)) which allows a claimant to specify in the claim for relief that the loss should be set only against the income of the person sustaining the loss, without extending to the income of that person's spouse.

Retirement annuity relief

TA 1970 s 227(1A) as amended by FA 1980 s 31 allows relief for qualifying retirement annuity premiums up to a maximum of $17\frac{1}{2}\%$ of net relevant earnings for the year of assessment. Net relevant earnings as defined in TA 1970 s 227(5) are determined after the deduction of losses brought forward. The effect on retirement annuity relief of alternative claims for loss relief against current total income or against future trading profits should be considered.

Interaction with other claims and elections

Many different claims and elections may affect the ability to set off losses to advantage:

(1) In the case of wife's earning elections the set-off of losses can remove the reason for the election. If an election has been made, the set-off of losses can be frustrated if the income of the spouse sustaining the loss is not sufficient to absorb the loss. The time limit for revoking the election will often have passed by the time relief under FA 1978 s 30 is claimed.

(2) An election under TA 1970 s 117 in respect of the second and third years of assessment in which a trade is carried on will affect the amount of loss relieved by aggregation: *IRC v Scott Adamson* (1932) 17 TC 679;

(3) FA 1978 s 28 provides relief for fluctuating profits of farmers and market gardeners (see **36.1** below). In computing the average profits, a loss is treated as a nil profit. No part of the loss is relieved by aggregation under s 28, and s 28(5)(a) allows full relief for any loss. The decision to average may, however, affect the rate of tax at which the loss is relieved.

(4) The possibility of a partial claim for first year allowances is considered at **4.5**.

Timing

The year of assessment in which losses arise and are relieved will often have a material effect on the amount of tax saved. It can be vitally important to have a loss in one period rather than another.

A trader is unlikely to have much control over the timing of revenues, but he will be abe to time his expenditure. Scope for the timing of expense items will be limited, but capital expenditure can often be planned. For a discussion of how this may be done see **4.2**.

The timing of loss relief can also be affected by the date to which accounts are drawn up. Where there is a permanent change of accounting date the Board of Inland Revenue have the power to determine the basis of assessment under TA 1970 s 115(2)(b). Although the Board's practice on a change of accounting date where there are assessable profits is well publicised, the Revenue retain total discretion where losses are concerned and it may be possible to negotiate increased relief.

Cessation, actual or contrived, may also have a part to play in loss planning. After the first three years of assessment in which a trade is carried on, the Inland Revenue will normally accept claims under TA 1970 s 168 on an accounts year basis rather than the strict fiscal year basis. On cessation, the Revenue's practice is not to withdraw relief given previously when making adjustments to the penultimate and pre-penultimate years under TA 1970 s 118(1)(b).

Summary

The object of loss planning should be to obtain the greatest possible relief in terms of tax. Except in the most straightforward cases planning will be complicated by the variety of reliefs available, personal allowances, the interaction of loss reliefs with other claims and elections and availability of repayment supplement. Until a satisfactory computer program capable of resolving these variables is available, voluminous calculations will be a feature of most loss planning exercises.

CORPORATION TAX

14 Incorporation

14.1 TIMING OF INCORPORATION

The transfer of an unincorporated trade to a company necessarily involves the cessation of the trade, so triggering the provisions of TA 1970 s 118 (see **8.13** above). Where trading profits are increasing, this may lead to additional assessments being raised under s 118(1)(b) for the penultimate and ante-penultimate years of assessment.

Where the possibility of incorporation is envisaged from the start, it may be possible to make use of parallel trading operations carried on by a company and a partnership (see **2.14** above). Otherwise, the timing of incorporation will be a fine decision depending on the figures of the case in question. It will generally be advantageous to defer incorporation so as to avoid having the first three years of assessment of unincorporated trading re-assessed on an actual basis rather than under the favourable opening year rules of TA 1970 s 115 (see **8.12** above). How long this deferral needs to be depends on the figures: it may be as little as three years if the results mean that s 118(1)(b) will not be relevant on a cessation, or up to six years where s 118(1)(b) is relevant.

For reasons set out at **2.4** above it will not generally be advantageous to incorporate a family business unless substantial profits are being earned and retained in the business. Even in a case where profits are being generated, there may be unrelieved losses available to the proprietors of the business which is to be incorporated. That fact alone need not be a cause for deferral of incorporation: TA 1970 s 172 allows such losses (and unrelieved trade charges) to be carried forward against income which the person entitled to the losses derives from the company. Relief under s 172 does not, however, extend to unused capital allowances or stock relief. If additional assessments are made under TA 1970 s 118(1)(b), an election for separate taxation of wife's earnings in one of the years involved may become beneficial. Unfortunately, the time limit for making such an election is twelve months after the end of the relevant year of assessment. Where s 118(1)(b) assessments are made it may be necessary to rely on the discretion of the Board of Inland Revenue to extend this time limit. The Board's sympathy for such an approach is likely to depend to a large extent on the speedy submission of the relevant claims and final accounts.

14.2 TRANSFER OF BUSINESS TO A COMPANY

The transfer of an unincorporated business to a company means that, because the company is a legal person separate from its owners, there must necessarily be a disposal of the business and assets transferred. If it were not for relieving provisions in the CGT and capital allowances legislation, chargeable gains and balancing charges would necessarily arise on the disposal by reference to the difference between cost or written down values of the assets transferred and their market value at the time they are transferred.

CGTA 1979 s 123

This is the legislative provision specifically designed to facilitate the transfer of a business to a company. It applies:

'where a person who is not a company transfers to a company a business as a going concern together with the whole of the assets of the business or the whole of those assets other than cash, and the business is so transferred wholly or partly in exchange for shares issued by the company to the person transferring the business' (CGTA 1979 s 123(1)).

Where the conditions are met, the chargeable gains arising on the transfer are rolled over against the cost of the shares in the transferee company, but:

(1) The amount rolled over cannot exceed the cost of the shares. Thus if a valuable chargeable asset is transferred, giving rise to a substantial gain, but the net value of the assets transferred is small because the company also assumes heavy liabilities, the amount of the gain rolled over into the shares will be restricted to the net value of the assets transferred.
(2) Where the consideration for the transfer is not wholly shares (eg where the company gives both shares and cash for the assets) the

rolled over gain is restricted to the fraction of the gain represented by:

$$\text{chargeable gain} \times \frac{\text{market value of shares issued}}{\text{value of whole consideration given for the transfer.}}$$

A number of points arising out of this legislation are worth particular consideration:

(1) Section 123(1) stipulates that the whole of the assets of the business, or the whole of the assets other than cash, must be transferred to the company if the relief is to be available.

(a) It will usually be sensible not to transfer cash. If the cash is transferred it can only be withdrawn at the cost of a tax charge (ie as remuneration, dividends or a loan to a participator). If, on the other hand, it is retained outside the company at the time of transfer, it can always be lent to the company afterwards if necessary. Indeed, it may be worthwhile to ensure that at the time of the transfer the business is as liquid as possible (by accelerating invoicing and debt collecting and deferring payments to creditors) to maximise the amount of cash available for retention. The legislation does not prohibit the transferor obtaining cash by borrowing on the business account to repay the balance on his capital account and transferring the liability to the company (but it is then necessary to ensure that roll-over is not restricted through an insufficiency of net assets as described above).

(b) The possibility that goodwill exists as a chargeable asset should not be overlooked.

(c) For reasons explained at **2.3** above, appreciating assets should not generally be transferred to a company because of the double charge to tax faced by a shareholder who wishes to get his hands on the proceeds of a subsequent sale of such an asset. It may be possible to avoid transferring a particular asset to the company by first transferring it out of the business, eg to a spouse who does not share in the ownership of the business. Such a course may, however, be perceived by the Inland Revenue as an abuse of the relief and be challenged under the new approach to tax avoidance outlined at **1.3** above.

(d) Capital duty is payable on the value of the shares issued as consideration for the assets acquired. Stamp duty is payable on land and debtors transferred to the company by reference to their market value.

(2) The transfer of land with development value can have major tax consequences quite apart from the general proposition that appreciating assets should not be transferred to a company. DLT is chargeable whenever development value is realised on disposal of

14.2 Transfer of business to a company

land or buildings (see Chapter 28 for a discussion of DLT planning in the context of a family business). The DLT legislation contains no roll-over relief equivalent to CGTA 1979 s 123. Accordingly, a transferor wishing to transfer land with development value to a company in order to obtain the benefit of s 123 will crystallise a DLT charge on the transfer. Under DLTA 1976 Sch 8 para 52 some or all of the resulting DLT liability may be deferred for up to eight years. The Board of Inland Revenue (or, on appeal, the Special Commissioners) decide how much DLT it is just and reasonable to defer, taking into account the proportion of the consideration for the transfer which comprises shares. If the shares are sold the DLT may become payable immediately; otherwise it is payable at the end of the eight years.

(3) TA 1970 s 137 applies to determine the value of stocks of a trade at the time of its discontinuance (in this context, the value of the stocks to be brought into the final accounts of the transferor at the date of the transfer to the company). Section 137(1)(a) states that:

'if the stock is sold or transferred for valuable consideration to a person who carries on or intends to carry on, a trade in the UK, and the cost therefore may be deducted by the purchaser as an expense in computing for any such purpose the profits or gains of that trade, the value thereof shall be taken to be the amount realised on the sale or *the value of the consideration given for the transfer*'.

A person transferring a trade to a company would normally prefer to transfer stock at cost (or market value only if lower) to minimise the income tax liability arising from the final period of unincorporated trading. However, where the consideration for the transfer is shares, it could be argued that in arriving at the value of the shares to be issued the stocks should be taken into account at their market value. In that case 'the value of the consideration given for the transfer' of the stocks will be their market value, not their cost, and they will have to be valued on that basis in the final accounts of the unincorporated business.

CGTA 1979 s 126

The hold-over relief for gifts of business assets can be used to transfer a business to a company whilst avoiding the undesirable consequences of CGTA 1979 s 123 in relation to:

(a) the condition of s 123 relief that all the assets (other than cash) must be transferred;

14 Incorporation

(b) TA 1970 s 137;
(c) stamp duty liabilities; and
(d) DLT.

The provisions of CGTA 1979 s 126 are summarised at **30.12** below. The mechanics of the use of s 126 are as follows. The company is formed and a small number of shares issued to the owners of the business. It is on this small issued capital that capital duty is payable. The owners of the business then sell to the company the goodwill (if any) for a nominal sum, and all the other assets that they wish to transfer at their base costs for CGT purposes. The consideration for the assets can be paid in cash or left outstanding on loan account. An election under s 126 is then made.

An arguable objection to the use of s 126 is that there is really no gift at all because the transfer of assets to the company at an undervalue increases the value of the shares previously issued to the owners of the business on the formation of the company, and that this increase in the value of the shares should be added to the actual consideration for the purposes of s 126(6). It is understood, however, that the Inland Revenue do not pursue this point.

Attention is drawn to the following features of the s 126 route to the incorporation of a family business:

(1) The transferor can choose which assets are transferred and which are retained outside the company. This overcomes the fundamental objection to s 123 where appreciating assets are used in the business.
(2) The DLT legislation contains no provisions for substituting market value for the actual consideration given. If, exceptionally, it is decided to transfer land with development value to the company, it can be transferred at cost so avoiding a DLT charge until it is disposed of or developed by the company. Alternatively, the consideration for the transfer can be fixed so as to utilise the £75,000 annual exemption of the transferor (note that where land is a partnership asset, the partnership is entitled to a single £75,000 exemption only). This course will be advisable if there is any likelihood of a disposal of the land within six years after the transfer, as DLTA 1976 s 12(5) denies the annual exemption on a disposal by a company of land acquired within the preceding six years from a connected person.
(3) The effect of a claim under s 126 is to roll over capital gains on the assets transferred against the company's base cost, whereas under s 123 it is the shareholder's base cost of the shares which is reduced. This will often be advantageous because

(a) it reduces the capital gains tax payable by the shareholder on a disposal of his shares; and

(b) the company will often be able to use replacement roll-over (see Chaper 26) to defer indefinitely any gains arising on the disposal of the assets transferred to it.

(4) The freedom s 126 affords to transfer only some of the assets makes it possible to avoid stamp duty on the value of debtors by arranging for the transferor to retain the legal title to the debts and to collect them as agent for the transferor.

(5) Stocks and work-in-progress can be transferred at cost without the problem described above in the context of a s 123 transfer.

Stamp duty

Apart from the stamp duty saving possibility outlined above in relation to debtors, stamp duty may be avoided in the following situations by ensuring that a stampable document is not used:

(1) Many assets (eg stocks and plant or machinery) can be transferred by delivery without the need for a stampable conveyance.

(2) Stamp duty is chargeable on a conveyance of land but not on a mere contract for its sale. It is possible to contract for the sale of land to a company, so transferring the beneficial ownership (which is sufficient for CGT purposes), but not convey the property and transfer the legal ownership with the attendant stamp duty liability.

15 Basic Strategy for the Proprietary Company

The companies at which this part of the book is directed are those distinguished by a close relationship, often identity, between the shareholders and directors. Difference of legal form aside, such companies are often mere extensions of their proprietors and managers who will see their own assets and those of the company as money in different pockets of the same coat. The objectives of the proprietors will be to minimise the extent to which the Revenue can relieve them of the contents of the coat as a whole, without being much concerned out of which pocket the bill is eventually paid. In meeting this overall objective, the aims of individual proprietors may differ: one shareholder with substantial income from outside the company may look for capital growth of his shares, another not so fortunate will require an income from the company.

Family companies will almost invariably be close within the definition at TA 1970, s 282 and **18.4** and **18.5** below deal with points arising out of the close company legislation.

The first step in planning to mitigate tax in a close company context is to obtain an overview not only of the affairs of the company but of its proprietors. Once that is done, it is probable that the interests of the proprietors will be well served if, in each period, the overall liabilities of the company and the individual proprietors taken together are minimised. The question of planning for the mitigation of capital taxes on the owners of the family business is considered in Part III.

16 Small companies rate relief

16.1 BACKGROUND

FA 1972 s 95 provides for the profits of a company to be taxed at a rate lower than the general rate of corporation tax where the profits fall below a lower limit and for a marginal relief where the profits fall between the lower limit and a prescribed upper limit. The calculation of the marginal relief is made by charging the company's taxable profits at the full rate of corporation tax and then reducing the amount of tax so calculated by an amount equal to

$$F \times \left[(M - P) \times \frac{I}{P} \right]$$

where F is the fraction specified in the Finance Act for the relevant financial year.
  M is the upper limit of the relief.
  P are the company's profits subject to corporation tax (including the relevant proportion of chargeable gains) plus its franked investment income (but excluding franked investment income or group income from any other companies in a group).
  I is the company's income, ie its profits exclusive of chargeable gains.

The effect of applying the marginal relief formula is that the effective rate of tax on profits falling between the lower and higher limits of relief suffer tax at a marginal rate in excess of the full rate of corporation tax.

In FA 1984 ss 18 and 20 the government has taken the unusual step of setting corporation tax rates and limits as far ahead as 1987. The lower and higher limits have been fixed at £100,000 and £500,000 for the financial years 1982 to 1986. The other relevant figures are tabulated below.

16 Small companies rate relief

Financial year	Full rate of tax	Small company rate	Small company fraction	Marginal rate of tax between lower and upper limits
1882	52%	38%	7/200	55.5%
1883	50%	30%	1/20	55.0%
1984	45%	30%	3/80	48.75%
1985	40%	30%	1/40	42.45%
1986	35%	30%	1/80	36.25%

The high rate of tax on profits falling into the range £100,000 to £500,000 relative to the rate of tax applicable to profits falling below the £100,000 lower limit indicates that a small reduction in taxable profits can have a disproportionate effect on the overall tax bill. The fact that tax rates will fall as 1986 approaches points towards a general strategy of deferring taxable income and accelerating deductible expenditure and the realisation of losses. This strategy is particularly applicable to expenditure on the provision of plant and machinery (discussed in Chapter 4 above) in view of the phasing out of first year allowances by 1 April 1986.

16.2 REDUCING TAXABLE PROFITS

Capital expenditure

Notwithstanding the anti-avoidance provisions at FA 1984 Sch 12 paras 5–8, discussed in detail at **4.2** above the acceleration of capital expenditure on plant and machinery or industrial buildings is likely to be the main method of minimising the impact of the high marginal rate of tax on profits falling between £100,000 and £500,000 in a 12-month period. The effect of the anti-avoidance provisions mentioned above is that whereas prior to 13 March 1984 it was possible to 'incur' expenditure for tax purposes simply by making a contract, it is now necessary that the contract should be completed before the whole of the expenditure is relieved. Nonetheless, if a company requires plant etc for use in its business, the tax savings to be generated by accelerating the date on which the plant is acquired and paid for will often outweigh the resulting cash-flow disadvantages.

EXAMPLE

Z Ltd expects taxable profits before capital allowances of £150,000 for each of the two years ending 31 March 1985 and 1986. It will require

16.2 Reducing taxable profits 99

new plant costing £50,000 to be available for use on 1 January 1986. Z Ltd pays 14% interest on its overdraft. No dividends are paid; mainstream corporation tax is paid on 31 December each year. There are no chargeable gains.

(1) If purchasing the plant is delayed until 1 January 1986 the company will pay:

corporation tax for the year to 31 March 1985 on profits of	£150,000	£ 61,875
corporation tax for the year to 31 March 1986 on profits of	£150,000	
less 50% first year allowance on £50,000	25,000	
	125,000	46,875
	Total	£108,750

(2) By comparison, if the company were to acquire the plant on 30 March 1985, the figures would be:

corporation tax for the year to 31 March 1985 on profits of	£150,000	
less 75% first year allowance	37,500	
	112,500	£ 41,719
corporation tax for the year to 31 March 1986 on profits of £150,000		
		58,750
		£100,469
interest on £50,000 for 9 months at 14% = £5,250		
less interest on tax postponed £20,156 (£61,875 − £41,719) for 12 months at 14% 2,822		
		2,428
	Total	£102,897

—a saving of £5,853. The greater the capital expenditure as a proportion of taxable profits, the greater will be the cash saving resulting from its acceleration.

Other methods

Other techniques for influencing taxable profits include:

(a) acceleration of payment of charges (see **20.2** below);
(b) ensuring that directors' remuneration is set at a tax-effective level (see **17.1** below);
(c) making a contribution to a company pension scheme (see Chapter 31 below). An initial contribution to fund the past service of

directors can give rise to a major once and for all tax saving;
(d) ensuring that all foreseeable losses or write-offs are fully reserved;
(e) deferral of the receipt of investment income, eg by using deep discount bonds as an alternative to interest-bearing investments, or arranging for overseas associated companies to defer declaring dividends.

Deferring or accelerating the realisation of a chargeable gain will sometimes be effective in increasing marginal small companies relief. The limits of relief in FA 1972 s 95 are set by reference to 'profits' as defined in s 95(7) to include chargeable gains and franked investment income (other than franked investment income from other group companies). By their nature substantial chargeable gains are likely to arise only from time to time, and care should be taken to see that, commercial considerations permitting, they are realised in periods when they will have the least adverse effect on small companies rate relief.

Where a company falls into the marginal small companies rate band, the effect of realising a chargeable gain can be even more marked. Apart from the possibility that realising a gain will cause the company's liability to exceed the lower limit of relief, the formula used to compute this marginal relief, $(M - P) \times I/P$ means that the inclusion of gains in the profits P can reduce significantly the relief available.

16.3 ASSOCIATED COMPANIES

FA 1972 s 95(3) provides that the lower and upper limits for small companies' rate relief are, where there are two or more companies under common control, to be divided by the number of such companies. In some cases this can result in one or more companies having taxable profits well below the lower limit and other companies having profits suffering the marginal or full corporation tax rates, whilst the group profits in total do not exceed the lower limit. Steps to be considered to avoid this situation include:

(a) arranging for intra-group management or other charges to equalise profits;
(b) where companies in the group have common directors, arranging for directors' fees to be paid from the appropriate companies. This route must be taken with caution, as it may be necessary for a paying company to demonstrate that payments were made wholly and exclusively for the purposes of its own trade, and not just to

benefit another group company (*Marshall Richards Machine Co Ltd v Jewitt* (1956) 36 TC 511);

(c) merger of group companies into one trading company, clearly a more drastic step, or at any rate the merger of any unprofitable subsidiary with a profitable company—s 95(3) makes no distinction between profitable and unprofitable associated companies when dividing the small companies' relief between companies;

(d) where intra-group trading takes place it may be possible to adjust inter-company transfer prices to equalise profits.

It is possible for a company with profits in excess of the upper limit for small companies' rate relief to derive some benefit from the operation of s 95. If the existing company forms a subsidiary to carry on a small part of its trade and arranges for the subsidiary to have profits close to £50,000 (the lower limit of relief ÷ 2) those profits will be taxed at 30% rather than 50%, an annual saving of £10,000. If the subsidiary's operations are kept simple, the saving achieved should outweigh the additional audit and administrative costs involved.

17 Remuneration of proprietors

17.1 GENERAL PRINCIPLES

An explained in chapter 15 above, the proprietors of a family company will be concerned to minimise the total tax bill suffered by the company and by the individual proprietors. They will not be much concerned whether the liability falls on the company or on themselves as individual taxpayers provided that each of the family units concerned has available sufficient money to meet their personal expenditure (subject, of course, to the company having sufficient funds, which in turn depends on the company earning sufficient profits in the long term).

Subject to the exception arising out of *Copeman v William Flood & Sons Ltd* (1940) 24 TC 53 (discussed below) it is self evident that remuneration paid to a director/proprietor of a family company and taxed in his hands will give rise to a like deduction in computing the company's taxable profits. This leads to the conclusion that the overall tax bill of the company and its proprietors will be minimised when each is being taxed at the same rate. The profits of many proprietary companies are likely to fall below the limit of £100,000 and so the 30% small companies rate will apply. This suggests that (purely from a tax minimising point of view) each director's remuneration should be set at a level such that his total income for the relevant year(s) of assessment will fall below £15,400. On the basis that a director will prefer to have money in his own pocket rather than in the company if that imposes no tax penalty, it is preferable to vote remuneration just below the £15,400 limit.

Where a company is paying tax at 50%, the tax-effective level of directors' remuneration increases to £30,600. As explained at **16.1** above, a company whose profits fall between £100,000 and £500,000 will suffer a comparatively high marginal rate of tax on the profits in excess of £100,000: in such a case it may be tax effective to pay remuneration of up to £38,100 for each family employee to reduce the company's profits to £100,000.

There will, of course, be circumstances in which the payment of remuneration will increase rather than reduce the overall tax bill. It is self evident that if the company has no corporation tax liability, payment of remuneration will increase the overall liability. More easily overlooked, however, is the joint employer's and employee's liability to account for Class I National Insurance contributions which together exceed 20% of the remuneration paid and which both fall on the proprietors of a private company in one capacity or another. Only when the upper limit of £13,000 (1984–85) has been exceeded does the payment of additional remuneration give rise to a tax saving without increasing the National Insurance contributions liability.

National Insurance contributions

Where directors' remuneration at the levels discussed above are concerned, the liability to pay Class I National Insurance contributions is likely to be immaterial in considering how much to pay, as all the payments will exceed the annual upper limit of liability. The practice of reducing Class I liabilities by paying a relatively low monthly salary to establish a monthly earnings period and voting occasional large bonuses which do not attract contributions on the excess over the monthly limit was made ineffective by SI 1983/10 which directs that all directors should be assessed by reference to an annual earnings period. The new rules do, however, open the possibility of avoiding some Class I National Insurance contributions by holding two annual general meetings of a company within one fiscal year. It is usual for directors to draw amounts on account of fees to be voted to them at a subsequent AGM. SI 1983/10 prescribes a twelve months 'earnings period' for assessing directors' remuneration for Class 1 National Insurance contributions purposes and directs that contributions shall be assessed on the amount of earnings *paid* in the earnings period. Earnings are deemed to be paid at the time they are voted and made available to the director concerned. Suppose, therefore, that a company makes up accounts to 31 December each year. It would be possible to hold the AGM and vote fees for the year to 31 December 1983 in May 1984; the fees so voted would be liable for contributions in 1984–85. If the AGM for the year to 31 December 1984 were to be held before 5 April 1985, any fees voted at that meeting would also fall into 1984–85 for contribution purposes. To the extent that the total fees voted in 1984–85 exceed the higher annual earnings limit for that year

(£13,000) the liability to account for National Insurance contributions will be avoided. Levels of Class I National Insurance contributions do, however, remain highly relevant when the question of dispersal of income to the families of a company's proprietors is being considered.

17.2 PAYING THE PROPRIETOR'S FAMILY

In general a company is free to pay whatever wages its directors decide to pay. Obtaining a tax deduction for those wages, may, however, prove to be more difficult. *Copeman v William Flood & Sons Ltd* (1940) 24 TC 53 is regarded by the Inland Revenue as authority for challenging the payment of what the inspector regards as excessive levels of remuneration in relation to the value of the work done by the recipient, on the grounds that the remuneration was not paid wholly and exclusively for the purposes of the trade, and so falls to be disallowed under TA 1970 s 130(a).

William Flood & Sons Ltd was a private company formed in 1937 to take over the pig-dealing business carried on by a Mr Flood. Mr Flood, his wife, two sons and a daughter were the directors and held all the shares. The daughter was then 17 years of age; her duties consisted of answering telephone enquiries. One of the sons, aged 23, called on farmers to purchase pigs. The daughter and son were each paid the substantial remuneration of £2,600 (about £36,000 at current prices) in respect of the first year of trading by the company. The daughter drew £70 and the son £277, leaving the balances in current accounts with the company. The Crown contended that it was open to the commissioners to consider whether the sums charged as remuneration were in fact wholly and exclusively laid out for the purposes of the company's trade and that, having regard to the age and duties of the son and daughter, the sums in question could not be so regarded. The commissioners declined to interfere with the deduction claimed by the company, but the High Court upheld the Crown's contention and remitted the case to the commissioners to determine what amounts were in fact expended wholly and exclusively for the purposes of the company's trade.

A similar principle was at stake in *Samuel Dracup & Sons Ltd v Dakin* (1957) 37 TC 377 in which no deduction was allowed for premiums paid to provide pensions for controlling directors. A more recent case, *Dollar v Lyon* [1981] STC 333 indicates that the question of whether payments to children fall within s 130(a) is a question of fact to be determined by the commissioners, and that in making their determination the commissioners are entitled to have regard to legal restrictions on the employment of young children. Mr and Mrs Dollar, who farmed in partnership, paid their children for working on the farm. The four children, aged 8 to 14, each did about fifteen hours work per week on the farm. They were paid £2 per week each in cash, and £250 of national savings certificates were purchased for each child; the total of £354 represented the minimum agricultural wage for the work done. The commissioners held that apart from the £104 cash paid to the eldest child the payments to the other children were in the nature of pocket money and not a deductible expense of the farming trade. In reaching their conclusion they took account of the fact that it would have been illegal to 'employ' the three younger children. The High Court held that the commissioners were entitled to find as they did, that they were correct in not deciding the appeal on the basis that employment of the younger children would have been illegal but that they were entitled to take account of the illegality of such employment 'since if two explanations of a given state of affairs is possible, one of which involves the doing of something illegal and the other not, the innocent explanation is, in general, to be preferred'.

The cases cited above are reason for moderation in paying wages or directors' fees to members of the families of proprietors who do not devote the whole of their time to the business of the company, but certainly do not preclude taking this route to achieve significant tax savings. In the first place, it is unlikely that inspectors would attack the payment of modest wages to children of the proprietor old enough to perform useful duties for the company, possibly at weekends or during school holidays. Payment of wages up to the limit of the single person's allowance to a child with no other income will save the company tax of £602 at 1984–85 rates, whilst not giving rise to any income tax liability. Secondly, in the case of more mature members of the proprietor's family, there may be factors which justify the payment of more substantial remuneration than the amount of time devoted to the company's business might appear to warrant. Directorship alone imposes legal obligations which justify adequate compensation. Where the principal directors have to be absent from the company's base, they will find it valuable to be able to arrange for someone they can trust to keep an eye on the company's business and to sign cheques etc in their absence. It is difficult to see how the Revenue could challenge successfully the payment of quite substantial remuneration in these circumstances. In the authors' experience, General Commissioners are very reluctant to substitute their own figure of allowable remuneration in place of the amount actually paid, unless the amounts paid were wholly unreasonable.

The directors of a proprietary company may wish to pay high levels of remuneration in the knowledge that the amounts paid may be challenged by the inspector as excessive. One consequence of a successful challenge by the inspector is that the company will not be allowed a deduction in computing its profits. The position of the recipient is less clear. The authors have seen cases where inspectors have maintained that the excess remuneration should be treated as a distribution, but the authors believe that this argument is untenable. Distributions are defined in TA 1970 s 233(2), and must generally be 'in respect of shares' (or securities). The absence of a direct link between the excess remuneration and the recipient's shareholding (if any)—it would be unwise to pay remuneration in proportion of members' shareholdings—takes the payment outside s 233(2). To use s 233(3), which treats as a distribution any transfer of a company's assets to a member in excess of the value given by the member in return, would require an unreasonable stretching of the words of the section. The same applies to TA 1970 s 284(2) which extends the definition of distributions in the case of close companies.

In many cases the problem of a successful challenge by the inspector can be mitigated by reliance on the Inland Revenue Press Statement of 13 July 1970, now incorporated in SP 5/1973. Where a disallowance of remuneration paid to the director of a close company has been negotiated with the inspector, the Schedule E liability of the director will be reduced by the amount of the disallowance, provided that the amount disallowed is formally waived and refunded to the company by the director. The requirement that the excess remuneration should be refunded suggests that if it is decided for tax planning reasons to pay what may be regarded as excessively high levels of remuneration, it will usually be desirable for the potential excess to be left on current account with the company, rather than being withdrawn, to ensure that the director can make the refund. For other matters relevant to the waiver of remuneration, see **17.4** below.

17.3 COMMERCIAL CONSTRAINTS

In planning levels of remuneration to be voted to directors and family employees, commercial constraints have to be kept in mind. Whilst it is not necessary for a director to draw any remuneration which has been credited to the current account, the company nonetheless has to hand over to the collector tax and National

Insurance contributions collected under the PAYE system when the remuneration is made available to the director, normally when it is either paid or credited to his account with the company, on terms that he has an unconditional right to draw it (*Garforth v Newsmith Stainless Ltd* [1979] STC 129). Although the company will have the benefit of a compensating reduction in its corporation tax liability, that benefit may not be felt for up to twenty one months after the company's year end. The resulting cash-flow disadvantage should not be overlooked. Readers may like to consider whether the *Newsmith* case means that liability to account for tax under PAYE on directors' remuneration can be deferred by making the right to draw the remuneration conditional on some future event.

Banks and other creditors of the company may not view with favour the voting of high levels of remuneration, even if little cash is actually withdrawn from the company. This and similar factors should be discussed with the directors before any final decision is made.

17.4 WAIVER OF REMUNERATION

A director's service agreement or the company's articles may entitle him to levels of remuneration which the company is unable to sustain or which would impose a tax penalty as would be the case, for instance, where a loss making company has no immediate corporation tax liability and any remuneration paid is liable to income tax (possibly at high rates) in the hands of the director. The cash-flow disadvantage referred to above may be particularly acute in this situation. It may also be desirable for a director to waive remuneration due to him to increase profits available for distribution to shareholders; following the abolition of the investment income surcharge, the payment of dividends can be an effective means of spreading income to family members who cannot be employed by the company (see **18.2** below).

It is understood that the Inland Revenue will accept a waiver of remuneration at any time before the Schedule E or corporation tax assessments affected by it have been determined under TMA 1970 ss 50 or 54 although, strictly, the waiver should be made before the remuneration is due under the terms of the service agreement etc. FA 1976 s 91 provides that a waiver of remuneration assessable under Schedule E is not a transfer of value as long as the waiver is taken into account in computing the profits of the payer. To avoid questions being raised in the future, the remuneration should be formally waived by deed.

17.5 ACCOUNTS BASIS

TA 1970 s 181 imposes tax under Schedule E Case 1 on 'any emoluments for the chargeable period (year of assessment)'. Following *Dracup v Radcliffe* (1946) 27 TC 88 the emoluments for a year of assessment are those earned in the year, irrespective of when they are paid. Where, as will usually be the case with a family company, a director's remuneration is determined at least partly by reference to the company's results, and the company's accounting year straddles a fiscal year end, there can be considerable delays in determining the remuneration assessable for each fiscal year.

For this reason the Inland Revenue will normally allow (and indeed encourage) the assessment of remuneration on the accounts year basis, which uses the remuneration shown in the company's accounts ending in the relevant year of assessment. The director can, however, insist on the use of the strict fiscal year basis, which must in any event be applied:

(1) for the first year in which emoluments are earned;
(2) for the second year if the company's accounting period ending in that year is shorter than twelve months;
(3) for the year of cessation and the penultimate year.

A taxpayer assessed on the accounts basis may revert to the strict fiscal year basis at any time, but the Revenue will normally resist any subsequent claim to change back to the accounts basis.

If total remuneration is expected to increase each year, the Schedule E assessments will be based on lower emoluments than were actually received during the fiscal year, with a resulting cash-flow benefit to the director. Adoption of the accounts year basis also simplifies tax calculations, and will generally be advantageous. If, however, remuneration is expected to vary widely from year to year, the accounts basis may result in a substantial charge to tax in a year in which the actual income is low. Where earnings fluctuate from year to year, the earnings basis will tend to even out the annual assessments and might save liability to higher rates of tax.

17.6 BENEFITS IN KIND

General principles

FA 1970 s 183(1) provides that emoluments chargeable to tax under Schedule E 'shall include all salaries, fees, wages, perquisites and

17.6 Benefits in kind

profits whatsoever'. *Tennant v Smith* (1892) 3 TC 158, HL established that a benefit in kind could be charged to tax under the general rules of Schedule E only if the employee receiving the benefit could turn it into money—the concept of 'money's worth'. *Heaton v Bell* (1969) 46 TC 211, HL established that if on giving up a benefit an employee is entitled to an increase in salary, the benefit can be turned into money and gives rise to a taxable emolument equal to the increased salary forgone whilst the benefit is enjoyed.

The rules for assessment of benefits-in-kind were extended by FA 1976 s 61 which charges to tax the cost to the employer of providing a wide range of benefits to a director or to any employee whose total emoluments (including any taxable benefit) are at a rate of £8,500 or more per year ('higher-paid employees'). The benefits mentioned in the legislation (s 61(2)) are accommodation (other than living accommodation which is taxed on a different basis), entertainment, domestic or other services and other benefits and facilities of whatsoever nature. There are specific rules for the taxation of car benefits, beneficial loan arrangements and employee share schemes.

The FA 1976 benefits legislation extends not only to benefits provided for a director or higher-paid employee, but also to members of his family or household (s 61(1)(a)). In the context of a family company it is likely that any 'family' employee who is not 'higher paid' or a director will be a member of the family or household of someone who is. Accordingly, this section is devoted to considering the way in which the use of benefits-in-kind rather than cash payments can be tax effective for director/proprietors of a family company.

The receipt of a benefit-in-kind as opposed to cash remuneration does not, of course, in itself confer any tax benefit on the recipient: the income tax payable on a taxable benefit costing £1,000 is the same as the tax on cash remuneration of a like amount. There are, however, certain benefits which are valued for tax purposes on a basis which does not reflect the full cost of providing the benefit; the use of such benefits creates a tax advantage when the tax paid by the company which provides the benefit and by the recipient are considered together. The cost of providing and running a relatively modest car today exceeds £3,000 annually. If that cost is deducted in computing the profits of a company charged to corporation tax at the 30% small companies rate the company will save tax of £900. The user (assuming that he uses the vehicles privately) of the car will suffer a scale charge on, say, £525 resulting in tax of £157.50 if he is a basic rate taxpayer. The net saving compared with paying the user an additional £3,000 out of which to run his car is thus £742.50.

17 Remuneration of proprietors

Provision of a car

For the reasons set out above, the provision of a car for each director/proprietor is likely to be a tax-efficient measure. The relevant legislation is at FA 1976 s 64 and Sch 7 and is not repeated here. However, aspects of the legislation provide planning opportunities:

(1) In most cases the scale charge applicable to the provision of a car is determined by the car's cylinder capacity. It is only when the original market value of the car (defined at FA 1976 s 75(5)(e) as the price, inclusive of customs duty, car tax and VAT, which the car might reasonably have been expected to fetch on a retail sale in the UK in the open market immediately before the date of its first registration) exceeds the prescribed limit (£16,000 for 1984–85) that cost becomes a relevant factor. Accordingly, it will generally be tax effective for the car provided to be of modest engine size, but there is no reason why every conceivable extra should not be fitted as long as the total cost is not pushed over £16,000. It is probably wise to ensure that the extras are fitted when the car is acquired by the company, as otherwise the Inland Revenue might seek to assess the value of the use of the extras as a separate benefit, although this will lead to car tax being payable on the extras as well as on the basic vehicle.

(2) As explained at (1) above, the original market value of a car is relevant to determine the scale charge where it exceeds £16,000 (1984–85). In arriving at this value, however, account can be taken of any discount generally offered by retailers on the sale of a single car of the type in question.

(3) If it is desired to provide a prestige car for a director/proprietor, it may be appropriate to consider the provision of a suitable secondhand vehicle. Depending on the age of the vehicle, it is likely that its original market value would not exceed £16,000 although its current value may be much higher, as would be the cost of its modern counterpart.

(4) FA 1976 Sch 7 para 3 reduces by half the scale charge where the business use of the car exceeds 18,000 miles in the fiscal year. Schedule 7 para 5 increases the charge by half where business mileage is 2,500 miles or less. Where it is likely that either of these limits will be relevant in a year of assessment, the car user should review his business mileage to see if it is worthwhile increasing it (perhaps by travelling by car rather than train) so that the relevant limit will be exceeded.

(5) Schedule 7 para 2 reduces the scale charge on a time basis where the motor car was not available for the employee's use throughout the year of assessment. Where the car was unavailable only by reason

of its being incapable of being used (probably because it was being repaired), the period of unavailability must extend to thirty or more consecutive days before relief is due. If a car user is in a position where he cannot use his company car, perhaps because he is abroad, it may be worth arranging for a board minute to be drawn up withdrawing authority to use the car. The car will then be deemed not to be available for his use and the taxable benefit will be reduced accordingly. In the case of taxpayers who travel abroad regularly, significant savings can be obtained by this means.

Car fuel benefit

From 6 April 1983 FA 1976 s 64A imposes a scale charge where an employer provides fuel for private motoring by an employee in a company car. (The scale charge does not apply to the provision of fuel for use in a car owned by the employee, which is taxed under the normal benefit rules on the cost to the employer.) The provisions of s 64A(3) effectively mean that the scale charge will apply however the employer goes about providing petrol for private use.

Attention is drawn to the following planning points:

(1) The 1984–85 scale charge for a car of 1300–1800 cc is £480. Assuming a petrol price of £1.85 and a car capable of 30 miles per gallon, it will be tax efficient for the family company to provide petrol for private use and for the car user to suffer the scale charge if the user's annual private mileage is 8,000 miles or more. Below that mileage it will be more efficient for the user to reimburse to the company the whole cost of any petrol provided for private use. It should be noted that s 64A(6)(a) requires that the *whole* of the expense incurred by the employer must be made good; partial reimbursement does not reduce the scale charge. On a strict interpretation of s 64A(6) the reimbursement should take place within the fiscal year in question; in practice the Inland Revenue do not appear to object if the reimbursement takes place within a reasonably short time of the year end.

(2) There is no 50% uplift in the scale charge where a second car is provided. This enhances the benefit of providing a second vehicle.

Living accommodation

FA 1977 s 33(1) imposes a charge to tax on all employees (not only directors or the higher paid) for whom living accommodation is provided by reason of their employment. The employee is charged to tax on the 'value to him' of the accommodation, which is defined in

17 Remuneration of proprietors

s 33(2) as the greater of:

(a) the rent which would have been payable for the period of occupation if the premises had been let to him at an annual rent equal to the gross annual value of the property. TA 1970 s 531 defines gross annual value in the same words as are used in the rating legislation, and inspectors invariably accept the gross rateable value of the property as the annual value for s 33 purposes; and
(b) the amount of rent actually paid by the employer.

Any amount reimbursed to the employer by the employee is deducted from the assessable benefit. It follows that if a family company rents a property and allows a director/proprietor (or a member of his household) to use it, no tax benefit will accrue. However, if the company buys a property and allows a director to occupy it, a substantial advantage can be derived. This is because the annual value on which the director is charged is likely to be substantially below the true commercial value to him of the accommodation provided. At present, a property carrying an annual commercial rent of £5,000 is likely to have a gross rateable value of less than one tenth of that amount.

EXAMPLE

Market rent for accommodation provided	£5,000
Gross rateable value	500
	£4,500

which at 30% is £1,350 which represents the overall saving in tax from the provision of accommodation by the employer compared with putting the employee in funds to pay the market rent.

A director/proprietor of a family company is most unlikely to be able to take advantage of the exemptions at FA 1977 s 33(4) which apply to representative occupiers, as s 33(5) excludes from the exemption any director of the company or of an associated company providing the accommodation, who alone or with his associates is able to control more than 5% of the share capital or income of the company. In the unusual case where this restriction does not apply the value of the accommodation benefit can be considerably enhanced if the company meets the costs of fuel, repairs, cleaning and the provision of furniture as FA 1976 s 63(A) restricts the assessable benefit arising from the provision of these benefits to 10% of the employees net emoluments, an amount which is likely to be considerably below the actual cost to the employer of providing the benefit.

17.6 Benefits in kind

Any decision to acquire a property costing more than £75,000 for occupation by an employee after 6 April 1984 must take account of FA 1977 s 33A, introduced by FA 1981 s 21. Section 33A imposes an additional annual charge by reference to a percentage of the excess cost over £75,000. The percentage used is the 'official rate of interest', for the purposes of FA 1976 s 66, currently 12%. The charge is additional to the charge under s 33; if the employee pays a rent in excess of the annual value of the property he may deduct it from the charge under s 33A. The cost of the property includes improvement expenditure as well as the original acquisition cost. If the property was acquired more than six years ago the market value at the date the employee first occupies the property is substituted for the cost.

The charge under s 33A reduces but certainly does not eliminate the tax benefit derived by an employee who occupies an expensive property owned by his employer. The charge applies only to the excess cost over £75,000 and the 12% notional interest rate is not very far removed from the rate of return a lessor might expect from an expensive property.

EXAMPLE

An employee occupies a house which cost his employer £100,000 and which has annual value of £1,250. The commercial rent would be £10,000 pa.
The employee will pay tax on
  annual value   £1,250
  + (£125,000 − £75,000) × 12% =   6,000
                                                         £7,250

which is £2,750 less than the market rent.

The decision to provide accommodation cannot be viewed in isolation. For the reasons explained above, it will generally be necessary for the company to buy the property and not to rent it. There may be good reasons why the company should not acquire a valuable and appreciating property. Conversely, the acquisition of a property may be a good use for funds which cannot otherwise be distributed without an unacceptable tax cost.

18 Distributions

18.1 GENERAL PRINCIPLES AND DEFINITIONS

In the context of tax planning a family company, the question of distributions is likely to arise in one of two ways:

(1) Is it tax-effective to pay dividends rather than, say, remuneration?
(2) The owners of a family company will often pay little regard to the legal distinction between property owned by the company and property which they own personally. A knowledge of the scope of the statutory definitions of distributions is necessary to ensure that they do not receive unplanned taxable distributions.

Definition

The principal statutory definition of transactions to be treated as distributions is at TA 1970 s 233, which provides that the term includes:

(1) Any dividend paid by a company, including a capital dividend but excluding a distribution made in respect of share capital on a winding up.
(2) Any other distribution out of the assets of the company (whether in cash or otherwise) in respect of shares in the company, except to the extent that it is a repayment of capital on the shares (unusual, except in the case of redeemable preference shares as most repayments of capital require the consent of the court under the Companies Act 1948 ss 66 and 67) or is matched by the receipt by the company of 'new consideration'. TA 1970 s 237(1) defines 'new consideration' as consideration not provided directly or indirectly out of the assets of the company.
(3) The issue of any redeemable shares, or any security (securities

18.1 General principles and definitions 115

are inherently redeemable), except to the extent that the company receives new consideration for the issue. This provision is designed to prevent the circumvention of the charge to income tax on distributions by a company issuing bonus shares and then redeeming them, which has the effect of putting distributable reserves in the hands of the shareholders. TA 1970 s 234 contains a complementary provision which taxes as a distribution any issue of share capital other than for new consideration which follows a repayment of share capital after 6 April 1965.

(4) Interest paid on securities which are:

(a) within (3) above; or

(b) securities which are convertible directly or indirectly into shares unless they are quoted securities or have been issued on terms comparable with those of quoted securities, securities which are otherwise 'connected with' shares of the company and securities issued by a UK resident company but held by a non-resident 75% associated company; or

(c) securities where the rate of return to the lender depends to any extent on the results of the company's business, but only (following FA 1982 s 60) to the extent that the interest paid exceeds a normal commercial rate.

(5) An amount equal to the difference between the value or benefit received by a shareholder on a transfer to him of assets or liabilities of a company and the amount or value of new consideration which he gives for it.

A family company will almost certainly be a close company. TA 1970 s 284 extends the definition of distribution in the case of a close company to any expense which the company incurs in connection with the provision for any participator, or associate of a participator, of 'living or other accommodation, of entertainment, of domestic or other services, or of other benefits or facilities of whatever nature', to the extent that the recipient does not make good the expense to the company. However, no charge arises under s 284 if the benefit provided by the company is assessable as a benefit-in-kind under FA 1976 Part III Chapter III or FA 1977 s 33 (see **17.6** above).

Whilst it is not, perhaps, too much to hope that the owners of a family company will not pay dividends, issue shares or securities or otherwise alter the company's capital structure without consulting their tax advisors, it is quite easy for them to undertake transactions which may amount to distributions within the extensive definitions at TA 1970 ss 233 and 284. It is arguable that s 233(3), which taxes transfers of assets to members at an undervalue and transfers of assets to a company at an overvalue, does not apply to a transfer to a single shareholder, but the Inland Revenue are unlikely to accept that interpretation. Where the company is a close company, CGTA 1979 s 75 imposes a further penalty in that the amount of undervalue is apportioned between the recipients and deducted from the cost of their shares on any subsequent disposal. The combined effect of these provisions can have a disastrous effect on transactions which the parties concerned may have undertaken for what are prima facie sensible commercial reasons. The following example was encountered in practice by one of the authors.

EXAMPLE

F carried on a chemists business which he transferred to a company in June 1965, acquiring 10,000 £1 shares as consideration for the transfer. The value of the company's premises at the date of transfer was £5,000. In August 1983 F decided to sell the business and retire. He had made no pension provision; in order to secure an income after the sale, he transferred the premises from the company to himself, paying their book value of £5,000; their market value was £75,000. He then sold the shares for £100,000.

F expected a tax bill of £27,000 (£100,000 − £10,000 at 30%). Instead he faced a bill of nearly £75,000, computed as follows:

(1) distribution of £70,000, being the difference between the book value of £5,000 and the current market value of £75,000, on which the tax was £44,780

(2) CGT on the sale of shares:
sale consideration £100,000
original cost £10,000
less undervalue 70,000
Nil
£100,000 at 30% 30,000
£74,780

Whilst this is an extreme case, it does illustrate the following tax planning points:

(a) taxpayers may not realise that book values are largely irrelevant for tax purposes—what matters is the current market value;
(b) as stressed at **1.3** above, the time to think about tax planning is as early as possible in the life of a business. If F had made proper pension provision in good time, he might not have made the disastrous transfer of the property.

Proprietors of family companies need to have stressed to them the fact that if they want the tax and commercial advantage of trading through a limited company, they must recognise that the company is

18.1 General principles and definitions

a separate legal person and that any transactions they have with the company are likely to have tax consequences.

Dividends as income

The imputation system of taxation is designed to be neutral so far as the decision whether to retain profits or pay dividends is concerned. ACT accounted for when distributions are made can be offset against mainstream corporation tax of the period of payment, assuming that the company has sufficient mainstream liability. Subject to the points made below, the abolition of the investment income surcharge and the 30% small companies rate of corporation tax introduced in FA 1984 mean it makes no difference to the proprietor of a company whether he receives income from the company as remuneration or dividends. Indeed, there may be a small cash-flow advantage in paying dividends; PAYE tax on remuneration is payable to the collector fourteen days after the end of the month in which the remuneration is paid, whereas ACT may not be payable for up to three months, and higher rate tax will not be due until 1 December after the end of the year of assessment. Payment of a dividend does not attract liability to National Insurance contributions.

EXAMPLE

Q Ltd makes profits of £70,000 for the year to 31 March 1985. P works full-time for the company and owns substantially all the shares. He wishes to pay himself £30,000 and has to decide whether to pay dividends or directors' remuneration.

(1) *directors' remuneration*
    Corporation tax is due on
    profits of   £70,000
    less remuneration   30,000
                              ───────
                              £40,000 at 30% =   £12,000
    P pays income tax on £30,000 of   11,395
                                              ─────────
                                    Total tax   £23,395
                                              ═════════

(2) *dividends*
    Corporation tax is due on profits of £70,000 at 30%   £21,000
    less ACT on dividend: £30,000 at 30%   9,000
                                                          ───────
                                                          £12,000
    P pays income tax on £30,000 as above   11,395
        (dividend of £21,000 and tax credit £9,000)   ─────────
                                            Total tax   £23,395
                                                        ═════════

In a family company context there are, however, drawbacks to the payment of dividends as compared with remuneration:

(1) In many family companies both spouses will be both directors and shareholders. Dividends paid to a wife will be aggregated with her husband's income, whereas if she is paid remuneration the couple will be able to elect for separate taxation of her earnings.
(2) The level of pension provision which directors can make for themselves is determined by the level of their relevant earnings from the company. Dividends are not relevant earnings for this purposes.
(3) Payment of dividends may have adverse effects on the value of minority shareholdings for capital taxes purposes. A majority holding will normally be valued on a net asset basis, but the value of minority holdings is almost entirely determined by the expectation of dividend income. When no dividends have been paid, the value of a minority holding is, therefore, confined to the remote possibility that income may one day be received, or that something will be received in the course of winding up the company at some indefinite future date.
(4) The payment of dividends is definitely contra-indicated where the company is likely to have insufficient mainstream corporation tax liability to absorb the related ACT: the fiscal neutrality between the payment of remuneration or of dividends illustrated in the example above depends on the company obtaining full ACT set-off.

18.2 DIVIDEND WAIVER

Because of the drawbacks to the payment of dividends mentioned above, it is likely that dividends will be paid only where:

(a) it is desired to provide income for a shareholder who is not in a position to work for the company and be paid remuneration; or
(b) where the level of remuneration is sufficiently low to make the saving of combined employer's and employee's National Insurance contributions worthwhile.

These conditions are unlikely to apply to all the shareholders in a family company. Unless the shareholders to whom dividends are to be paid hold a special class of shares not held by the other shareholders, it is not possible for a company to pay dividends to one shareholder and not to pay another, unless the shareholder who is not to receive a dividend takes action to waive that dividend.

To avoid the possibility that a dividend waiver might be regarded as a transfer of value for CTT purposes, the waiver must be made within the twelve months before the dividend is declared (FA 1976 s 92) and should be effected by the execution of a formal deed.

18.3 TIMING OF DIVIDEND PAYMENTS

To derive the maximum cash-flow benefit from the operation of the imputation system, dividends should be declared in the latest possible quarterly return period within an accounting period, and as late as possible within the return period. As with income tax deducted from charges, a few days' delay in paying a dividend may result in a delay of three months in accounting for the ACT. Postponing the payment of dividends until towards the end of an accounting period will in appropriate cases allow accumulation of franked investment income; the attached tax credits can be used to frank dividend payments, thus avoiding the cash-flow disadvantages of accounting for ACT in one return period and receiving credit for the tax credits only when a subsequent quarterly return has been submitted.

Where a company expects to have corporation tax liability for the current accounting period, it will not normally be advisable to postpone payment of a dividend until after the end of the period: payment should be made during the period to obtain relief for ACT against mainstream corporation tax as early as possible.

Where the timing of a dividend payment is material for tax planning purposes, it is necessary to ensure that the necessary legal formalities are observed. TA 1970 s 527(3) provides that 'for all purposes of the Corporation Tax Acts dividends shall be treated as paid on the date when they become due and payable'. A dividend is due and payable when it has been declared and becomes payable in accordance with the articles of association of the company. Most family companies will have adopted the articles at Table A of the Companies Act 1948, which provide that

(a) the directors may from time to time declare interim dividends (Article 115); and
(b) the company in general meeting may declare (final) dividends, but the amount so declared is not to exceed the amount recommended by the directors (Article 114).

A final dividend is due and payable on the date it is declared, unless the resolution declaring it specifies some other date (*Hurll v*

18　Distributions

IRC (1922) 8 TC 292). An interim dividend, however, remains subject to review by the directors and may be rescinded by the directors at any time until it is actually paid; accordingly an interim dividend only becomes due and payable when it is paid (*Potel v IRC* (1970) 46 TC 658).

18.4　APPORTIONMENT

FA 1972 Sch 16 (as amended) allows an inspector to apportion the income of a close company among the participators in the company. Apportionment is by reference to the excess of the company's relevant income of an accounting period over its distributions for that period (not necessarily the distributions made in the period; FA 1972 Sch 16 para 10(1)). Relevant income, defined in FA 1972 Sch 16 para 8, comprises:

(a) in the case of a trading company or member of a trading group, so much of its distributable income other than trading income for the period as can be distributed without prejudice to the requirements of the company's business; and
(b) in the case of any other company, all its distributable income other than estate or trading income which cannot be distributed without prejudice to the activities or assets giving rise to that estate or trading income.

Most of the terms used above are defined at para 10. The fundamental computational rules of the apportionment legislation are outside the scope of this book; the authors have sought to concentrate on aspects of Schedule 16 which may require planning action.

Reducing distributable income

FA 1972 Sch 16 para 1(2) compares a company's distributable income with the level of its distributions. Reducing the level of distributable income may be a viable alternative to making distributions. Techniques applicable when it is desired to reduce distributable income include:

(a) timing capital expenditure to create trading losses available for relief against investment income under TA 1970 s 177(2);
(b) paying additional directors' remuneration or pension scheme contributions to create losses as at (1);
(c) accelerating or deferring the payment of charges, which in the

apportionment computation are set against investment income before other income or gains;
(d) selling investments producing income to realise a capital gain rather than receiving the income.

In the case of a trading company, the measures at (a) and (b) will not be effective (except in so far as they have a secondary effect on the company's liquidity and so its ability to pay dividends) unless they create a loss available for offset against investment income: trading income of a trading company is not subject to apportionment (FA 1972 Sch 16 para 8(1)). It is likely that any argument with the inspector about apportionment will not come to a head until well into the company's next accounting period, by which time the company should be able to forecast results for that period. Where losses available for carry back under s 177(2) are likely to arise, the approach to the inspector should be slanted accordingly.

Requirements of the business

Since 26 March 1980, the trading income of a trading company has not been subject to apportionment (FA 1980 s 44(1) and (3) and Sch 9 para 1). A trading company's other distributable income is likely to be small in relation to the trading results, and it will usually be possible to argue successfully that none of the investment income can be distributed without prejudice to the company's business. Points to be borne in mind in this connection include:

(1) FA 1972 Sch 16 para 8(3) (added by FA 1978 s 36(2) and Sch 5 para 1) allows a company to have regard not only to the requirements of its current trade but also to 'any other requirements necessary or advisable for the acquisition of a trade or a controlling interest in a trading company or in a company which is a member of a trading group'. (FA 1972 Sch 16 para 12A, however, excludes from this relaxation the purchase of a trade or assets from a company which at any time within the previous twelve months was an associated company). The decision in *Wilson and Garden Ltd v IRC* [1982] STC 597, HL, moreover, indicates that even before FA 1978 the requirements of a business could include diversification into a new trade.
(2) *IRC v Thompson Bros (London) Ltd* [1974] STC 16 established that the business requirements of the company are to be determined at the date when the accounts are considered by the directors and the decision whether to pay a dividend is made. In his judgment in the *Wilson and Garden Ltd* case referred to above, Lord Roskill approved the principle that developments between the company's year end

and the date of the decision about dividends should be taken into account in determining business requirements.

(3) The liquidity position of the company at the time of the dividend decision is highly material. A profitable company with a fast expanding business will often be short of funds for financing working capital; this is likely to be particularly true in the early years of a company's existence. However, *MacTaggart Scott & Co Ltd v IRC* [1973] STC 180 establishes that account must be taken of funds likely to become available in the course of the company's trading activities. Where the arguments against apportionment depend on lack of liquidity, detailed cash-flow forecasts will probably be required.

(4) In difficult economic times and in businesses known to have a high risk of failure, a prudent decision not to pay dividend can often be especially justified.

(5) Plans for future capital expenditure or expansion may be taken into account, and it is helpful if previous plans have been implemented. It is essential that such plans are included in board minutes or the chairman's report, and the amounts involved should bear some relation to the figures disclosed in the accounts as capital expenditure contracted for or authorised by the directors.

(6) Once the company has stated its requirements, *IRC v White Bros Ltd* (1956) 36 TC 587 establishes that the onus is on the inspector to show that the requirements are excessive.

Cessation or liquidation

FA 1972 Sch 16 para 13 provides that where a close company ceases to trade or to hold investments, no regard need be paid to the requirements of the company's business for any accounting period ending on or within twelve months of the cessation. All the distributable income (apart from trading income of a trading company) is subject to apportionment, except to the extent that distributions could not be made without prejudicing the claims of the company's creditors. The 50% abatement of the estate or trading income of non trading companies at FA 1972 Sch 16 para 9(1) is also withdrawn.

These provisions lead to the conclusion that where possible a close company should go into liquidation or cease trading or holding investments as soon as possible after the end of an accounting period. A company going into liquidation just before the end of its annual accounting period will be liable to apportionment for the current period and the whole of the preceding period. Delaying the liquidation until a few days into the next period would restrict the liability to those few days and the previous twelve months only.

Distribution or apportionment

If a company cannot sustain its argument that it has no excess of relevant income over distributions, it is faced with the decision whether to accept apportionment or make a distribution. In most cases it will be preferable to make a distribution, otherwise the participators will find themselves faced with a liability without having received the funds to meet it. If the company decides to distribute, it is possible to use dividend waivers (see **18.2** above) to direct the dividends to shareholders with the lower rates of tax; apportionment, however, would follow strictly the relative shareholdings.

A further disadvantage of accepting apportionment is that funds retained in the company will tend to increase share values for the future, whilst an immediate liability to tax will still have been incurred. Although future CGT computations may be adjusted to take account of the apportionment, to avoid problems of identification distribution may be preferable. Against this, however, the effect of paying dividends on the values of minority shareholdings should be considered.

Clearance

FA 1972 Sch 16 para 18 lays down a procedure for obtaining a statement from the inspector as to whether he intends to make an apportionment for an accounting period. Where a company is not a trading company or a member of a trading group, or has significant investment income, it is prudent to apply for clearance as a matter of routine.

18.5 LOANS TO PARTICIPATORS

TA 1970 s 286 provides that, subject to certain exceptions, when a close company makes a loan to a participator there is assessed and recoverable from the company notional ACT, calculated as though the amount of the loan was the amount of a distribution. Section 286(2) extends the meaning of loan to prevent avoidance. The notional ACT cannot be credited against the mainstream liability. If the loan is repaid, the notional ACT suffered is repaid to the company.

The exceptions at s 286(3) are unlikely to have much relevance in the case of family companies, as they depend on the borrower not having a material interest in the company, as defined in s 285 (broadly, 5% of the ordinary share capital).

It will normally be advantageous to ensure that a company does not make loans falling within s 286, and the period end review should be extended to an examination of the company's accounts with its directors. Where necessary, it may be appropriate to vote further remuneration to eliminate any debit balance on a director's current account, but the other tax consequences should be considered. In some cases it may be advantageous to accept a charge under s 286. With the basic rate of income tax at 30%, the effective tax charge on a loan to which s 286 applies is 42.86%. This may be well below the rate of income tax which would have been suffered by the recipient if a like amount had been drawn as remuneration. Moreover, the notional ACT is repayable if the loan is subsequently repaid. If it is decided to accept s 286 liability, the provisions of the Companies Act 1980 ss 49–53, which relate to loans to directors should be examined to ensure that the loan is not illegal and that proper disclosure is made in the accounts.

If a loan to a participator is waived or written off, s 287 provides that the participator is treated as having received the amount written off as though it was income received after deduction of basic rate income tax. This may involve liability to higher rates of income tax. Although it is arguable that s 287 may be circumvented by arranging for the company to be not close on the day the loan is written off, it will normally be preferable to make other arrangements, particularly if the waiver is in connection with the termination of a directorship or employment with the company (see **35.2** below).

19 Financing the family company

19.1 SHARES OR LOANS?

The proprietor of a family business who is about to invest funds in a family company may do so either by subscribing for shares in the company or by lending cash to the company by way of a loan. Both courses offer advantages and disadvantages.

Shares

Shares form part of the permanent capital of the company and the capital invested is not, except in the case of redeemable shares (almost invariably redeemable preference shares) repayable except when the company is wound up. The company obtains no relief for the legal costs involved in a share issue, and suffers capital duty at 1% on the nominal value of the issue. Dividends are not deductible in computing the company's profits, although, as explained at **18.1** above, where the choice is between paying dividends and paying remuneration or interest either method will produce the same overall tax bill, provided that

(a) the payment of remuneration results in a reduction in the company's taxable profits (as opposed to creating or augmenting a loss); and
(b) the company can obtain full offset of the ACT payable in respect of the dividend.

FA 1980 s 37 provides relief against income under TA 1970 s 168 for a capital loss arising to an individual on the disposal after 5 April 1980 of shares in an unquoted trading company where the disposal is:

(1) an arm's length sale for full consideration; or

19 Financing the family company

(2) in the course of a liquidation; or
(3) a deemed disposal on a claim under CGTA 1979 s 22(2) that the value of the shares has become negligible.

It is to be hoped that this provision will be of little relevance to the proprietors of a family business: for the reasons set out at **2.3** above a family business should only be incorporated if it is profitable and likely to remain so. Shares issued in such circumstances are unlikely ever to be worth less than their value on issue.

An issue of shares is the only way in which investment can be obtained under the business expansion scheme; see **19.4** below.

Loans

Unless there is a written agreement for a term loan, which would be most unusual in the case of a loan by a proprietor of a family company, money lent to a company by its proprietors is repayable at their discretion. Following the abolition of the investment income surcharge in FA 1984, it will generally make no difference whether a company pays interest or additional directors' remuneration; indeed, where the total payment to a participator is below the upper limit for National Insurance contributions, there will be an advantage in paying interest.

FA 1980 s 38 provides relief as a trading expense of expenses incidental to the obtaining of loan finance (a loan or loan stock) where the interest payable on the loan is allowable for tax purposes. The loan or loan stock must not be convertible into, or carry the right to the acquisition of, shares within three years from the date when the loan finance was obtained. If the loan does carry conversion rights, relief for the costs is deferred until the end of the three year period and is then given only if the rights have not been exercised during that period.

CGTA 1979 s 136 allows a lender to obtain loss relief for CGT (but not against income) where he makes a loan to, or guarantees the lending of, a UK resident trader who uses the money wholly for the purpose of his trade, profession or vocation, and the loan becomes irrecoverable or a payment is made under the guarantee. If any of the amount relieved is subsequently recovered, a corresponding chargeable gain arises in the year of receipt.

Summary

The relative advantages of shares and loans in the financial structure of a family company are summarised in the table below.

19.1 Shares or loans?

Shares	Loans
1 Shares are part of the fixed capital of the company and cannot be repaid except on liquidation.	Loans can be repaid at any time without any tax consequences.
2 Dividends are not deductible in computing profits. It may not always be possible to obtain full set-off of ACT, particularly where the company's profits include chargeable gains.	Interest is deductible in computing profits.
3 Losses on shares in an unquoted company may be relieved against the shareholder's total income.	Losses on loans etc to trading companies qualify for CGT relief only.
4 There is no relief for the incidental costs of raising share capital.	The incidental costs of raising loan finance for a trading company are deductible as a trading expense.
5 Shares are relevant business property for capital transfer tax.	Loans are not relevant business property.
6 Shares entitle the shareholder to the growth in the capital value of the company. Retained profits can be extracted at capital gains tax rates on liquidation.	Loan capital does not participate in capital growth.

When a profitable business is incorporated it will usually be sensible for the proprietors to ensure that sufficient shares are issued to enable each shareholder to hold enough shares to facilitate capital taxes planning: a share capital comprising two £1 shares can be somewhat restrictive for this purpose. Apart from the foregoing, commercial considerations may dictate that capital should be introduced in the form of shares. Outside commercial institutions may wish to see a fixed capital commitment from the proprietors as a condition of their involvement. Where large sums of outside money are required, the proprietors of the business may wish to seek investment from a business expansion scheme fund even though this involves giving up a share in the capital growth in the company's value, in which case a share issue will be necessary.

Where these conditions do not obtain, it will generally be preferable to opt for loan finance. Where this is obtained from outside sources, it offers the advantage that the lender does not share in the capital growth of the company. Where the proprietors themselves have money to invest, they should lend it to the company: as the company makes profits and generates cash surpluses the loans can be repaid, putting money back into the pockets of the proprietors without any tax liability being incurred. In the longer term, however, it is desirable that any amounts lent to the company by its proprietors should be small in relation to the value of the lenders' shareholding: shares are business property for CTT purposes but loans are not.

19.2 WHO SHOULD HOLD THE SHARES?

Capital taxes planning for the proprietors of a family business is considered in Part III. The intention in this section is to draw attention to the fact that the time to make family dispositions of shares is at, or soon after, the issue of the shares when the shares are likely to be worth little more than their par value or at any rate considerably less than they will be worth after a period of profitable trading. Among the points to be considered are:

(1) Who will control the company? Commercial considerations aside, this question is relevant in determining whether the 50% business property relief available to a controlling shareholder is available; minority interests qualify for relief only at 30%. Where shares are held by a trust the first named trustee will normally be able to exercise the votes attaching to those shares.

(2) The disposition of the shares is also relevant in determining whether the company is a shareholder's 'family company' for the purposes of retirement relief and hold-over relief for gifts of business assets.

(3) The use of different classes of shares can be a useful means of severing voting control from income and capital rights.

19.3 RELIEF FOR INTEREST PAID

An individual who borrows money to invest in a company or in assets to be used by that company will wish to structure his

19.3 Relief for interest paid

borrowings so that he obtains relief for the interest he pays. The relevant provisions are at FA 1972 s 75 and Sch 9 and are summarised below.

Loans to acquire an interest in a close company

Relief is available for interest paid on a loan to an individual applied:

(a) in purchasing ordinary shares in a close company; or
(b) in lending money to a close company which is used wholly and exclusively for the purposes of the business of the company or any associated company;
(c) in paying off another loan, interest on which would have been eligible for relief (FA 1974 Sch 1 para 9(1)).

The company must have been a close company for tax purposes throughout the period from the application of the loan to the payment of the interest. Furthermore, the close company must be:

(a) a trading company; or
(b) a member of a trading group; or
(c) a company whose income consists of more than 75% of estate or trading income

To be entitled to relief the individual must:
(1) have a material interest in the company when the interest is paid; or
(2) hold some ordinary shares in the company when the interest is paid and, in the period from the application of the loan to the payment of the interest, have worked for the greater part of his time in the management of the company or an associated company (FA 1974 Sch 1 para 10).

Where the individual resides in a property owned by a property or investment company, it is not sufficient for him to have a material interest in the company; he must also have worked for the greater part of his time in the actual management of the company or of an associated company. (FA 1974 Sch 1 para 10(1)). 'Material interest' means broadly more than 5% of the ordinary share capital (TA 1970 s 285).

If the individual recovers any of the money which he has put into the company, he is treated as using that amount to repay a corresponding part of the loan, whether in fact he does so or not, so that the interest qualifying for relief is reduced (FA 1974 Sch 1 para 13). He is treated as recovering money if:

(a) he sells, exchanges or assigns any part of the share capital or it is repaid to him; or

(b) the company repays a loan from him; or
(c) he assigns his rights as a creditor of the company (FA 1974 Sch 1 para 14).

Two planning points arise out of these provisions:

(a) a shareholder borrowing money to invest in a company should ensure that he obtains at least 5% of the ordinary share capital of the company or will work for the greater part of his time in the management of the company; and
(b) The shareholder should ensure that subsequent changes in shareholding (eg the introduction of institutional equity investment) do not result in the company ceasing to be 'close' within the definition at TA 1970 s 282.

Loans to purchase machinery or plant

Where an employee borrows money to buy machinery or plant (eg a motor car) which he uses for the purposes of his employment, he is entitled to relief on the loan interest payable during the three tax years after the end of the year of assessment in which the loan was obtained (FA 1972 Sch 9 para 12).

Similar relief is available to a partner who borrows money to buy a car or other item of machinery or plant for use for the purposes of the firm's business (FA 1972 Sch 9 para 10).

Loans to purchase to improve land let at a commercial rent

FA 1974 Sch 1 para 4 provides for tax relief for interest paid on a loan taken out to acquire or improve property which is let. The property must be let at a commercial rent for more than twenty-six weeks out of any period of fifty-two weeks falling wholly or partly within the year of assessment. For the rest of the fifty-two week period if it is not let it must be:

(a) available for letting; or
(b) used as an only or main residence of the borrower, his divorced or separated spouse or a dependent relative; or
(c) prevented from being so let or used by any construction or repair work (FA 1974 Sch 1 para 4(1)(b)).

The practical effect of these requirements is that, where a property is purchased with a view to letting, the letting must commence within six months of the first payment of interest if tax relief on that interest payment is to be obtained.

Relief is given only against income from lettings, whether of that property or any other. It is not allowed against the borrower's general income. If in any year interest paid exceeds the letting income the excess can be carried forward and set against letting income of future years provided the property is still eligible for relief (FA 1974 Sch 1 para 7).

19.4 BUSINESS EXPANSION SCHEME

Reference has been made at **19.1** above to the possibility of obtaining investments in a family company under the business expansion scheme introduced by F(No 2)A 1983 s 26 and Sch 5. The scheme is considered from the point of view of an investor at **33.3** below. It is unlikely that a proprietor of a family company will be able to obtain relief for his investment in the company under the scheme because the relief is conditional on the investor not being 'connected with' the company. A person is connected with a company if he:

(a) is a paid director or employee of the company; or
(b) he and his associates control, or can acquire control of, more than 30% of the company's capital (shares and borrowings) or voting power.

These conditions apply for a period of five years from the issue of the shares. Note, however, that an investor may, without becoming connected with a company, receive:

(a) dividends and interest which do not exceed a normal return on the investment;
(b) payment or reimbursement of expenses wholly, exclusively and necessarily incurred by him or his associate in the performance of his duties as a director of the company;
(c) reasonable and necessary payments for services rendered to the company in the course of a trade or profession (not being secretarial or managerial services or services of a kind provided by the company itself) where the payments received are taken into account in computing the profits of the recipient under Schedule D Case I or II.

Accordingly, relief may be obtained by a person who carries on a trade or profession and invests in a company with which he will have a trading connection so that he can receive a return on his investment through that connection. Following the abolition of the investment income surcharge it is possible to visualise a situation where an investor wanting only a part-time involvement in a family company will be satisfied with the return he gets from the reimbursement of his expenses, a commercial rate of dividends and the prospect of capital growth in the value of his shares until the five year qualifying period has elapsed. It remains true, however, that the participator in a family company who relies on the company for his main source of income is most unlikely to be able to qualify for business expansion scheme relief.

The scheme may nonetheless be of interest to a family company seeking external equity finance. Such finance is likely to come in one or two forms:

(a) as a direct investment by an individual investor; or
(b) from a business expansion scheme fund.

Individual investments under the scheme are unusual, although the matching services offered by some financial institutions, notably ICFC Ltd, may change the picture. The lower limit of investments by a fund is likely to be in the region of £100,000; below that figure incidental costs become disproportionately high. To qualify for investment under the scheme, the company must:

(a) carry on a 'qualifying trade' or be a holding company whose subsidiaries carry on qualifying trades or start to carry on such a trade within two years. 'Qualifying trade' means any trade which does not to 'any substantial extent' consist of:

   (i) dealing in commodities, futures, shares, securities or land;
   (ii) farming;
   (iii) dealing in goods otherwise than in the course of an ordinary trade of wholesale or retail distribution;
   (iv) banking, insurance, money-lending, debt factoring, hire-purchase financing or other financial activities;
   (v) leasing or receiving royalties or licence fees;
   (vi) providing legal or accountancy services;
   (vii) providing services to any business controlled by the person controlling the company which includes any of the above activities;

(b) be under the control of an individual who has acquired that control after 5 April 1983 and who in the period of two years before and five years after the share issue has, or has had, a controlling interest in another trade;
(c) not have in issue shares which are not fully paid up.

There are numerous other conditions to be complied with during a period of five years from the issue of the shares; investors will normally seek comprehensive indemnities against any action of the company or the controlling shareholders causing a withdrawal of relief. Fund managers will also insist on stringent financial disciplines to protect their investment. Nonetheless, were substantial funds are required and the controlling shareholders will accept some reduction in their share of the equity and freedom of action, business expansion scheme investment can be a very cost-effective way of obtaining the funds.

19.5 PURCHASE BY A COMPANY OF ITS OWN SHARES

The Companies Act 1981, partially to comply with various EEC directives, introduced significant changes in the law relating to the share capital of companies. The Act permits limited companies to buy their own shares. The intention of this change was to make it easier for companies, particularly private ones, to obtain funds or restructure their capital.

At first sight, it may not be immediately obvious what the advantages are to a company. So far as private companies are concerned the main economic advantage is that, by having the company as a potential purchaser, an incoming member will be less likely to be locked into the company. Freer flows of capital into the company are thus encouraged. Indeed, an option to sell shares back to the company might be given to a potential incoming member as an inducement. Equity funding reduces the risk entailed in having to fund expansion through loan capital at potentially high interest rates. Proprietors may be more encouraged, as well as enabled, to seek equity funds for expansion if permanent equity need not be given up, as it can now be bought back at a later date.

Secondly, family control can be retained while still buying out principal shareholders on their death or retirement. This reduces the tendency towards concentration of corporate ownership which seems almost inevitable in times of economic downturn when few external investors, except financial institutions and public companies, can afford to buy shares, and those who do are likely to demand a significant or controlling interest.

Thirdly, small shareholdings in companies can be dealt with more economically. Apathetic or dissident minorities may be bought out. Small holdings may be disposed of more efficiently by selling them to the company rather than by transferring them to existing members or attempting to find an external purchaser.

The operation of the Companies Act 1981 provisions in the absence of the legislation introduced by FA 1982 would have penal tax consequences. If for example a company had proceeded to purchase some of its own shares from an individual shareholder, it is probable that the proceeds would have been classed as a distribution within the meaning of TA 1970 s 233 in so far as they exceeded the original capital subscribed. The company would then have been liable to ACT and even if it was able to set this off against its mainstream liability there would have been a serious cash-flow disadvantage. Capital allowances, stock relief and the present economic conditions would probably mean that the company could not make immediate use of the ACT. Should the purchase not be classed as a distribution within TA 1970 s 233, the Inland Revenue would be likely to attack the transaction under the anti-avoidance provisions of TA 1970 s 460 with similar results to the taxpayer (see **35.4** below). It is to counter these inequities that FA 1982 ss 53 and 56 and Sch 9 were introduced.

The problems of distribution definitions under TA 1970 s 233 are immediately recognised by s 53 in that both subsections (1) and (2) commence 'References in the Corporation Taxes Acts to distributions of a company shall *not* include references to ...'.

Section 53 deals with payments made by a company after 5 April 1982 on the redemption, repayment or purchase of its own shares (hereafter these are all referred to as a 'purchase'). The section is split into two quite distinct parts and it is important to recognise the reasons for the different treatments:

(1) s 53(1) applies to transactions generally and Sch 9 sets out the applicable conditions.
(2) s 53(2) applies only where funds are needed to satisfy CTT liabilities on death and the conditions are far less stringent than those under s 53(1).

Section 53(1) purchases

The section lays down numerous and complex conditions, all of which have to be met:

(1) The company purchasing the shares must be *unquoted* and either be a *trading* company or a holding company of a trading group. For this purpose a company whose shares do not have a full stock exchange quotation but are quoted on the Unlisted Securities Market is regarded as unquoted (SP18/80). 51% subsidiaries of a quoted company are not regarded as unquoted. 'Trading' naturally excludes investment companies but specifically excluded are dealers in shares, or securities or land or commodity futures. Moreover the business must consist wholly or mainly of the carrying on of a trade

19.5 Purchase by a company of its own shares

and for groups the company and its 75% subsidiaries must meet these requirements.

A holding company is one whose business (disregarding any trade carried on by it) consists wholly or mainly of holding shares or securities in its 75% subsidiaries.

(2) The purchase is made wholly or mainly for the purpose of *benefiting a trade* carried on by the purchaser.

It may at first sight appear difficult to say that it is to the benefit of a company's trade for the company to buy back its own shares and thereby either deplete its bank balance or increase its overdraft. However, it appears that the legislation is looking for a good commercial reason that will outweigh this temporary depletion and be of substantial longer-term benefit. The removal of a dissentient director shareholder might be sufficient reason.

When the legislation was first introduced there was a great deal of uncertainty as to what the Inland Revenue's attitude would be. In the hope that it would help matters the Inland Revenue has issued a Statement of Practice (SP2/82). In it are set out examples of what is considered to be benefiting a trade. These examples are:

(a) boardroom disagreements (although where the disagreement is over the question whether the company should discontinue trading and become an investment company and the shareholder being bought out advocated the continuance of trading, the Inland Revenue would not regard that as meeting the requirements);

(b) an outside shareholder withdrawing his investment;

(c) the retirement of the proprietor to make way for new management;

(d) a shareholder has died and the beneficiaries do not want to keep the shares.

It is now clear that only in special circumstances will the Inland Revenue agree that a purchase is for the benefit of the trade if there is not a full disposal of shares by the vendor.

A retiring director retaining a few shares to keep an interest in the company is, however, acceptable. Experience to date is that the Revenue are generally reasonably helpful in the application of the legislation.

(3) Not unexpectedly, the purchase must not form part of a *scheme or arrangement* the main purpose of which is to enable the vendor to participate in the profits of the company without receiving a dividend or to avoid tax.

FA 1982 Sch 9 introduces a number of other conditions that must be met particularly as they affect the vendor.

Sch 9 conditions

(1) *Residence* (para 1)   The vendor must, in the year of assessment in which the sale took place, have been resident and ordinarily resident in the UK.

(2) *Period of ownership* (para 2)   The shares being sold must have been held by the vendor for five years prior to the date of sale. In calculating the five year period it is possible, where shares were transferred to the vendor by the spouse, to count the period of the spouse's ownership provided they were living together both when the transfer was originally made and, if not deceased, also when the shares are sold to the company.

The previous owner's period of ownership also counts where the vendor has acquired the shares under the will or intestacy of the previous owner and where the vendor is the personal representative of the previous owner and in these two cases the combined period of ownership is reduced to three years.

Where shares of the same class are acquired over a period the rules for identifying acquisitions and disposals are drafted in the most favourable way for the shareholder. Shares acquired earlier are taken into account before shares acquired later (FIFO). Previous disposals are treated as having been made out of shares acquired later rather than earlier (LIFO). Generally shares acquired in a reorganisation are regarded as being acquired when the original share capital which is subject to the reorganisation was acquired.

(3) *Substantial reduction of shares* (para 3)   In theory it is not necessary for the vendor to dispose of all his shares but if he does not the Inland Revenue may not accept any 'benefit of trade'. The legislation refers only to a substantial reduction in his interest. A substantial reduction takes place where the interests immediately after the transaction do not exceed 75% of what they were immediately before. As the sale will mean a reduction in the shares in issue it will be necessary to dispose of more than 25% of the original holding to meet this condition.

(4) *Associates* (para 4)   If *immediately after the purchase* any associate of the vendor owns shares of the company, then their combined interests as shareholders must be substantially reduced. Associates are specifically defined in Sch 9 para 14 but this definition is less onerous than the general definition of associate in TA 1970 s 303. For the purposes of Sch 9, the following are associates:

(a) a husband and wife living together;

19.5 Purchase by a company of its own shares

(b) a minor child and its parents;
(c) a company, any company it controls and any person connected with the first company;
(d) a trustee holding shares of the company; and
  (i) a settlor; and
  (ii) an associate of the settlor within (a) or (b) above;
(e) a trustee holding shares of the company and a person who is or may become beneficially entitled to a 'significant interest' in the shares;
(f) personal representatives of an estate which includes shares of the company and any person who is or may become beneficially entitled to a significant interest in the shares comprised in the estate;
(g) a person who is accustomed to act on the directions of another person in relation to the affairs of the company and that other. This definition would appear to associate a managing director with all his employees. Fortunately the Inland Revenue has confirmed that this will not usually 'be regarded as applying to the normal relationships between an employee and someone set over him in a company' (SP2/82).

A person's interest in (e) and (f) above is significant if its value exceeds 5% of the value of all the property held on the trusts or comprised in the estate excluding any property in which he is not and can not become beneficially entitled to an interest. Therefore, where all the shares issued by a company are held by associates that company cannot purchase any shares and obtain the protection from distributions made available by s 53(1).

(5) *Groups of companies* (para 5) Where the company making the purchase is a member of a 51% group of companies immediately before the purchase, the substantial reduction of the vendor's interest is determined on a group basis. This test is applied by taking the relevant interest of each group company and averaging the interests without any regard to the size or values of the individual companies. The average immediately after the purchase must be 75% or less than the average immediately before the purchase. It is also necessary to consider companies which have left the group but where arrangements are in force which could mean them rejoining the group at a later date.

(6) *No continuing connections* (para 7) Paragraph 7 states that:

'the vendor must not immediately after the purchase be connected with the company making the purchase or with any company which is a member of the same group as that company'.

The term 'connected with a company' is defined by para 15 and covers the situations where a person and his associates have or can acquire control of it or more than 30% of:

(a) the issued ordinary share capital; or
(b) the loan capital and issued share capital; or
(c) the voting power of the company; or
(d) the assets available for distribution to equity holders on a winding-up.

The term 'loan capital' is defined to cover most forms of indebtedness but where a person acquires or becomes entitled to acquire loan capital of the company in the ordinary course of his business, which includes the lending of money, that loan capital is disregarded for these purposes provided the person takes no part in the management or conduct of the company.

Section 53(2) purchases

The conditions required by s 53(2) are far less arduous than those of s 53(1) and only require that:

(a) the company be unquoted and trading, or the holding company of a trading group. This is identical to the first condition for s 53 (1) which was fully covered earlier;
(b) the whole or substantially the whole of the payment is applied by the vendor in discharging a liability of his for CTT charged on death and is so applied within two years after the death. The payment referred to above is after taking account of any CGT that arises on the purchase.
In SP2/82 the Inland Revenue has indicated that they consider '"substantially the whole" means nearly all'. They have yet to define 'nearly all'!
(c) undue hardship would otherwise occur. Although undue hardship has not been defined it will be expected that where an estate has sufficient cash or ready realisable assets to meet any CTT liability, it will not meet the requirement if it chose instead to sell unquoted shares in a company. It would also seem that the section will only apply up to the amount needed to satisfy the CTT liability and amounts in excess will be treated as distributions.

Clearance procedure

Fortunately the legislation includes a clearance procedure and the Inland Revenue in SP2/82 has included full instructions on the form the application should take.

19.5 Purchase by a company of its own shares

TA 1970 s 460 (see **35.4** below) may well be applicable to the transaction and in these circumstances a clearance application under TA 1970 s 464 can be made at the same time.

It is also possible under FA 1982 Sch 9 para 10(2) to make an application that the exemptions do *not* apply if this is what is required.

Provision is also made for returns of payments; in particular where a payment is regarded as falling within the exemption a return of the payment must be made by the company within 60 days (FA 1982 Sch 9 para 11). The Inland Revenue also has various powers to obtain information (FA 1982 Sch 9 para 12).

Planning points

(1) Before a company can purchase its shares, (or issue redeemable shares) suitable powers must exist in the articles of association. Few articles adopted by existing companies contain powers of this nature and shareholders may want to take steps to amend the articles. This requires the passing of a special resolution which could place minority shareholders at some risk. It is possible that, armed with sufficient votes, a large shareholder could arrange for his shares to be purchased by the company leaving a small shareholder in control, perhaps without the benefit of sufficient expertise and with the company stripped of liquid funds. The retention of pre-emption rights or other safeguards should be considered.

(2) Shares in private companies must frequently be valued for CGT, CTT and stamp duty purposes. When valuing minority holdings in such companies the lack of an effective market for the shares is often a crucial factor supporting a reduced valuation. Amendment of the company's articles to allow it to purchase the shares could have a considerable effect on valuation—this possibility should be carefully examined before changing restrictive articles. In some cases it may be best not to make any change until a proposed share purchase is imminent; in others it may be appropriate to exclude any possibility of purchase.

(3) A shareholding in an unquoted trading company is 'relevant business property' for the purposes of business property relief, enabling the value transferred to be reduced by 50% or 30%. This deduction will no longer be available if a holding of shares is replaced by cash.

(4) The purchase of shares by a company will increase the percentage shareholdings retained by the remaining shareholders, as a result of the reduction in issued share capital. A minority shareholding existing before the purchase may become a controlling interest,

possibly reflecting increased value not offset by the availability of business property relief.

(5) FA 1982 Sch 9 para 8 requires that the purchase of shares must not be part of a scheme or arrangement whereby the vendor meets the requirement that his holding shall be 'substantially reduced' after the purchase, and subsequently enjoys a greater interest. Specifically, a transaction occurring within twelve months after the purchase is deemed to be part of such a scheme. The section applies if the arrangement was designed for this purpose, or *was likely to* have such an effect—the test is therefore objective.

(6) Husband and wife are associates only as long as they are living together. In the case of separation or divorce it is often necessary to deal with holdings of shares in a closely controlled company when attempting to reach a financial settlement, and a solution may be linked with FA 1982 s 53 (1) in the knowledge that the parties are no longer associates. To take an extreme case, a company with only two shareholders who are husband and wife can never use s 52(1) as it is impossible for their associated holdings to be 'substantially reduced'. If they separate, however, it is possible for one to remain in control of the company and for the other to sell his or her shares to the company. However, experience to date suggests that this solution may not always find favour with the Revenue where the principal benefit is a divorce settlement rather than a benefit to the trade of the company.

(7) It will generally be desirable that the price the company pays for the shares it acquires should approximate to their market value. If the price significantly exceeds market value it is likely that the Revenue will refuse clearance on the grounds that the proposed purchase in nothing more than a scheme for extracting funds from the company. If the price falls significantly short of the market value, then:

(a) there is a danger that the value shifting provisions of CGTA 1979 s 25 may apply. Section 25 provides that if a person having control of a company exercises his control so that value passes out of shares in the company owned by him or a person with whom he is connected, or out of rights over the company exercisable by him or by a person with whom he is connected, and passes into other shares in or rights over the company, that shall be a disposal of the shares or rights out of which the value passes by the person by whom they were owned or exercisable. Such a disposal is deemed to be a transaction not at arm's length and the consideration given is deemed to be the market value of what is acquired by the person to whom the value has shifted. In the present context, therefore, if a controlling shareholder were to procure that the company purchased his shares for less than their market value, the shortfall in value received by him would be reflected in an increase in the value of the shares held by the other shareholders, situation clearly within s 25.

(b) There may be a settlement within the very broad definition at TA 1970 s 454 (3) which includes 'any disposition, trust, covenant, agreement, or arrangement'; a person is a settlor if 'he has provided.... funds directly or indirectly for the purposes of the settlement'. In the situation described at (a) above, the majority shareholder has probably made a disposition or entered into an arrangement and has provided funds indirectly through the company share purchase. Whether s 454 applies will depend on whether there was any element of bounty in the transactions undertaken (see, for instance, *Bulmer v IRC* (1966) 44 TC 1).

20 Interest and charges

20.1 INTEREST—TRADING EXPENSE OR CHARGE ON PROFITS?

TA 1970 s 251(2) and (3) prevent a company from deducting interest paid in computing its income from any source unless the interest is paid to a bank carrying on a bona fide banking business in the UK. TA 1970 s 248 allows a company to deduct charges paid in an accounting period from the total profits of the period as reduced by any other relief other than group relief. The definitions of charges at s 248(3) includes:

(a) any yearly interest, annuity or annual payment within s 52(2) of the 1970 Act;
(b) any other interest payable in the UK to a UK bank, member of a UK stock exchange or discount house.

Section 248(2), however, excludes from the definition of charges any payment, which is deductible in computing profits' for the purposes of corporation tax.

It used to be thought that the effect of these provisions was that a company could choose to treat interest either as a trading deduction or as a charge; in any event, the Inland Revenue very rarely challenged either treatment. However the matter was finally considered in *Wilcock v Frigate Investments Ltd* [1982] STC 198. With slight adjustments to the figures in the interests of simplicity, the position in that case was that during the year to 30 June 1975 the appellant company had:

(a) a trading profit of £7,000 from property dealing;
(b) trading losses brought forward of £5,500;
(c) rental income of £3,500; and
(d) paid interest of £6,000 on a loan to acquire the property providing the rental income.

20.1 Interest—trading expense or charge on profits?

The company contended that the corporation tax computation should be

trading income	£7,000	
less losses s 177(1)	5,500	£1,500
rental income		3,500
		5,000
less charges paid		5,000
assessable profits		Nil

The High Court, however, decided that, based on a finding of fact by the Commissioners, the interest paid was 'deductible' on normal commercial principles in computing the company's trading profits, with the result that the computation become:

trading income (£7,000–£6,000)	£1,000
less brought forward	1,000
	—
rental income	3,500
assessable profits	£3,500

losses carried forward £4,500.

The court rejected the company's contention that a payment is 'deductible' in computing profits only if a deduction is claimed. The court refused to consider whether on normal commercial principles the interest was deductible from the rental income rather than in computing trading profits, as the appellant had not raised this point before the commissioners.

In many cases it will make no difference whether interest is treated as a trading deduction or as a charge. In situations such as the *Frigate Investments* case, however, the different treatments can have a major effect on the tax payable. The same principles would have applied if Frigate had had chargeable gains rather than rental income. Where a company has trading losses which include stock relief brought forward, the treatment of interest as a charge rather than as a trading deduction will use the stock relief (the carry-forward of which is limited to six years) more rapidly. TA 1970 s 248(1) directs that charges are to be relieved after all other reliefs. Trading losses brought forward under TA 1970 s 177(1) are, therefore, relieved before current charges. If interest is treated as a charge rather than as a trading deduction, losses brought forward will be utilised. Any excess of the charges over the remaining profits can be carried forward without time limit under s 177(8).

If a trading company can see a significant advantage in having interest paid treated as a charge, how is this to be achieved? The most straightforward answer is probably to avoid paying interest direct to a UK bank etc by routing it through another company. That will bring the interest within the prohibition on deductions at TA 1970 s 251(2) with the result that it will be treated as a charge.

20.2 TIMING OF PAYMENT OF CHARGES

Under the provisions of TA 1970 s 248(1) charges are deductible in computing the profits of the accounting period in which they are paid. It will sometimes be desirable to ensure that a payment falls into one period rather than another. This may be because it is desired to adjust taxable profits in a period, eg to maximise small companies' rate relief, or to take account of the fact that where charges exceed the total profits of an accounting period, TA 1970 s 177(8) allows the carry forward only of charges incurred wholly and exclusively for trade purposes, and that excess charges carried forward are available only against future trading profits. For example it would be possible for a company to have unrelieved charges in one period and a trading profit and chargeable gains expected in the next period. If the excess charges are trade charges they may be carried forward to extinguish the trading profit, but the chargeable gains might still lead to the payment of tax. The payment might be avoided by deferring the excess charges until the later period, when they would be available for offset against the gains.

In the context of the deferral or acceleration of the payment of charges, it should be noted that TA 1970 s 248(3) provides that interest paid to a bank, member of The Stock Exchange or discount house is treated as being paid when it is debited to the paying company's account in the books of the person to whom it is payable. Where these classes of payees are concerned, therefore, the payee's co-operation will be required if payment dates are to be adjusted. In the case of charges other than interest paid to a bank etc, the question of when payment is made can be difficult to resolve. It is probable that the courts would follow commercial practice, as for instance, where an accountant would normally regard a payment as made when a cheque is drawn rather than when it is presented to a bank; this would apply particularly where business is normally transacted by post, in which case the date of posting is normally regarded as the date of the transaction. To be on the safe side, however, it is prudent to arrange that the due dates for payment of charges are fixed to ensure that, allowing for normal commercial delays or the possibility of oversight, payment is actually made before the end of an accounting period.

The effect of the date of payment of charges on the company's liability to account for income tax under FA 1972 Sch 20 should not be overlooked. Where the company does not receive significant amounts of income from which income tax has been deducted, postponement of an interest or other payment due at or shortly before a quarter end until the beginning of the next quarter will defer the liability to account for the income tax deducted from the payment by up to three months. If the company has significant taxed income, the cash flow benefits of deferral may be even greater, by allowing the immediate offset of tax suffered against tax due to the Revenue.

21 Company chargeable gains

21.1 GENERAL PRINCIPLES

TA 1970 s 238(1) charges corporation tax on company 'profits', defined at s 238(4) as including income and chargeable gains. TA 1970 s 265(2) directs that company chargeable gains are to be computed in accordance with the CGT legislation. FA 1972 s 93 restricts the corporation tax charge on chargeable gains to that fraction of those gains which results in the gains, when charged to tax at the full corporation tax rate, suffering tax only at the rate applicable to capital gains. The general rules for computing capital gains are outside the scope of this book; this chapter covers planning points relevant to mitigating the tax effects of company chargeable gains.

Now that artificial tax avoidance schemes have been effectively outlawed by the *Ramsay* and *Furniss* decisions (see **1.3** above), there is little that a company can do to reduce the amount of any chargeable gain to be brought into its corporation tax computation. What the company may be able to do, however, is to influence the timing of the realisation of the gain. The accounting period in which the gain is realised can have an effect on:

(a) the application of the small companies rate of corporation tax to the company's profits, because of the inclusion of chargeable gains in profits P in the formula $(M - P) = I/P$ (see **16.2** above);
(b) the effective utilisation of capital losses;
(c) the effective utilisation of trading losses against chargeable gains.

Where the timing of a disposal is important, it should be noted that CGTA 1979 s 27 provides that the time of disposal is the contract date and not, if different, the time at which the asset is conveyed. If the contract is conditional, the date of disposal is the time at which the condition is satisfied.

21.2 USE OF CAPITAL LOSSES

TA 1970 s 265(1) provides for the carry-forward of capital losses, but there is no provision allowing such losses to be carried back. Where a chargeable gain has been realised during an accounting period and has not been extinguished by losses brought forward, the company's plans for future disposals should be reviewed to see if there are any planned disposals likely to generate losses. If there are, the disposals may be brought forward in time, or the period of account extended to cover the date of the later disposal. Any extension of the period of account should be considered in the light of the comments at **22.3** below.

As an alternative, the possibility of a claim under CGTA 1979 s 22 should be considered if the value of any asset (for instance, a trade investment) has become negligible. Notwithstanding the recent case of *Williams v Bullivant* [1983] STC 107, SP12/75 indicates that it is the practice of the Inland Revenue to accept claims under s 22 up to two years after the end of the accounting period in which it is desired to crystallise the loss.

21.3 RELIEF FOR TRADING LOSSES

TA 1970 s 177(2) and (3A) allows a company to set current trading losses against profits; as mentioned at **21.1** above, TA 1970 s 238(4)(a) defines profits as including chargeable gains. FA 1972 s 93(2) means that the trading loss is set against the whole gain. Trading losses brought forward under s 177(1) may not be set against chargeable gains. Where a company is making trading losses, the realisation of chargeable gains should be timed to make best use of those losses by ensuring that as far as possible disposals take place in a period when losses arise rather than in a subsequent period.

22 Company losses

22.1 STATUTORY PROVISIONS

This chapter is concerned with planning how best to obtain relief for trading losses, using the relevant provisions of TA 1970, which are set out below together with the relevant time limits, concentrating on planning aspects rather than on the fundamentals of the relief. References are to TA 1970.

s 177(1)	Carry forward to future periods.	Six years from the end of the accounting period in which the loss is incurred.
s 177(2), (3A)	Relief against total profits of current and past periods.	Two years from the end of the accounting period in which the loss is incurred.
s 177(8)	Carry forward to trade charges.	As for s 177(1).
s 178	Terminal losses.	Six years from the date of cessation of trading.
s 254	Relief against franked investment income.	As for s 177(2), extended to six years for management expenses and charges.
ss 258–264	Group relief.	Two years from the end of the accounting period of the surrendering company

Two points of practice arise out of these time limits:

(1) Where a claim is to be made under s 177(2) for the carry-back to a current accounting period of losses expected to arise in a subse-

quent period, it is not necessary that the loss of the later period should have been quantified at the time the claim was made.
(2) Where the loss of a company surrendering losses by way of group relief is unlikely to be agreed before the expiry of the two year time limit, a provisional claim may be made. The claim may, however, be provisional only as to the amount of the relief and the remaining information should be specified as in the case of a substantive claim and notification of consent.

22.2 STRATEGY

It will be clear that a company which has incurred a trading loss will normally benefit most from obtaining relief for that loss as soon as possible. The normal strategy will therefore be to offset the loss against any other profits of the accounting period under TA 190 s 177(2), then against profits of earlier periods under s 177(2) and (3A). Any balance of loss will then be carried forward. The circumstances in which this strategy may have to be varied are few, but include cases where:

(1) A claim under s 177(2) or (3A) will displace non-trade charges, which cannot be carried forward, and for which no relief will therefore be obtained.
(2) A company has suffered a temporary set-back in its trade, and expects to be taxable at the full 50% corporation tax rate in the next accounting period. Relief against other profits of the accounting period or against profits of earlier periods may be at only 30%, in which case it may be preferable to carry forward the losses. In making this decision, however, it will be necessary to bear in mind not only the company's cash position (in a period of difficult trading an immediate cash repayment may be more valuable than a larger but future tax saving) but also the possible receipt of repayment supplement. The falling rates of corporation tax set out in FA 1984 mean that it will be increasingly unlikely that any deferral of relief will be beneficial.

Repayment supplement

Repayment supplement will be a feature of many claims under s 177(2) and, more especially, s 177(3A). F(No 2)A 1975 s 48 provides that the supplement is payable from the later of twelve months after the date of payment or twelve months after the due date of payment of the tax now being repaid to the end of the tax month in which the repayment is made. A tax month runs from the 6th of one month to the 5th of the next. Two planning points arise:

(1) Particularly, in the case of a claim under s 177(2) against the profits of the previous accounting period, it may be beneficial to delay claiming the relief until twelve months have elapsed since the tax for the previous accounting period was due or paid. Section 177(10) provides for a claim under s 177(2) to be made up to two years after the end of the accounting period in which the loss arose.
(2) Submission of a claim should be timed so that it is likely that the Revenue will make the repayment early in the next tax month rather than late in the current month. A few days' delay in repayment can lead to a full month's supplement being due. Where repayment is received after the 6th of a month, the calculation of the supplement should be checked to ensure that the additional months have been included.

Effect on other reliefs

In making a claim under s 177(2) and (3A), the fact that the loss relief may affect relief for ACT, stock relief and double tax relief should not be overlooked. Where losses are carried back under s 177(3A) for three years, the surplus ACT position for up to five years may be affected. FA 1972 s 85(3) requires that a claim for carry-back of ACT to be made within two years of the end of the accounting period in which the surplus arises, which means that it will not normally be possible to carry back surplus ACT to periods not affected by the s 177(3A) claim.

In the case of stock relief, FA 1981 Sch 9 para 17(1) limits the carry forward of unused relief to six years. This carry-forward is unaffected by the abolition of stock relief in FA 1984. Components of that loss are deemed to be relieved against profits in the order:

(1) In the current accounting period
 (a) against losses apart from current capital allowances and stock relief;
 (b) against current capital allowances;
 (c) against current stock relief.
(2) In subsequent accounting periods
 (a) against capital allowances brought forward from periods ending after 13 November 1980;
 (b) against new scheme stock relief on a first in, first out basis
 (c) losses brought forward from periods ending after 13 November 1980;
 (d) other losses, capital allowances or stock relief.

When losses attributable to first year allowances are carried back under s 177(3A), FA 1972 Sch 9 para 17(4) provides that the additional losses in the period to which the allowances are carried back attributable to the allowances are treated as capital allowances and so set off in priority to stock relief for the period. This may result in stock relief not being set against profits within the six year time limit and so being lost.

Double taxation relief cannot be carried forward, and may be lost if trading losses are set against the profits of the accounting period so as to extinguish the corporation tax liability for the accounting period.

TA 1970 s 254

The final relief to be considered in this section is the set-off of losses against surplus franked investment income under TA 1970 s 254. A claim under this section gives rise to an immediate repayment, but losses so relieved are relieved only at the ACT rate and not at the rate of corporation tax applicable to profits. This disadvantage is alleviated only if the company has a surplus of distributions over franked investment income in a later period, in which case s 254(5) provides that the losses relieved under s 254(1) are reinstated and relieved against trading profits, and the ACT relief otherwise available is restricted by the tax credits repaid.

It follows from these provisions that a claim under s 254 will normally be beneficial where a company is likely to have a surplus of distributions over franked investment income in the fairly near future, so reinstating for relief at corporation tax rates losses relieved at the ACT rate. This situation is likely to arise when a company has experienced a temporary downturn in its fortunes, and can turn the tax credits repaid to good account in helping its recovery. On recovery the company will be in a position to resume dividend payments, thus creating a surplus of distributions over franked investment income.

Where a company is not likely to have a surplus of distributions over franked investment income in the future, the benefits of a s 254 claim are more equivocal. It is necessary to weigh the benefits of an immediate repayment against the loss of possible future relief at corporation tax rates. A claim should normally be made where it is unlikely that future profits and unfranked investment income will be sufficient to use foreseeable losses. In such a case, moreover, the company should consider switching from investments producing franked income to those producing unfranked income.

A minor planning point arises out of the order of set-off prescribed by s 254(2). There is a choice of set-offs in the case of trading losses and capital allowances given by way of discharge or repayment of tax. These losses etc must first be set against total profits of the accounting period in which they arise (s 254(3)). The claimant then has a choice whether to claim relief for the losses or allowances in the current period under s 254, leaving any balance to be carried back under s 177(2) or (3A), or to make the s 177(2) claim followed by a s 254 claim for the current period in relation to any unrelieved balance. It is necessary to calculate the overall relief (including repayment supplement) resulting from each claim in order to see which is more beneficial. Any balance remaining after either claim has been made can be relieved under s 254 against profits of a preceding period equal in length to the period in which the surplus franked investment arose, or carried forward under s 177(1).

22.3 CHANGE OF ACCOUNTING DATE

On the basis that tax deferred is tax saved, it will sometimes be beneficial to terminate an accounting period early to accelerate loss relief. For example if a company has suffered a temporary business setback resulting in losses for a period after which profits are expected, it may be beneficial to produce accounts for the short period of loss only and obtain an immediate repayment of tax under TA 1970 s 177(2). Similar considerations apply where a profitable company has incurred substantial capital expenditure qualifying for first year allowances or has set up a pension scheme early in an accounting period: immediate relief can be obtained by terminating the accounting period as soon as the expenditure has been incurred.

Changes of accounting date should also be considered in certain circumstances to maximise group relief. TA 1970 s 261 sets out the rules concerning 'corresponding accounting periods', which are not repeated here. Two planning points arise out of these rules:

(1) Section 259(1) provides that the loss of the surrendering company for its accounting period may be set off against the total profit of the claimant company for its corresponding accounting period. The wording of the subsection indicates that the limitation of group relief to that appropriate to the corresponding accounting period applies only to the claimant company. This means that, although s 261(2) limits the amount which can be set against the profits of a claimant company to a proportion of the loss of the surrendering company, each of several claimant companies in the group can claim an appropriate proportion of the loss subject only to the overriding restriction in s 263(2) that the total relief given cannot exceed the total loss of the surrendering company.

22.3 Change of accounting date

(2) Section 259(6) brings excess charges within the scope of group relief. Relief is normally given by reference to the charges paid by the surrendering company in its accounting period, but where that accounting period does not correspond with the claimant's accounting period, the charges are time apportioned to arrive at the amount available for relief and the actual date of payment is disregarded. In appropriate cases it may be beneficial to ensure that the accounting periods of surrendering and claimant companies do not correspond, so that charges are time apportioned to a period when group relief is more useful than it would be if the timing of the relief were to be determined by the date of payment of the charges.

TA 1970 s 262 provides that group relief can be claimed only in respect of losses arising whilst both the surrendering and claimant companies are members of the group. Where the accounting periods of the two companies do not coincide, losses and the profits against which they may be set are time apportioned. If a loss-making company is acquired by a group it may be beneficial to extend the accounting period of the loss-making company so that more of the loss is time apportioned to the period when both companies are members of the group. Changes of accounting date to mitigate tax in the case of companies' chargeable gains are considered at **21.2**.

Although the freedom of a company to choose its accounting date within the constraints imposed by TA 1970 s 247 is a valuable planning tool, it is necessary to sound several notes of caution:

(1) Company law imposes restrictions on a company's freedom to change its accounting date. CA 1976 s 3(1) directs that a company's accounting reference date can be changed only if notice is given during the accounting reference period; s 3(5) does not allow an accounting reference period to be extended beyond eighteen months; and s 3(6) does not allow an accounting reference period to be extended more than once in five years unless the extension is in order to bring into line the accounting reference dates of companies in a group. This last exception can provide a means of avoiding the effect of s 3(6) by purchasing an off the shelf subsidiary company with the desired year end and changing the accounting reference date of other group companies to coincide with the new company's year end.

(2) Section 177(2) provides for losses to the carried back against profits of a period equal in length to the period in which the losses have arisen. Unless the losses of a short accounting period arise from first year allowances and can be relieved under s 177(3A) as discussed above, the adoption of a short accounting period may restrict relief available under s 177(2).

(3) *Marshall Hus & Partners Ltd v Bolton* [1981] STC 18 is authority for an inspector to apportion profits between accounting periods comprised in a period of account of more than twelve months on the basis of the timing of transactions within the period of account rather than by simple time apportionment. This may negate the anticipated benefit of spreading profits, etc over a longer period.

23 Receivership and liquidation

23.1 RECEIVERSHIP

A full review of the rights and duties of a receiver or liquidator with regard to taxation liabilities is outside the scope of this book. This chapter is aimed at giving a broad outline of the provisions of the Taxes Acts as they affect receivers and liquidators, and to draw attention to some planning opportunities.

The appointment of a receiver does not of itself cause the end of an accounting period of the company, unless the receiver ceases to trade when he is appointed (TA 1970 s 247(3)(c)). Commercial considerations aside, it may often be beneficial for the receiver to continue to trade, albeit perhaps on a reduced scale, to obtain relief for current trading losses against any gains arising from the disposal of assets (see **21.3** above). In any event, if some disposals are expected to produce gains and others losses, the receiver should ensure that losses are realised before, or in the same accounting period as, gains to ensure that gains and losses are fully offset (see **21.2** above).

In general, a receiver has available to him the full range of corporate tax planning devices, including:

(a) group dividend and interest elections under TA 1970 s 256—see **24.2** below;
(b) group relief for losses under TA 1970 ss 258–264-see **24.3** below;
(c) intra-group transfers of assets and roll-over relief under TA 1970 ss 273 and 276–see **25.3** below;
(d) set-off and surrender under FA 1972 ss 85 and 92—see **24.4** below;
(e) company reconstructions without change of ownership under TA 1970 s 252–see **25.4** below. This last provision can be extremely useful to a receiver or liquidator wishing to sell the trade or part of the trade. Any potential purchaser to likely to be unwilling to risk

taking on any liabilities which may be associated with the vendor company. To avoid this situation the receiver can 'hive down' the trade with a new company formed for the purpose, so giving the purchaser the benefit of a 'clean' company.

23.2 LIQUIDATION

In contrast to the position of a receiver, the appointment of a liquidator in itself triggers certain statutory provisions. TA 1970 s 24(7) provides that an accounting period shall end and a new one begin on the passing by the company of resolution for winding-up or on the presentation of a winding-up petition on which a winding-up order is made. Subsequent accounting periods run to the anniversary of the commencement of the winding-up.

The rate of tax for a financial year is fixed in arrear and but for the rules in TA 1970 s 245(2) and (3), it would be impossible for a liquidator to complete a winding-up as he would not be able to determine how much tax he owed to the Inland Revenue. The rules referred to provide that tax for the final accounting period is to be charged at the rate laid down for the penultimate financial year, unless, before the affairs of the company have been completely would up, the rate for the current year has been fixed, in which case that rate is used. FA 1984 ss 18 and 20 has fixed the corporation tax rates up to the financial year 1986, with the result that liquidators will know what rates of tax are applicable up to 31 March 1987.

The appointment of a liquidator removes a company from any group of companies of which it may be a member for the purposes of group dividend and interest elections under TA 1970 s 256 and group relief for losses under ss 258–264, but the company remains a member of any CGT group under TA 1970 s 273. Under FA 1972 s 92(4) it appears that where a company has received the benefit of surrendered ACT from its parent and the parent or subsidiary subsequently goes into liquidation, the surrendered ACT can be set against profits only up to the date of the commencement of the winding-up. This is a point to be borne in mind when the timing of a voluntary winding up is being considered.

The effect of the appointment of a liquidator on a company's liability to apportionment under FA 1972 Sch 16 is considered at **18.4** above.

24 Groups of companies—income and distributions

24.1 GENERAL PRINCIPLES

For reasons set out at **2.3** above, the authors do not generally favour a group of companies as a trading vehicle, preferring a divisional structure where a company carries on several activities. Accordingly, in this chapter we have dealt with provisions relating to groups in outline only, concentrating on planning opportunities and pitfalls arising from the legislation.

The tax legislation recognises that in most cases a group of companies is, in reality, a single commercial entity. Accordingly, a number of provisions are provided to reflect this commercial reality to some extent. These provisions include rules dealing with:

(a) group relief for losses;
(b) intra-group dividends and interest;
(c) surrender of ACT;
(d) group reconstructions;
(e) intra-group transfers of assets.

Intra-group asset transfers are discussed at **26.1** below; the other provisions are considered in this chapter.

24.2 GROUP RELIEF FOR LOSSES

Group relief under TA 1970 ss 258–264 is available where a loss is made by a member of a 75% group: the loss can be surrendered to any other member of the group. In this context a 75% group comprises a parent company and any subsidiary in which the parent owns beneficially 75% or more of the issued share capital. All the companies must be resident in the UK. Section 259(6) extends the definition of loss available for group relief to include excess charges on income. Attention is drawn to the following planning points:

(1) The effect of the decision in *Pilkington Bros Ltd v IRC* [1982] STC 103, HL is that to be certain that group relief will be available without having to rely on concessionary treatment by the Inland Revenue, it is necessary to ensure that a group is organised with all the subsidiaries being held by a single parent company and without the intervention of any sub-holding company.

(2) Group relief is given only in respect of the 'corresponding accounting periods' of the companies concerned (s 261). For a discussion of changes in accounting dates to minimise the effect of these provisions, see **22.3** above.

(3) Section 262 provides that group relief is available only if the claimant and surrendering companies are members of the same group throughout the whole of the relevant accounting periods of each company. When a company joins or leaves the group, an accounting period is treated as starting or ending, so preserving relief for losses during the period in which the group relationship existed. Any necessary apportionments of profits or losses are made on a time basis unless 'it appears that that method would work unreasonably or unjustly' in which case 'such other method shall be used as appears just and reasonable'. Either the taxpayer or the Revenue can claim to use some basis other than time apportionment. However, FA 1973 s 29 provides that where arrangements are in existence whereby a company *could* cease to be a member of group, that company shall be treated as though it were not a member of the group. This is a point to be watched where the sale of a group company is contemplated. The accounting period of the company being sold should be terminated before any 'arrangements' (for which see SP 5/80) come into existence: that will preserve relief for losses up to the new accounting date.

(4) A claim under TA 1970 s 177(2) or (3A) will usually be more beneficial than the surrender of current losses to another company because of the tax-free repayment supplement likely to arise where losses are carried back.

(5) Where a group contains more than one company which could benefit from the surrender of losses, the choice should take account of:

    (a) the dates on which each company is due to pay corporation tax (see **24.6** below);

    (b) the extent to which each company's profits exceed the £100,000 limit for the small companies rate of tax; and

(c) where overseas income is received, the possibility that double tax relief will be lost if losses are surrendered.

24.3 GROUP DIVIDENDS AND INTEREST

TA 1970 ss 256 and 257 allow a parent company and its 51% subsidiaries (defined in the same terms as apply to a 75% subsidiary for group relief—see **24.2** above) to elect that intra-group dividends shall be paid without the need to acount for ACT under the imputation system, and to pay interest without deduction of income tax.

Most groups of companies are likely to have taken advantage of these provisions and will be paying dividends from subsidiaries to the parent as group income. Section 256(1) (proviso) allows a company which has elected under s 257 to notify the collector that the election is not to apply to a particular dividend payment. If a subsidiary has franked investment income, a cash-flow advantage may be derived if the subsidiary pays a dividend to its parent outside the s 257 election, thus transferring to the parent the benefit of this franked investment income for off-set against the ACT due on its own dividend payments. This procedure may also be useful in reducing or eliminating unrelieved surplus ACT in the parent company. ACT surrendered by a parent company cannot be carried back by a subsidiary; where the group situation warrants it, payment of a dividend by a subsidiary outside the group election will generate ACT in the subsidiary available for carry back against the subsidiary's mainstrean liablity for earlier years.

24.4 SURRENDER OF ACT

In addition, or as an alternative, to the carry-back or forwards of surplus ACT, a parent company in a 51% group may surrender ACT (not only surplus ACT) to its subsidiaries, as provided by FA 1972 s 92. Under s 92(3) the subsidiary is treated as having paid a dividend on the same day as it was paid by the parent, and so can set the ACT against its own mainstream liability for the period in which the dividend is paid. Section 92(3A) prevents the subsidiary from carrying back surrendered ACT under FA 1972 s 85(3), but surrendered ACT is set against the current liability before ACT paid by the subsidiary, releasing any ACT on dividends paid by the subsidiary free for carry-back. The following points should be borne in mind when considering a claim to surrender ACT to a subsidiary:

24 Groups of companies—income and distributions

(1) If a previously profitable group makes a loss in the current period, but nonetheless pays a dividend, it may be beneficial for the parent company to surrender the ACT of the previous accounting period to the subsidiaries (assuming they have sufficient liability to use it), thus reviving a mainstream liability in the parent for the previous period against which the current surplus ACT may be setoff.

(2) A loss-making parent company may be advised to surrender ACT to subsidiaries likely to make profits in the future, even if they have no mainstream liabilities for the current period; the resulting surplus ACT in the subsidiaries is then carried forward.

(3) A parent company which has overseas income which has suffered foreign tax at a rate in excess of 20% will normally find it beneficial to surrender ACT to a subsidiary to avoid any restriction of double tax relief.

(4) Section 92(4) provides that ACT can be surrendered to a subsidiary only where the recipient company has been a subsidiary throughout its accounting period. When a subsidiary is acquired, consideration should be given to terminating one company's accounting period at the date of acquisition so that full surrender of ACT is possible thereafter.

24.5 RECONSTRUCTIONS

TA 1970 s 252(1) as extended by (7) provides that where, on a company ceasing to carry on a trade or part of a trade, another company begins to carry on that trade or that part thereof as its trade or as part of its trade, and:

(a) on or at any time within two years after that event the trade or part thereof, or any other trade of which the activities comprise the activities of that trade or part thereof, or any interest amounting to not less than a three-fourths share in either the trade, the part thereof or the other trade belongs to the same persons as any of them or such an interest in any of them belonged to at some time within a year before that event; and

(b) the trade or part thereof or any other trade such as is mentioned in paragraph (a) above is not, within the period taken for the comparison under paragraph (a) above, carried on otherwise than by a company which is within the charge to tax in respect of it;

then the transfer of the trade does not cause the trade to be permanently discontinued and a new trade set up.

The wording above is tortuous and difficult to follow; it is set out

24.5 Reconstructions

in full because it will sometimes be necessary to refer to the legislation itself and it is hoped that readers will find it helpful to see the combined effect of the words of s 252(1) and (7). What s 252 means is that a transfer of a trade or part of a trade from one company to another does not cause the trade to be permanently discontinued and a new trade set up, provided that at some time within two years after the transfer the trade or the company owning the trade are at least 75% owned by the same persons as owned them at some time in the year preceding the transfer.

The new company inherits the capital allowances written down values of the old company, as well as any trading losses brought forward. Note, however, that non-trading (eg capital) losses are not carried forward.

Section 252 can be very useful when reorganising the affairs of a group, for instance when bringing trades previously carried on by a number of group companies into one company.

Assuming, as is likely to be the case, that there will be no change in the ownership of the companies merely as a result of the reconstruction, the important factors are that:

(a) the old company should transfer the whole or part of its trade; and
(b) the activities transferred should amount to a trade or part of a trade to be carried on by the company to which the transfer is made.

There is a wealth of case law on the distinction between transferring a trade and merely transferring the assets with which the trade is carried on. In *Watson Bros v Lothian* (1902) 4 TC 441 the court held that for a shipping trade to be transferred it was necessary for the debts and customer lists of a shipping company as well as the ships to be transferred. On the other hand, *James Shipstone & Sons Ltd v Morris* (1929) 14 TC 413 indicates that it is not necessary for all the assets and liabilities to be transferred. In *Thomson and Balfour v Le Page* (1923) 8 TC 541 the purchaser of a business took over only the plant, a few employees and goodwill and not the books, debtors or management staff. The vendors wrote to their customers advising them that the purchasers had succeeded to their trade, and the court held that the commissioners were entitled to find that there had been a succession. Finally, in *Wadsworth Morton Ltd v Jenkinson* (1966) 43 TC 479 the directors of a company in liquidation began to trade again with their existing customers through a new company. The courts approved the directors' contention that the key factors in considering whether there had been a succession were:

(a) whether the profit making apparatus of the old company had been transferred and continued in an identifiable form;

(b) the nature of the trade;
(c) identity of customers;
(d) the place where the trade is carried on;
(e) identity of employees.

Applying these principles in practice, it is suggested that a transfer within s 252 should be carried out as follows:

(1) The plant and equipment should be transferred (by delivery to avoid stamp duty) at the written down value shown in the accounts.
(2) The employees concerned should be given new contracts of employment.
(3) Stocks should be transferred at cost.
(4) Ideally, work-in-progress should be transferred at cost. However, as the contractual liability is between the old company and its customers it may be impractical to novate the contracts. If that is the case, it is suggested that the work-in-progress should be transferred for accounts purposes, and that Board minutes should record that the transferee company is completing the work as agent for the transferor and that any profits or losses on completion are to belong to the transferee.
(5) Existing customers should be circularised to the effect that the transferee is taking over the trade of the transferor.
(6) Debtors and creditors should be transferred at book value. To avoid stamp duty on the assignment of the debts, Board minutes should record that from the date of the transfer the transferor will collect debts as agent for the transferee and will satify the creditors out of the sums received from the transferee.
(7) There is no objection to the purchase consideration being left outstanding on an inter-company loan account.

In several of the cases quoted above in which there was held to be a transfer of a trade, the successor purchased goodwill from the predecessor. Indeed in the *Thomson and Balfour* case goodwill was about all that was purchased apart from the plant. However, whilst the purchase of goodwill is in itself a strong indication that a trade has been transferred, it is not a necessary feature of a transfer of trade if the other important factors are present.

24.6 PAYMENT OF TAX

Corporation tax is generally payable nine months after the end of an accounting period (TA 1970 s 243(4)). Where, however, a company was trading before 1 April 1965, the due date for payment of corporation tax is extended to the same interval from the end of each accounting period as there was between the end of the basis period for the 1965–66 income tax assessment and 1 January 1966; the interval cannot be less than nine months and may be as long as twenty-one months. To retain the favourable payment date, the company must have remained within the charge to corporation tax in respect to its trade since the financial year 1965

The opportunity to defer the payment of tax by up to twelve months is clearly valuable, and leads to the following planning conclusions:

(1) In a group of companies, profits should be channelled into a company with a favourable payment date; conversely, losses should be realised in other companies. If, for instance, a company with a favourable payment date has trading losses and other income, it will generally be better to surrender the losses to other companies through group relief, rather than to setoff the losses against the other income under TA 1970 s 177(2).

(2) In any group reorganisation, care should be taken to preserve the trade of a company with a favourable payment date. Section 244 does not deprive a company of its favourable payment date if it begins to carry on other trades, as long as the trade carried on at 1 April 1965 continues.

25 Groups of companies—chargeable gains

25.1 INTRA-GROUP TRANSFERS OF ASSETS

For reasons set out at **2.3** above, the authors do not generally favour a group of companies as a trading vehicle, preferring a divisional structure within one limited company where a company carries on several activities. Accordingly, in this chapter we have dealt in outline only with the chargeable gains of companies in a group, concentrating on planning opportunities and pitfalls arising from the legislation.

TA 1970 s 273 provides that where capital assets are transferred between companies in a group, the transfer is deemed to take place for such consideration as will result in the transferor company making neither a gain nor a loss; in other words, the transferee inherits the base cost of the transferor. A group is defined for this purpose in TA 1970 s 272 as the principal company of the group and all its 75% subsidiaries, that is, subsidiaries of which it owns beneficially 75% or more of the share capital directly or indirectly (TA 1970 s 532).

If a company leaves a 75% group, TA 1970 s 278 provides that any assets owned by the company leaving the group which have been acquired by that company from another group company within the previous six years are treated as having disposed of and immediately reacquired by the owner company at their open market value at the time the company leaves the group. Note that this provision does not merely crystallise the gain deferred on the intra-group transfer; it also charges any gain arising since the transfer.

Attention is drawn to the following planning points arising out of the group chargeable gains legislation:

(1) The Inland Revenue can be expected to resist attempts to use the legislation to avoid liability to tax through transactions which have no commerical justification, following the principles established in

the *Ramsay*, *Burmah* and *Furniss* cases (see **1.3** above). In particular, the authors are aware that the Inland Revenue are currently attacking schemes involving the acquisition by a group of capital loss companies to shelter gains arising elsewhere in the group. The Revenue's attitude to the routing of disposals of chargeable assets through one company in a group to ensure that losses and gains are matched within the same company (and for no other commercial reason) is not yet apparent. Until the Revenue's attitude does become clear, the authors suggest that the scheme should normally be continued, notwithstanding the double charge to stamp duty where the group companies concerned are not in a 90% group relationship.

(2) Section 278(1) excludes from the general charge when a company leaves a group 'cases where a company ceases to be a member of a group by being wound up or dissolved or in consequence of another member of the group being wound up or dissolved'. This provision was used in *Burman v Hedges and Butler Ltd* [1979] STC 136 to avoid tax on a transfer between groups, but any such attempt in future is likely to be attacked using the *Ramsay* principle.

(3) An intra-group transfer of land is within the scope of TA 1970 s 488, and s 273 affords no relief from any liability under s 488. (For an outline of the scope of s 488, see **37.7** below). Where an intra-group transfer of land takes place prior to a sale outside the group, it is prudent to ensure that the transfer is at market value so that the transferee company cannot be held to have acquired the land with the sole or main object of realising a gain from its disposal.

25.2 ROLL-OVER RELIEF

TA 1970 s 276 provides that for roll-over relief purposes all the trades carried on by companies within a group are to be treated as a single trade, with the result that gains arising in one trading company can be rolled over against acquisitions in another such company. Attention is drawn to the following planning points:

(1) The relief provided by TA 1970 s 276 means that the search for qualifying 'new assets' must extend to all group companies carrying on trades (see **26.2** below).

(2) It may sometimes be possible to obtain roll-over relief on an asset which has been held by a group company but not used for the

purposes of a trade. If the company transfers the asset to another group company, TA 1970 s 273 ensures that no gain arises at that point. If the new company then uses the asset for the purposes of its trade before disposing of it outside the group, it will qualify for roll-over relief if it has used the asset 'throughout the period of (its) ownership' of the asset (CGTA 1979 s 115(1)).

(3) Shares (for instance, in a subsidiary) are not within the class of assets at CGTA 1979 s 118 qualifying for roll-over relief. If, therefore, a group plans to liquidate a subsidiary, any assets within the subsidiary likely to give rise to chargeable gains should be transferred to other group companies before the liquidation is effected; if the assets are used by the transferee companies for trade purposes they may then be sold out of the group if desired, and roll-over relief claimed on any gains.

(4) Section 273 is commonly used to allow assets on which a gain is likely to arise to be transferred to group companies with capital losses. Where the losses are not sufficient wholly to extinguish the gain, care should be taken to ensure that the acquiring company uses the assets for the purposes of its trade before disposing of them outside the group, otherwise no roll-over relief can be claimed for the balance of the loss.

(5) CGTA 1979 s 116 restricts roll-over where not all of the proceeds of disposal of the old asset are applied in acquiring new assets; where the cost of the new assets is less than the base value of the old asset, no roll-over is possible. Where this last situation is likely to arise, the effects of s 116 can be mitigated if the company holding and intending to dispose of the old asset first transfers a share in the asset to another group company; the two companies then jointly dispose of the asset outside the group. The second company will inherit a proportionate share of the base cost of the asset to be set against its share of the disposal proceeds; this part of the gain will probably be taxable immediately as it is unlikely that the second company will use the share of the old asset in its trade. The first company will have a reduced base value for s 116 and may be able to achieve full roll-over. A similar arrangement is possible between husband and wife, using CGTA 1979 s 44. This scheme is not, however, likely to be attractive where the asset involved is land with development value. DLTA 1976 s 12(4) and (5) as amended by FA 1980 s 116(2) removes the £75,000 exemption where an asset is sold outside a group and a previous intra-group disposal was a part disposal and not a disposal of the entire asset.

CAPITAL GAINS TAX

26 Roll-over relief

26.1 GENERAL PRINCIPLES

CGTA 1979 ss 115–121 provide for a valuable deferral of tax on chargeable gains where the proceeds from the sale of a qualifying asset are reinvested in the acquisition of other qualifying assets. The classes of qualifying assets (ss 118 and 119) are as follows:

(1) Any land or building 'occupied (as well as used) only for the purposes of the trade', but excluding land etc used in a trade of dealing in or developing land or of providing services to the occupier of land in which the person carrying on the trade (and making the disposal) has an estate or interest. It is interesting that the legislation specifically severs a building from the land on which it stands and treats it as a separate asset, contrary to the general rule of law which treats a building and the land on which it stands as one asset. The question of whether land is occupied for the purposes of a trade can raise complex legal issues; for instance in *Temperley v Visibell Ltd* [1974] STC 64 ownership and the intention to occupy land without any actual use being made of the land (because it was sold and other land acquired) was held not to amount to occupation for the purposes of s 118. Whether land or a building occupied by an employee or partner of the business qualifies for relief depends on whether the property can be shown to be in representative occupation (*Anderton v Lamb* [1981] STC 43). This will normally be difficult to establish in the context of a family business.

(2) Fixed plant or machinery which does not form part of a building. It was established in *Williams v Evans* [1982] STC 498 that this category includes only fixed plant and fixed machinery and not, as the appellant in that case had contended, fixed plant and any machinery.

(3) Ships, aircraft and hovercraft.

(4) Goodwill.

The asset disposed of and the asset acquired need not be within the same class as long as each is a qualifying asset.

The effect of claiming the relief is that any gain arising on the disposal of the old asset is deducted from the base cost of the new asset to be taken into account on any subsequent disposal. Where only part of the consideration received for the old asset is used to acquire new assets partial roll-over is available provided that the part which is not applied is less than the gross gain on the disposal (before time apportionment etc to take account of any period of ownership prior to 6 April 1965).

Where the old asset was used only partly for business purposes the disposal consideration capable of being rolled-over is apportioned:

(a) in the case of land or buildings where identifiable parts were or were not used for business purposes, by treating the parts as separate assets (s 115(5));

(b) where the whole asset was used for trade purposes for only part of the period of ownership by the disponor, on a time basis (s 115(6)).

Where apportionment on a time basis is necessary, it is the practice of the Inland Revenue to consider the business and non-business use of the asset only during the period after 6 April 1965.

Any apportionment agreed between buyer and seller in an arm's length transaction will normally be conclusive for tax purposes (*EV Booth (Holdings) Ltd v Buckwell* [1980] STC 578).

If a taxpayer carries on two trades, either consecutively or concurrently, both trades are treated as one and gains on assets used in one trade can be rolled over against acquisitions in the other (s 115 (7)). SP8/81 states that the Inland Revenue are prepared to treat trades as carried on successively where the interval between the cessation of one trade and the commencement of another does not exceed three years.

Where the new asset acquired is a depreciating asset, that is an asset with a predictable life not exceeding fifty years, or will become a depreciating asset within ten years, full roll-over relief is not available (s 117). Instead, any gain is held over until

(a) the depreciating asset is disposed of by the trader; or
(b) the depreciating asset ceases to be used for the purposes of a trade carried on by him; or
(c) the tenth anniversary of the acquisition of the depreciating asset.

If, however, the trader acquires another non-depreciating asset whilst the original gain is still held over, he can claim that the held over gain should be wholly or partly rolled over against the cost of the new non-depreciating asssset.

Section 121 extends roll-over relief to assets owned by an individual and used in a trade carried on by his 'family company'. The definition of family company is considered in Chapter 29 below. There is no requirement that the company should have been his family company for any minimum period. Note, however, that an individual cannot roll over a gain on such an asset into an asset bought by him for a trade of his own, or vice versa, not can he roll it into an asset he buys for use by a different family company or into an asset which is bought by the company.

Gains can be rolled over only against acquisitions which take place within a period beginning twelve months before the disposal giving rise to the gain and ending three years after the disposal (s 115(3)). An unconditional contract for an acquisition within the specified period is sufficient; if the contract is not in fact completed any necessary adjustments are made when the situation is finalised. The Board of Inland Revenue have discretion to extend the time limit, and are generally helpful in this respect where the failure to replace assets within the time limit arises from circumstances outside the taxpayers control.

Roll-over relief in the case of groups of companies is considered at 25.2 above.

26.2 STRATEGY

Subject to commercial considerations, a trader disposing of business assets giving rise to a chargeable gain should plan to buy, within the time limit for relief, new qualifying assets into which the gain is rolled over. Where the purchase of specific assets is not possible or desirable, the trader's advisers should review periodically the capital expenditure of the business during the twelve months before and the three years after the disposal, to ensure that all assets to which roll-over relief may apply are made the subject of a claim. In this connection the existence of relief for fixed plant or machinery should not be overlooked. Fixed plant is not defined in the legislation or case law, with the result that the phrase must be given its normal English meaning (*IT Special Comrs v Pemsel* (1891) 3 TC 53, HL). The authors suggest that any plant or machinery requiring attachment to the fabric of the business premises or to its plumbing or wiring (other than simply putting a plug in a socket) should be regarded as fixed. The Revenue will usually accept that items of plant and machinery which are fixed in the sense that they are normally kept in one place such as a factory or workshop and are unsuitable to be moved about easily are to be regarded as fixed plant.

Roll-over relief applies only where the consideration received for the first asset is used 'to *acquire*' a new asset. Strictly, as land and buildings constitute one asset, the land, the construction of a building on land already owned by the trader does not involve the acquisition in legal terms of a new asset. Similarly, if the land and an existing building are acquired and the expenditure is merely on alterations and improvements, no new asset is acquired and roll-over is not available on the capital cost of those works.

It is understood, however, that the Revenue are prepared to treat the construction of a new building and works of improvement or alteration to an existing building as the acquisition of a new asset for roll-over purposes. The works involved would only be those which could be said to result in some change to the building, that is, to the actual fabric of the building or to the fixtures and fittings which will be landlord's fixtures and fittings, irrespective of whether they are also plant and machinery and qualify for capital allowances as such. Expenditure on moveable items, eg carpets, furniture and other tenant's fittings, would not qualify.

The use of the word 'assets' (in the plural) in CGTA 1979 s 115 indicates that a gain can be rolled over against the cost of more than one new asset. The legislation is silent on the manner in which the gain is to be related to the new assets and their costs reduced for future disposals. The authors' view is that the wording of s 115(1) ('on making a claim as respects the consideration which has been so applied') allows a claimant to claim the relief in the way which is most advantageous, not necessarily in the order in which the new assets are acquired. Where possible, for instance, gains should not be rolled over against the cost of depreciating assets. As a general rule, gains should be rolled into assets least likely to be sold in the future. If there is insufficient expenditure on new assets to cover all gains, gains which are large in relation to the sale proceeds should be rolled over before gains which are small in relation to the sale proceeds.

Where gains are rolled over against depreciating assets, the provision of CGTA 1979 s 117(3), (4) and (5) should be borne in mind throughout the period of ten years after the acquisition of the depreciating asset or until it has been sold. It will usually be advantageous to transfer the roll-over relief from the depreciating asset to any non-depreciating asset acquired during the qualifying period. The acquisition of a depreciating asset may, however, be a useful stepping-stone to full roll-over relief if other non-depreciating assets cannot be acquired within three years of the original disposal. Once the depreciating asset has been acquired, the trader has up to ten years to acquire non-depreciating assets and achieve full roll-over.

26.3 DEEMED DISPOSALS AND DEEMED CONSIDERATION

Many transactions undertaken in a family business context will involve capital gains being levied by reference to a deemed rather than an actual disposal or acquisition (eg where an asset is acquired on the death of a previous owner) or the substitution of a deemed consideration for the actual consideration given (eg where market value is substituted when the disponer and acquirer are connected persons).

CGTA 1979 s 115(8) provides that any provision of CGTA 1979 'fixing the amount of the consideration deemed to be given for the acquisition or disposal of assets shall be applied before this section is applied'. Accordingly, roll-over relief is given on the gain computed by reference to the deemed consideration and not by reference to any actual consideration.

The position on a deemed disposal or acquisition is less clear. Section 115(1) refers to the consideration which a trader *obtains* from the disposal of an asset which is *applied* by him in acquiring another asset. If, on a deemed disposal, no actual consideration passes, it can be argued that no consideration has been 'obtained' or 'applied'. It is Inland Revenue practice, however, to allow roll-over relief on gains calculated by reference to deemed disposal proceeds, so that, for instance, a gain on a gift can be rolled over under s 115 if gifts roll-over under CGTA 1979 s 126 or FA 1980 s 79 is not claimed. On the other hand, the Revenue do not appear to allow gains to be rolled over against a deemed acquisition where no consideration is actually given by the acquirer.

Where the old asset is exchanged for a new asset, on a strict interpretation of the legislation no roll-over relief is due: s 115(1) refers to the consideration for the old asset being 'applied in acquiring' the new asset whereas in the case of an exchange the consideration for the old asset *is* the new asset. However, the Inland Revenue have confirmed to the CCAB that roll-over relief is available where assets are exchanged.

27 Partnership capital gains

27.1 PARTNERSHIP ASSETS

Where two or more persons carry on a business in partnership, CGTA 1979 s 60 provides that:

'(a) tax in respect of chargeable gains accruing to them on the disposal of any partnership assets shall ... be assessed and charged on them separately, and
(b) any partnership dealings shall be treated as dealings by the partners and not by the firm as such.'

The cornerstone of current CGT treatment of partnerships is the Inland Revenue Statement of Practice of 17 January 1975 (SP 1/75). This statement provides that where an asset is disposed of by a partnership to an outside party each of the partners will be treated as disposing of his fractional share of the asset. Similarly, if a partnership makes a part disposal of an asset each partner will be treated as making a part disposal of his fractional share. In computing gains or losses the proceeds of disposal will be allocated between the partners in the ratio of their shares in asset surpluses at the time of the disposal. Where this is not specifically laid down the allocation will follow the actual destination of the surplus as shown in the partnership accounts; regard will, of course, have to be paid to any agreement outside the accounts. If the surplus is not allocated among the partners but, for example, put to a common reserve, regard will be had to the ordinary profit-sharing ratio in the absence of a specified asset-surplus-sharing ratio. Expenditure on the acquisition of assets by a partnership will be allocated between the partners in the same way at the time of the acquisition. This allocation may require adjustment, however, if there is a subsequent change in the partnership sharing ratios. The Revenue practice of dividing acquisition costs and disposal consideration in accordance with capital profit-sharing ratios at the relevant times may not be wholly in accordance with the statute, but in practice it gives a sensible result and is universally adopted.

27.2 TRANSACTIONS BETWEEN PARTNERS

This is an area where the 1975 Statement of Practice really comes into its own. Revenue practice is founded on the contention that CGTA 1979 s 60 treats any partnership dealings in chargeable assets for CGT purposes as dealings by the individual partners rather than by the firm as such. Each partner has, therefore, to be regarded as owning a fractional share of each of the partnership assets and not for this purpose an interest in the partnership. Where it is necessary to ascertain the market value of a partner's share in a partnership asset for CGT purposes, it will be taken as a fraction of the value of the total partnership interest in the asset without any discount for the size of his share. If for example, a partnership owned all the issued shares in a company, the value of the interest in that holding of a partner with a one tenth share would be one tenth of the value of the partnership's 100% holding.

The Revenue practice is almost certainly incorrect in two respects:
(1) It ignores the fact that each partner has an asset, his partnership share, which is a chose in action distinct from his interest in the partnership assets.
(2) A fractional share in an asset is in fact likely to be worth less than a strict apportionment of the whole value of the asset would suggest. A half interest in land, for instance, is likely to be worth in the region 40% of the value of the whole. The Revenue statement specifically excludes any such discount.

Despite these errors of principle the computational rules set out in the Revenue statement are generally sensible. The chances of persuading the Revenue to accept computations prepared on some other basis without recourse to the courts are slim, with the effect that whatever its shortcomings the Statement of Practice effectively has the force of law in almost all cases. For that reason, the rest of this section concentrates on the main provisions of the statement as they apply to different situations which may arise during the life of a partnership.

Changes in partners or partnership sharing ratios

An occasion of charge arises when there is a change in partnership sharing ratios including changes arising from a partner joining or leaving the partnership. In these circumstances a partner who reduces or gives up his share in asset surpluses will be treated as disposing of part, or the whole, of his share in each of the partnership assets and a partner who increases his share will be treated as making a similar acquisition. The disposal consideration will be a fraction (equal to the fractional share changing hands) of the current balance sheet value of each chargeable asset provided that there is no direct payment of consideration outside the partnership. Where no adjustment is made through the partnership accounts (eg by revaluation of the assets coupled with a corresponding increase or decrease in the partner's current or capital account at some date between the partner's acquisition and the reduction in his share) the disposal is treated as made for a consideration equal to his CGT cost and thus there will be neither a chargeable gain nor an allowable loss at that point. A partner whose share reduces will carry forward a smaller proportion of cost to set against a subsequent disposal of the asset, and a partner whose share increases will carry forward a larger proportion of cost.

The general rules set out above require modification, however, where:

(a) the partners are connected persons for reasons other than the fact that they are partners; or
(b) where partnership assets are revalued in the accounts; or
(c) where, on a change in partnership profit-sharing-arrangement payments are made between partners outside the framework of the accounts.

Transfers between connected persons

CGTA 1979 s 63(4) provides that a person is 'connected' with any person with whom he is in partnership, except in relation to acquisitions or disposals of partnership assets pursuant to bona fide commercial arrangements. A change in partnership sharing arrangements will normally fall within the exception. In a family business, however, it is likely that partners will be connected by virtue of relationships other than partnership. In such a case CGTA 1979 s 62 applies to treat transactions between them as being otherwise than by way of a bargain at arm's length, with the result that CGTA 1979 s 29A(1) deems the transactions to have taken place at market value. The statement of practice, however, provides that market value will not be substituted if nothing would have been paid had the parties been at arm's length. Similarly, if consideration of less than market value passes between partners connected other than by partnership or otherwise not at arm's length, the transfer will be regarded as having been made for full market value only if the consideration

27.2 Transactions between partners

actually paid was less than that which would have been paid by parties at arm's length. Where a transfer has to be treated as if it had taken place for market value, the deemed disposal proceeds will fall to be treated in the same way as payments outside the accounts (see below).

Adjustments through the accounts

Where a partnership asset is revalued a partner will be credited in his current or capital account with a sum equal to his fractional share of the increase in value. An upward revaluation of chargeable assets is not itself an occasion of charge. If, however, there were to be a subsequent reduction in the partner's asset-surplus share, the effect would be to reduce his potential liability to CGT on the eventual disposal of the assets without an equivalent reduction of the credit he has received in the accounts. Consequently, at the time of the reduction in profit-sharing ratio he will be regarded as disposing of the fractional share of the partnership asset, represented by the difference between his old and his new share, for a consideration equal to that fraction of the increased value at the revaluation. The partner whose share correspondingly increases will have his acquisition cost to be carried forward for the asset increased by the same amount. The same principles will be applied in the case of a downward revaluation.

Payments outside the accounts

Where on a change of partnership sharing ratios, payments are made directly between two or more partners outside the framework of the partnership accounts, the payments represent consideration for the disposal of the whole or part of a partner's share in partnership assets in addition to any consideration calculated on the bases above. Often such payments will be for goodwill not included in the balance sheet. In such cases the partner receiving the payment will have no CGT cost to set against it unless he made a similar payment for his share in the asset (eg on entering the partnership) or elects to have the market value at 6 April 1965 treated as his acquisition cost. The partner making the payment will only be allowed to deduct the amount in computing gains or losses on a subsequent disposal of his share in the asset. He will be able to claim a loss when he finally leaves the partnership or when his share is reduced provided that he then receives either no consideration or a lesser consideration for his share of the asset. Where the payment clearly constitutes payment for a share in assets included in the partnership accounts, the partner receiving it will be able to deduct the amount of the partnership acquisition cost represented by the fraction he is disposing of.

Partnership assets dividend in kind among the partners

Where a partnership distributes an asset in kind to one or more of the partners, eg on dissolution, a partner who receives the asset will not be regarded as disposing of his fractional share in it. A computation will first be necessary of the gains which would be chargeable on the individual partners if the asset had been disposed of at its current market value. Where this results in a gain being attributed to a partner not receiving the asset the gain will be charged at the time of the distribution of the asset. Where, however, the gain is allocated to a partner receiving the asset concerned there will be no charge on distribution. Instead, his CGT cost to be carried forward will be on the market value of the asset at the date of distribution as reduced by the amount of his gain. The same principles will be applied where the computation results in a loss.

Summary

It is a well-known legal maxim that every case depends on its facts. In some cases the attempt by the Inland Revenue to lay down computational rules will lead to anomalous results, in which case the taxpayer should consider the computation in the light of the general provisions of the CGT legislation; many inspectors of taxes appear to be prepared to accept any basis of computation which gives a sensible result and which does not actually contradict the statement of practice. Attention is drawn to the following points arising out of the Revenue statement of practice:

(1) Where a partner is admitted to or leaves the firm, or partnership sharing ratios are changed, an immediate charge to CGT can be avoided if:
    (a) there is no adjustment in the partnership accounts to reflect increases in the value of partnership assets; and
    (b) no payment passes; and
    (c) where a partnership share is transferred for no consideration or for a consideration below market value between persons who are connected other than through the partnership, the parties can demonstrate that no payment would have been made had the parties been at arm's length.

It may be difficult to demonstrate that condition (c) is satisfied; the

argument will be assisted if:
  (i) unconnected partners have been admitted on similar terms; and
  (ii) the partner being admitted has professional or other qualifications such that the value of his services to the partnership business justifies his admission without payment.

(2) Where a charge to tax cannot be avoided on the admission of a 'family' partner without payment, the gain can be deferred by using the general relief for gifts at FA 1980 s 79, thus putting the parties in the position they would have been if the conditions at (1) had been satisfied.

(3) A transfer between partners' capital accounts (by debiting the account of one partner and crediting the account of another) will give rise to a capital gain only if the partnership assets have been revalued since the acquisition. The effect of such a transfer is to pass over the ownership of a proportionate part of the transferor's share in the balance sheet value of the partnership assets. Provided that partners are aware of the current values of the partnership assets (so that they do not, for instance, exceed annual or other exemptions when making gifts of partnership capital) there is generally no good reason to revalue assets on a partnership balance sheet.

28 Development Land Tax

DLTA 1976 s 1 charges development land tax (DLT) on realised development value occurring on the disposal of an interest in land in the UK. As well as actual disposals, the tax is chargeable on a deemed disposal when a project of material development is begun. Realised development value means the proceeds of the disposal net of costs of disposal (or the market value of the land at the commencement of a project of material development) less the base value of the land calculated on one of three alternative bases. The tax is charged at a flat rate of 60%.

The intention of the legislation is to tax only the development value of land, that is the increase in value attributable to the prospect of development. Any increase in value which relates to the increase in the value of the land for its current use (before development) is chargeable to CGT. Where development has been carried out the part of the gain attributable to the value of the building work is chargeable as part of the developer's trading profits or capital gains; this follows from the fact that the legislation deems the gain to arise immediately before development starts, so that value added by subsequent work is excluded.

A full review of the legislation and the way in which realised development value is calculated is outside the scope of this book. In this chapter the authors have sought to concentrate on the way in which the tax is likely to effect a family business, and how that effect may be minimised.

The proprietors of a family business may encounter DLT:

(a) on an actual disposal of land with development value; or
(b) if they start a project of material development on land which they own.

Many businessmen are aware that DLT is levied on a disposal, but the charge on the commencement of a project of material development is often overlooked and does not come to light until it is too late to take any effective tax planning action. Material development may be defined broadly as any development for which planning permission is required under the Town and Country Planning Act 1971 other than development falling into one of the categories set out in DLTA 1976 Sch 4 Pt II, viz:

(a) the carrying out of work for the maintenance, improvement, enlargement or other alteration of any building, so long as the cubic content of the original building is not exceeded by more than one-third;
(b) rebuilding a building destroyed or demolished as part of the development or within the previous ten years, so long as the cubic content of the original building is not exceeded by more than one-tenth;
(c) the carrying out on any land used for the purposes of agriculture or forestry of any building or other operations required for the purposes of that use;
(d) the carrying out of operations on land for, or the use of land for, the display of an advertisement;
(e) the carrying out of operations for, or the use of land for, car parking, provided that such use shall not exced six years;
(f) the use of a dwelling house, office/retail shop manufacturing, storage or processing premises, or premises which were last used for such purposes before they became vacant for the same class of purpose as that for which they were last used (ie a factory making typewriters can be used as a factory to make shoes, but a change of use to a warehouse would not be within the exception);
(g) where part of a building or land is used for a particular purpose, the use of not more than one-tenth of the cubic content of the buildings or of the area of the land for that purpose;
(h) the resumption of the last previous use of land which has been temporarily used for another purpose or which has been unoccupied.

It is important to note that a change of use as well as the commencement of construction work can amount to material development.

A project of material development is began when any 'specified operations' are begun. Specified operations are defined at DLTA 1976 Sch 1 para 2:

'(a) any work of construction in the course of the erection of a building;
(b) the digging of a trench which is to contain the foundations, or part of the foundations, of a building;

(c) the laying of any underground main or pipe to the foundations, or part of the foundations, of a building or to any such trench as is mentioned in paragraph (b) above;
(d) any operation in the course of laying out or constructing a road or part of a road;
(e) any operation in the course of winning or working minerals ... ;
(f) any change in the use of any land, where that change constitutes development.'

These definitions are important because it is possible to influence the timing of a charge to DLT by varying the time at which one or more of those operations is undertaken.

The basis of any DLT planning in relation to a family business is likely to be DLTA 1975 s 12 (amended by FA 1984 s 118) which provides an important exemption for the first £75,000 of gains realised in a financial year (which runs from 1 April to 31 March, for individuals as well as companies; the 5 April year end for individuals has no relevance for DLT). Attention is drawn to the following planning points relevant to maximising the use of this exemption:

(1) Section 12(3) provides that where a person makes more than one disposal in a year, gains on earlier sales are to be relieved in priority to those on later sales.

(2) Section 12(4) and (5) denies this exemption where the taxpayer acquired his interest from a connected person (as defined in CGTA 1979 s 63) within the twelve months prior to the disposal. Where a DLT liability can be foreseen well in advance there is scope for fragmentation of the interest in the land between individuals more than twelve months before the disposal, perhaps among members of a family.

(3) FA 1980 s 116(2) denies the exemption where the disposal was by a person other than an individual and the interest was acquired both:

(a) from a connected person within six years of the disposal for no consideration or for a consideration below market value; and
(b) as a result of a disposal of less than the whole interest in the land concerned within the previous six years by a connected person.

This section is effective in preventing belated fragmentation of an interest in land within a group to obtain a number of £75,000 exemptions, but it does provide scope for a company owning two distinct sites on which development is to start within the same year to sell one site to a connected company and obtain two £75,000 exemptions.

(4) Neither (2) nor (3) above prevent fragmentation of land at the time of purchase by arranging for a number of related persons to acquire the land in separate blocks, but note that s 12(9) treats a partnership as a single person for DLT purposes.
(5) Wherever possible, disposals should be made in tranches of £75,000 in successive years.
(6) Where that is not possible, the use of cross-options should be considered. By this means the first tranche of land can be disposed of absolutely in the first year with the attendant £75,000 exemption and the remainder is disposed of subject to cross-options which are not exercised until a later year. The disposal of the remainder is deferred to the later year because DLTA 1976 s 45(2)(a) deems a disposal to take place when the option is exercised. The parties are in a very similar position to that which would obtain if the balance of the land had been sold outright, as either party can force the other to complete the transaction. The fact that the position is so similar may lead the Inland Revenue to attempt to apply the principles established in *Furniss v Dawson* (see **1.3** above) to disregard the options and to treat the transactions as a single disposal. In the authors' view, even if the options can be disregarded it will not result in the second disposal occurring when the options are granted (ie at the same time as the first disposal). To disregard the options and yet to look at their grant to determine the time of disposal is fundamentally illogical.
(7) In the case of a project of material development, it may be possible to start the development on different parts of the land each year and to obtain the £ 75,000 exemption on the start of each phase. Before doing this, however, the effect of inflation and of the completion of the initial phases on the value of the remaining land should be taken into account.

DLTA 1976 s 18 as amended by FA 1981 s 131 exempts the gain arising on the commencement of a project of material development if:

(a) the owner acquired the interest in land being developed within the three years prior to the commencement of the development; and
(b) the owner had begun development immediately on acquisition, no significant amount of realised development value would have accrued to him.

The provision was intended as an administrative convenience, but it affords a valuable relief to a trader developing land for his own use. If land is bought with the benefit of planning permission at a price reflecting that permission, any increase in the value of the land between acquisition and the commencement of development is excluded from the DLT charge provided that development commences within three years of the acquisition. It is essential to observe the three year time limit for the commencement of material development. Section 18(3) lays down a procedure by which the developer can obtain clearance that the Inland Revenue are satisfied that the s 18 exemption applies. It will normally be advisable to seek this clearance as soon as possible after the acquisition of development land.

DLTA 1976 ss 19 and 19A provide valuable deferral of DLT liability where a person develops land for his own use. Under s 19, a person who carries on a trade and develops land used for the 'industrial purposes' of that trade may defer any DLT payable on the commencement of the development until either

(a) he disposes of his interest in the land (other than by way of a deemed disposal on the commencement of further development or an intra-group transfer), or
(b) the building ceases to be used for the industrial purposes of a trade carried on by the taxpayer and he either ceases to trade altogether or uses the building for a non-qualifying purpose. Thus the right of deferral is not lost if the taxpayer ceases to use a building for a non-qualifying purpose. Further, the right of deferral is not lost if the taxpayer ceases to use a building in one trade and beings to use it in another. A non-qualifying use is established if for twelve months or more in any period of twenty-four months it is used otherwise than for a qualifying purposes.

There are provisions dealing with part deferral where part only of the building is used for industrial purposes, and specific rules covering sale and leaseback transactions. The definition of 'industrial purposes' is wide and includes use in the course of a trade for the carrying on of any process (other than a process carried on in a dwelling house or retail shop) for, or incidental to, the generation of electricity or any of the activities specified in DLTA 1976 Sch 4 para 7 Class E, viz

(a) the making of any articles or part of an article, or the production of any substance;
(b) the altering, repairing, ornamenting, finishing, cleaning, washing, freezing, packing or canning, or adapting for sale, or breaking up or demolishing of any article; or
(c) the getting or dressing of minerals.

Note, however, that storage and warehousing are not in themselves qualifying purposes and buildings used for such purposes and will not qualify unless they are part of some larger qualifying building and are used for a purpose indicated to the main qualifying activity (eg for storing newly manufactured products).

Section 19A (as amended by the FA 1984 s 119) provides a deferral of tax where a landowner commences a project of material development for his own use after 10 March 1981. The provision covers any development provided that the land is owned by the intending occupier at the time of the commencement of the development and the full planning permission is in force when the development is begun. The deferral ceases if the development interest in the land is disposed of other than by way of:

(a) a sale or leaseback (the subsequent sale of the lease will crystallise the deferred liability);
(b) a deemed disposal on the commencement of further development;
(c) an intra-group transfer;
(d) the granting of a lease for twelve months or less;
(e) the grant of a lease whereby the premises become tied premises.

The 1984 amendments limit the carry forward of the deferred liability to a period of twelve years beginning with the date of the original deemed disposal on the commencement of development. If the tax charge does not crystallise during that period, the liability is extinguished.

The twelve year limit on carry forward of liability means that deferral under s 19A is to be preferred to deferral under s 19 where both reliefs are available. The application of one or other of the provisions is mandatory when the conditions are met (the legislation says that liability 'shall' be deferred) but neither section specifies which is to take priority over the other. In the authors' view this means that a taxpayer who qualifies under s 19A will have his liability extinguished after twelve years regardless of whether he also qualifies under s 19. For a discussion of the DLT consequences of the transfer of development land to a company as part of the transfer of a trade on incorporation, see **14.2** above.

PART III

The owners of the business

29 Retirement relief
30 Gifts
31 Providing for retirement
32 The use of trusts
33 Sheltering income
34 Handing on the business
35 Selling the family company

29 Retirement relief

The relief from CGT on the sale or gift of a business or part of a business, or shares or securities in a company, given by CGTA 1979 s 124, is very valuable, especially now that it is proposed in FA 1984 to double the maximum relief to £100,000 for disposals on or after 6 April 1983. Other things being equal, taxpayers should try to plan their affairs so as to take full advantage of it.

'Other things being equal' is a necessary caveat because there will be circumstances where the opportunity to obtain retirement relief may have to be forgone in order to obtain a greater benefit. For example, it may be desirable for the purposes of CTT planning to give away assets before reaching the age of 60, the minimum age for retirement relief.

It is not intended to explain the legislation in any detail but to draw attention to the tax planning opportunities which retirement relief presents. References are to CGTA 1979 unless otherwise stated:

(1) The maximum relief is available only on reaching the age of 65 (s 124(3)). Other things being equal, it would be better for a taxpayer who owns a business or shares in a family trading company, to wait, if possible, until he reaches that age before disposing of his business or shares. Certainly he would want to pass the age of 60, since otherwise he would not be entitled to any relief at all (s 124(1)).

(2) The maximum relief can be obtained only if the ownership conditions specified in s 124(2) are met throughout a period of ten years ending with the disposal. Where the qualifying period is less than ten years a percentage reduction is made on a time basis to a minimum of 10% for a minimum qualifying period of one year (s 124(3)). Here again, other things being equal, it would be beneficial for the taxpayer to postpone the disposal of his business or shares in a family trading company in order to increase the qualifying period up to the maximum ten years.

In this connection, any businesses previously owned by the taxpayer or his family companies should be considered to see whether the period of ownership can be extended backwards by treating such businesses as the same one under Extra-Statutory Concession D8.

(3) The relief applies to sales or gifts (s 124(1)). It is doubtful if an exchange would qualify, and where an exchange is contemplated it should be restructured as a sale followed by a purchase.

(4) In the case of the disposal of a business, care should be taken to avoid a disposal of mere assets. The disposal of a business asset on its own will not qualify for relief unless, perhaps, it is of such a size or value in relation to the business as to lead to the inference that part of the business has been disposed of (*McGregor v Adcock* [1977] STC 206).

In the case of farmers, it seems that relief will be given where 50% or more of the land is disposed of, or where part of the farm can be identified separately, eg as a dairy farm (see *Country Landowner*, February/March (1981) p 36).

Whether there has been a disposal of a business or merely business assets must be a question of fact having regard to all the circumstances, including the way in which the disposal was structured and the wording of the sale agreement or other documents. Wherever possible, the disposal should be so arranged as to include part of the business, perhaps by the inclusion of some stock in trade and goodwill (eg by allowing the purchaser to use the business name and approach former customers of the business). If the purchaser is really interested in the assets rather than the business he should nevertheless be persuaded, if possible, to acquire the business and close it down himself.

(5) The family company requirements set out in s 124(8) should be watched and care taken to ensure that, other things being equal, the taxpayer does not make a disposal of shares in his family trading company which would result in the company no longer qualifying as his family company (see *Davenport v Hasslacher* [1977] STC 254).

At least 25% of the voting rights of the company must be exercisable by the taxpayer (or at least 51% by the taxpayer and his family, of which 5% must be exercisable by the taxpayer). Whether voting rights have actually been exercised or not is irrelevant (*Hepworth v William Smith Group* [1981] STC 354).

Where the taxpayer owns voting shares in company X, not directly, but through the medium of another company Y which he controls, there seems to be some doubt as to whether or not those voting rights are exercisable by him. The point would be relevant if, eg the taxpayer was disposing of non-voting shares in company X held by him directly. If the point does arise the advice must be to argue that those voting rights are exercisable by him.

This discussion will serve as a reminder that it is not necessary that the disposal in question should be a disposal of the taxpayer's voting shares. For example, a disposal of non-voting preference shares or loan stock would be eligible for relief as long as the company qualifies as his family company.

(6) In the case of a family trading company, the taxpayer must be a full-time working director of it, ie a director who is required to devote substantially the whole of his time to the service of the company in a managerial or technical capacity (s 124(2), (8) and see *IRC v D Devine & Sons Ltd* (1963) 41 TC 210 for a discussion of the meaning of the phrase for profits tax purposes). This is in contrast to an unincorporated business, where there is no requirement that the taxpayer must devote all, or indeed any, of his time to it.

Where a director works for more than one company the requirements for concessionary relief under Extra-Statutory Concession D9 should be carefully noted. If he divides his time between companies which are not in a group for corporation tax purposes or do not carry on complementary businesses no relief will be due.

(7) Particular care should be taken where it is proposed to incorporate a business because this can lead to loss of retirement relief in certain cases. For example, a husband and wife partnership where the wife does not work in the business, or a partnership of five unrelated persons each taking up 20% of the shares in the company.

(8) Special care needs to be taken to preserve retirement relief where there is an interval of time between the closing down of a business and the sale of the business assets or, in the case of a company liquidation, the making of a capital distribution to the shareholders. The conditions for relief cannot correctly be met in these circumstances. However, by Extra-Statutory Concession D14 relief will be given provided certain conditions are met. The points to note are:

(a) in the case of an unincorporated business, the business assets must be disposed of within three years of the closure;
(b) in the case of an individual shareholder, the capital distribution must be received within three years of the closure;
(c) the business assets belonging to the individual or to the company must not be used or leased for any purpose during the intervening period from the closure of the business to the disposal.

In each case the relief will be calculated by reference to the taxpayer's age at the date of closure.

Any chargeable business assets sold by the company in anticipation of liquidation may be included amongst the chargeable business assets and the total chargeable assets at the time of disposal of the shares (Extra-Statutory Concession D13). This suggests that, if possible, non-business chargeable assets should be sold before chargeable business assets, so as to increase the proportion of the gain eligible for relief.

(9) There can be a problem where the owners of a family company decide to sell out by exchanging their shares for shares in another company on a take-over. There will be no CGT liability on the exchange (CGTA 1979 s 85) but no retirement relief will be available on a subsequent disposal of the new shares. In these circumstances, it might be considered beneficial to arrange the take-over for shares plus cash of sufficient amount to enable the maximum retirement relief to be taken.

(10) Relief is given only in respect of chargeable business assets, ie assets (including goodwill but not including shares or securities or other assets held as investments) which are used for the purposes of a trade, profession or vocation (s 124(4) and for definition s 124(8); see also *Temperley v Visibell Ltd* [1974] STC 64 for 'used for the purposes of the trade').

It is not required that the assets are used *only* for the purposes of the business. Where, therefore, the disposal includes a dwelling house occupied by the taxpayer himself, which he uses for business purposes, and to which the private residence relief under CGTA 1979 s 101 does not apply, (eg because it is not his main residence), it should be maintained that the gain is eligible for retirement relief.

Nor is it necessary for an asset to be used for the purposes of the business throughout the whole period of the taxpayer's ownership. Where, therefore, the taxpayer has a non-business asset which is likely to show a substantial gain on disposal he might, in appropriate circumstances, begin to make use of it for business purposes and dispose of it as part of the business.

(11) In the case of a disposal of shares of a company, the gains eligible for relief are reduced in the same proportion as the company's chargeable business assets bear to the total chargeable assets (s 124(5)). A chargeable asset is defined as being every asset except one on the disposal of which no chargeable gain would accrue. This would seem to suggest that an asset which would show an allowable loss on disposal is not a chargeable asset. However, in June 1978, the then Chief Secretary to the Treasury stated that the definition did include assets which would show an allowable loss on disposal.

(Report of Standing Committee A, Hansard 13 June 1978, col 1047). This appears to be the Revenue view, though as long as there remains any doubt on the question the taxpaper is entitled to argue for whichever construction is to his advantage.

There is no requirement that the individual assets of the company are held for a minimum length of time. Where, therefore, it is commercially feasible, the gains qualifying for retirement relief can be increased by switching the assets prior to disposal so as to increase the ratio of chargeable business assets to total chargeable assets, eg the purchase of plant and machinery for cash.

(12) The chargeable business assets/chargeable assets formula bears particularly heavily in the case of shares in a parent company because shares in subsidiary companies will be chargeable assets but not chargeable business assets. Of course, shares in a pure holding company will not be eligible for relief anyway because it will not be a trading company. If, however, the parent company is a trading company, there are ways in which the retirement relief can be increased.

One possibility is to transfer the shares in the existing subsidiary to a new subsidiary specially formed for the purpose, leaving the sale price outstanding on loan. The parent company will then own the shares in the new subsidiary company, which will be worth little, and a debt due by the subsidiary company, which will not be a chargeable asset (CGTA 1979 s 134(1)).

A sale of the subsidiary to an outsider for cash, which is not a chargeable asset, might also be appropriate in some circumstances, eg where the shares in the subsidiary are held purely as an investment. Of course, regard would have to be paid to the potential charge to corporation tax on the sale.

Another way out of the difficulty might be for the subsidiary to pay the maximum possible dividend to the parent company, thus reducing the value of the subsidiary company. The extent to which the dividend may be subject to apportionment in the hands of the parent company should be examined, but in considering the parent company's requirements, the requirements of the group as a whole can be taken into account (CCAB Memorandum TR 508, 9 June 1983). Another point to watch is that the receipt of this dividend does not result in the parent company ceasing to be a trading company as defined in FA 1972 Sch 16 para 11(1).

Even in the case of a pure investment holding company all is not lost because it may be possible to transfer the trade of the subsidiary to it so that the holding company now qualifies as a trading company.

(13) It is well known that, notwithstanding the headnote to s 124, retirement relief is not confined only to retirement and could be available where the individual starts a new business after selling his old one. In these circumstances, the interaction of retirement relief with roll-over relief for the replacement of business assets under CGTA 1979 s 115 should be watched carefully. Although the matter is not entirely free from doubt, it does seem on the wording of the legislation that roll-over relief is given in priority to retirement relief because, when a roll-over claim is made, the disposal is deemed to be for a consideration that gives rise to neither gain nor loss (s 115(1)). If there is no gain, there can be no retirement relief.

In these circumstances, the decision whether or not to make a roll-over claim needs to be considered carefully having regard to the future intentions of the taxpayer and the likelihood of his making gains in the future which will qualify for retirement relief.

(14) Retirement relief does, however, taken precedence over roll-over relief for gifts under FA 1980 s 79 and the relief for gifts of business assets under CGTA 1979 s 126. Where, therefore, the taxpayer is proposing to make both sales and gifts, and the retirement relief will not be sufficient to cover the gains arising on both, the disposals should, if possible, be carefully timed to ensure that retirement relief is given against the gains arising on sales rather than on gifts, since the latter will normally be eligible for roll-over relief in any event.

(15) Where an asset is owned by a partner personally but used for the purposes of a business carried on by the partnership, the Revenue are prepared to accept that retirement relief is available on the disposal of the asset if it is associated with the disposal of the business or part of the business and provided the other conditions for relief are satisfied. Where, however, the partnership has paid rent for it, the asset is treated as an investment—and thus excluded from relief—except for a fraction of it proportionate to the partner's share of the rent. A larger fraction of the asset may qualify if the rent was clearly less than market value (Inland Revenue Statement of Practice 4 January 1973—see STI 1973 p 2). In order to maximise retirement relief, the partner should consider taking a larger profit share in lieu of rent.

(16) A similar point arises where a shareholder owns an asset personally which is used by the company. Strictly no retirement relief is due, except in the unusual case of the disposal of an asset held for the purposes of an office or employment by the person exercising that office or employment (see *Smethurst v Cowtan* [1977] STC 60). However, by Extra-Statutory Concession D11, the dis-

29 Retirement relief

posal of the asset will be regarded as qualifying for relief, subject to certain conditions. The important points to note are:
(a) the disposal of the asset must be associated with a disposal of his shares (but not, it seems, securities) in that company;
(b) if the taxpayer has charged a market rent for use of the asset no relief will be given; to the extent that the rent was clearly less than market rent a proportion of the gain will qualify for relief.

It would be better if the shareholder took a higher salary from his company instead of rent.

(17) Husband and wife are each entitled to the full retirement relief. Where it is proposed to transfer a business or shares in a company from one to the other, the two periods of ownership may be aggregated in calculating the length of ownership of the transferee spouse in certain circumstances (Extra-Statutory Concession D7).

The precise terms of the Concession should be examined where this situation arises. The really important point to note is that the transferor spouse must transfer his or her entire interest in the business or entire holding of shares in the company if the Concession is to apply. It would not, for instance, be possible for a husband to transfer half his business to his wife shortly before sale and expect to attract an additional amount of retirement relief against the wife's half share of the gain.

(18) Even so, a transfer of shares between husband and wife before disposing of them to a third party can sometimes be very beneficial. This arises from the fact that there is no condition that the actual shares disposed of must have been owned for any minimum period. So, eg a husband and wife might each own 50% of the shares of a trading company of which only the husband is a full-time working director. If the company is sold only the husband's gain would be eligible for retirement relief, but if, before the sale, the wife transfers her shares to her husband, the entire gain will qualify for relief. This would be an attractive proposition only if the husband has retirement relief available in excess of the gain on his original 50% shareholding. It is necessary to add a warning that a scheme such as this may well be vulnerable under the *Ramsay* doctrine (*W T Ramsay Ltd v IRC* [1981] STC 174, HL).

(19) Where a husband and wife jointly own an asset but only one of them carries on the business it seems that, strictly, only 50% of the gain will be eligible for relief. A guest house run by the wife as a sole trader is a common example. To ensure full relief, it would be better if the business is carried on as a partnership; the husband need take only a nominal share of profits.

29 Retirement relief

Finally, readers are reminded that, on 22 March 1984, the Inland Revenue issued a consultative document about possible changes in the retirement relief (see STI 1984 p 279 and TPT 4 April 1984, p 53). Some of the above planning points may, therefore, soon become out of date.

30 Gifts

30.1 GENERAL RELIEF FOR GIFTS (FA 1980 s 79)

Roll-over relief is available for gifts, including transfers of assets at less than market value. The relief originally applied only to transfers by an individual to an individual resident or ordinarily resident in the UK, but it has since been extended twice; firstly, to gifts by individuals to trustees (FA 1981 s 78) and secondly, to transfers by trustees either to individuals or other trustees (FA 1982 s 82).

The relief must be claimed by both transferor and transferee, except in the case of a transfer to trustees when a claim by the transferor alone is sufficient (FA 1982 s 82(1)). The claim must be made within six years after the end of the tax year in which the gift is made (TMA 1970 s 43(1)).

The effect of the relief is that the transferor's gain is rolled over against the transferee's acquisition cost (FA 1980 s 79(1)). Where, however, some actual consideration is received in excess of the transferor's base cost, the relief will be restricted (FA 1980 s 79(3)). Any CTT paid on the gift is a deductible expense in computing the donee's gain on a subsequent disposal of the asset (FA 1980 s 79(5)).

Planning points

(1) In theory, roll-over relief is only a postponement of tax, not a complete exemption, and the liability will arise if and when the donee sells the asset. If the donor were to retain the asset until his death, there would be no CGT liability and the donee would have an uplifted acquisition value equal to market value at the date of death. On the other hand, the rates of CTT payable on death are much higher than for lifetime transfers and the asset will probably have increased in value.

In practice, roll-over relief often leads to complete avoidance of tax, as, eg where the donee has CGT losses sufficient to cover the gain, or where he is likely to retain the asset until his death.

All this indicates that it is necessary to consider very carefully whether or not to claim the relief, though generally it will be beneficial to do so.

(2) Where a taxpayer is proposing to sell an asset pregnant with gain, he should consider making a gift of the asset prior to sale. For example, he might first give the asset to a member of his family who has available CGT losses sufficient to cover the gain, or he might give shares in the asset to one or more of his children, so as to make use of their exempt bands. It is now necessary to add the warning that such schemes may be vulnerable under the *Ramsay* doctrine (*W T Ramsay v IRC* [1981] STC 174, HL). The impact of CTT should also be taken into account, having regard particularly to the mutual gifts legislation in FA 1976 ss 86 and 87 if it is intended that the donee gives the proceeds back.

(3) Where a taxpayer is considering making a cash gift, he should consider, instead, the possibility of making a gift of an asset which shows a gain and claiming roll-over relief.

(4) Another occasion on which roll-over would be useful is where the taxpayer has a second home which is not his main residence and which he wishes to give to, say, his son. Provided the son then occupies the house as his main residence, any gain he makes on a subsequent sale of the house, including the held-over gain, will be exempt from CGT under CGTA 1979 s 101.

(5) A gift of a business on the basis that the donee takes over the liabilities makes the transaction a sale at an undervalue. The liabilities will be apportioned rateably between the assets and this could result in a considerable reduction in the gains eligible for roll-over (see FA 1980 s 79(3)). It would be better in these circumstances to arrange for the gift in two parts, so that the liabilities can be apportioned as far as possible to the assets on which no chargeable gains will, in any event, arise. It seems unlikely that an arrangement of this sort could be attacked by the Revenue under CGTA 1979 s 43(4) or under the *Ramsay* doctrine.

(6) The interaction of the general relief for gifts with retirement relief has already been noted in the previous chapter. This is a reminder that, where both sales and gifts of assets which qualify for retirement relief are envisaged, the sales should be made first, if possible.

(7) Where an asset is acquired before 6 April 1965 and sold at an undervalue, it may be advantageous to elect for 6 April 1965 value even though this would produce a larger gain than the time apportionment method. The reason for this is that the effect of FA 1980 s 79(3) is to match the consideration received against the cost of

30.1 General relief for gifts (FA 1980 s 79)

acquisition so far as possible. The balance of the consideration is matched with the chargeable gain and that part of the gain cannot be rolled over. Where the market value at 6 April 1965 is higher than the original cost, a correspondingly larger part of the consideration can be matched against it, so that the balance of the consideration to be matched with the chargeable gain is reduced. The result is that a larger part of the gain can be rolled over.

(8) A loss made on a disposal to a connected person can be set only against gains made on a future disposal to the same person (CGTA 1979 s 62(3)). Where, therefore, a person is proposing to make a gift to a connected person on which a CGT loss will arise, he should consider instead selling the asset for cash and giving away the proceeds. In this way he will have an allowable loss which he can set against gains generally without restriction.

(9) To the extent that a taxpayer's gains are within the annual exemption (£5,600 for 1984–85) a roll-over claim would be pointless and, indeed, disadvantageous to the donee since his base value would be reduced to no purpose. Where the gains are materially in excess of the exempt limit there is a problem because it is not possible to make a partial claim for roll-over relief. In these circumstances, the taxpayer might consider selling the asset to the intended donee at a price equal to his base cost plus £5,600 and they would then claim roll-over relief on the gain less £5,600 in accordance with FA 1980 s 79(3). The sale price would be left outstanding and in due course the debt would be written off.

To reduce the risk of an attack by the Revenue under the *Ramsay* doctrine it would be advisable to leave a reasonable interval between the sale and the release of the debt. Unfortunately, this might increase the CTT liability because the effect of the associated operations rules in FA 1975 s 44 is to treat the gift as being made at the time when the debt is released and at the value of the gift at that time. This must be weighed against the CGT advantage before embarking on the scheme.

(10) The existence of CGT losses brought forward from earlier years does not prevent a claim for roll-over relief being made. In general, one would advise making a claim, thus preserving the losses for carry forward against future gains, unless, of course, there is little likelihood of there being any.

(11) It should be remembered that the donee is entitled to the indexation allowance only after he has held the asset for twelve months.

(12) The extension of the relief by FA 1981 s 78 to include gifts to trustees is very useful where owners of family companies may wish to settle shares for the benefit of their children.

(13) Donors should be warned that if the donee becomes non-resident within six years after the gift, without having disposed of the asset, the held-over gain becomes chargeable, and if the donee does not pay the tax the donor may be assessed (FA 1981 s 79). If there is any real risk of this happening, the donor might consider taking some security from the donee.

30.2 GIFTS OF BUSINESS ASSETS (CGTA 1979 s 126)

The general relief for gifts under FA 1980 s 79 just considered has, to a large extent, replaced the earlier relief for gifts of business assets under CGTA 1979 s 126, so that s 126 relief is now relevant only in the case of a gift to a UK resident company. This is the practical result of CGTA 1979 s 26(1) and FA 1980 s 79(4) as amended by FA 1981 s 78(3) and FA 1982 s 82(2).

The relief, which must be claimed by both parties, works in a similar way to the general relief for gifts. Unlike the general relief, however, the CTT payable on the gift is not deductible in computing the donee's tax liability on a subsequent disposal of the asset.

Planning points

(1) To qualify for relief the asset must be used for the purposes of a trade etc but, unlike retirement relief, there is no requirement that the business, or part of the business, itself must be disposed of. Nor is there any minimum qualifying period for ownership of the asset though, if it has not been used for the purpose of the trade etc throughout the period of ownership, only part of the gain qualifies (CGTA 1979 Sch 4 para 5). This suggests that, where the taxpayer has a non-business asset which is likely to show a gain on disposal, he might begin to use it for the purposes of his business, so that at least part of the gain will qualify for relief.

(2) The trade etc must be carried on either by the transferor or his family company, and shares qualify for relief if they are shares in a trading company which is the transferor's family company. The family company requirements are the same as for retirement relief (CGTA 1979 ss 126(7) and 124(8)), but there is no minimum qualifying period; it suffices that the conditions are fulfilled at the time of the gift. Where, therefore, the transferor does not have enough shares to qualify, he may be able to buy the additional shares he needs immediately prior to the disposal of the asset. It should also be noted that in contrast to retirement relief, the transferor does not have to be a full-time working director of the company.

30.2 Gifts of business assets (CGTA 1979 s 126)

(3) In the case of shares in a family trading company, the rules relating to restriction of relief by reference to the company's chargeable business assets are virtually the same as for retirement relief. The reader is referred to chapter 29, points (11) and (12) for a discussion of the action which can be taken to maximise the relief.

(4) The effect of a disposal of shares on subsequent posssible gifts should not be overlooked. If the taxpayer reduces his holding below 25% (assuming that members of his family do not hold any shares), he would no longer qualify for roll-over relief for business assets (nor, for that matter, retirement relief and replacement roll-over relief) on subsequent gifts.

(5) For a discussion of the use of s 126 on the transfer of a business to a company see **14.2** ante.

31 Providing for retirement

31.1 RETIREMENT ANNUITIES (TA 1970 ss 226–229)

There is no doubt that the payment of premiums into a retirement annuity policy is one of the most tax efficient forms of investment that a self-employed person (or person in non-pensionable employment) can make. He gets tax relief at his top rate of tax on the whole of his premiums (within the prescribed limits), the pension fund itself is completely exempt from tax and he can, if he wishes, commute a substantial part of his pension (up to three times the remaining annuity) for a tax-free capital sum. The pension is taxed as earned income, but, with the abolition of the investment income surcharge from 1984–85, this is no longer of any special significance.

Types of contract

The most common type of contract is one which is intended to provide a retirement annuity for the individual himself (s 226(1)). The annuity can commence at any age between 60 and 75, and can be guaranteed for up to ten years. In the event of the individual's death after retirement, an annuity can be paid to the individual's widow or widower, but must not exceed the annuity paid to the individual. In the event of death before retirement, the premiums paid, with or without interest, or the value of the accumulated fund, can be returned to his estate (s 226(2)).

Under s 226A, a contract can be effected to provide an annuity for the individual's wife or husband, or his dependants, or to provide a lump sum on death before the age of 75. Since FA 1980 these policies can now be written in trust, which has obvious CTT advantages if the beneficiary is other than the surviving spouse.

31.1 Retirement annuities (TA 1970 ss 226–229)

Nature and amount of relief

The fundamental rule is that, unless an election is made under the carry back provisions dealt with below, relief for premiums paid, up to the maximum permitted limit, is given as a deduction from relevant earnings for the year of assessment in which the premiums are actually paid (s 227(1)). Since 1980–81, the maximum permitted limit is $17\frac{1}{2}$% of the taxpayer's net relevant earnings (15% before 1980–81) if he was born after 1933. If he was born in 1933 or earlier, the maximum percentage limit is increased according to the year of birth as follows:

Year of birth	1980–81 and 1981–82	1982–83 onward
1916 to 1933	$17\frac{1}{2}$	20
1914 or 1915	$20\frac{1}{2}$	21
1912 or 1913	$23\frac{1}{2}$	24
1910 or 1911	$26\frac{1}{2}$	$26\frac{1}{2}$
1908 or 1909	$29\frac{1}{2}$	$29\frac{1}{2}$
1907	$32\frac{1}{2}$	$32\frac{1}{2}$

The maximum limit on premiums paid under s 226A policies is 5% of net relevant earnings, which must come out of the maximum limits set out above, thus reducing the amount available for normal retirement annuities. However, this might be thought well worthwhile when it is considered that the premiums on a s 226A contract attract relief at the taxpayer's marginal rate of tax (presently up to 60%) as compared with life assurance relief of 15% (which has now been withdrawn for new policies effected after 13 March 1984).

An individual must start to draw his annuity by the age of 75, so no premiums can be paid after that age. This means that premiums cannot be paid in the current year 1984–85 by individuals born in 1908 or earlier.

Carry back of premiums

The taxpayer may elect that a premium paid in a year of assessment shall be treated as paid in the last preceding year of assessment or, if he had no relevant earnings in that year, in the year before that (s 227(1BB)). An election may be made whether or not there are any relevant earnings in the year in which the premium is paid and without any regard to the qualifying limits for that year.

Strictly, the election to carry back a premium should be made before the end of the year of assessment in which the premium is paid, but it is understood that in practice the Revenue may accept an election if made by 5 July in the following year of assessment (see *Tolley's Practical Tax* (1983) p 94 and *Taxation Practitioner* October (1983) p 279). However, in a letter published in *Taxation Practitioner* January (1984) p 28, Mr J P O Lewis of the Inland Revenue Press Office stated that this 'extension' does not entail the granting of any new concession or any change in existing practice so far as taxpayers are concerned. The change that has taken place is that local tax districts have been given discretion to accept certain late elections without reference to the Superannuation Funds Office. This discretion applies to late elections in respect to premiums paid in 1982–83 onwards. The letter goes on to say that the Revenue would not accept that this recent change in their procedures involves extension of time limits or any change in the Revenue's attitude to late elections.

In view of this letter it would appear to be unwise to rely on any extension of the time limit and the 5 April deadline should be observed wherever possible. In any event, it should be particularly noted that there has been no concession relating to the time for payment of the premiums—they must still be paid by 5 April.

Where an election is made, the relief for the relevant preceding year on the carried back premium plus any premiums actually already paid in and claimed for the preceding year will still be subject to the maximum permitted limit for that year.

This ability to carry back premiums is intended to help taxpayers who do not know the amount of their earnings until after the end of the year of assessment. A carry back to the last preceding year of assessment but one will be relevant when earnings cease on retirement or for other reasons; premiums could then be paid in the two years after cessation and carried back to the final year of earnings.

Carry forward of unused relief

Where the premiums actually paid (or treated as having been paid under the carry back rules) in any year of assessment are less than the maximum permitted limit for that year, the unused relief can be carried forward for up to six years. In any of these six years, the taxpayer may, if he wishes, and provided he has already paid premiums in that year up to the maximum permitted limit, pay an additional premium up to the amount of the unused relief brought forward. Where there is unused relief for more than one year, relief

31.1 Retirement annuities (TA 1970 ss 226–229)

for an earlier year is treated as being absorbed before relief for a later year, ie on a 'first in, first out' basis (s 227A(1) and (2)).

For the avoidance of doubt three points must be emphasised. First, unused relief is given in the year of assessment in which the additional premium is actually paid (or deemed to be paid by carry back).

Secondly, the additional premiums paid to absorb unused relief are not subject to the maximum permitted percentage limit in the year of payment or deemed payment; on the contrary, premiums must have been paid (or treated as paid by carry back) up to the maximum limit before additional premiums can start to mop up unused relief. There must, therefore, be sufficient net relevant earnings in the year in which additional premiums are paid (or treated as paid by carry back) from which the premiums can be deducted, so having unused relief does not guarantee relief for premiums paid.

Thirdly, the amount of unused relief is calculated according to the limits applying for the years in which the unused relief arose.

At the time of writing it is not too late to absorb any unused relief for the years 1977–78 onwards. For example, any unused relief for 1977–78 has to be used in 1983–84 or it will be lost altogether. It can be so used by the payment and carry back of an additional premium in 1984–85 or, indeed in 1985–86 if there are no net relevant earnings in 1984–85. But readers are reminded again that the maximum percentage limit for 1983–84 must be used before any additional premium can count against unused relief.

Late assessments

Where an assessment on relevant earnings for a year of assessment becomes final and conciusive more than six years after the end of that year and, as a result of that assessment, there is unused relief, the six year carry forward period will have elapsed. The taxpayer may, however, within a period of six months from the date on which the assessment becomes final and conclusive, elect that the unused relief be given in respect of so much of any qualifying premiums paid in that period as exceeds the maximum permitted limit for the year of payment. In other words, the normal rules apply and the permitted maximum limit must be used first before further premiums can count against the unused relief (s 227A(3)).

In a Statement of Practice (SP9/80) the Revenue have stated that if a back duty investigation is concluded by the acceptance of an offer in respect of tax, interest and penalties, claims under s 227A(3) will be accepted even though no assessment is actually issued if:

(a) the settlement includes tax on relevant earnings for a year ended more than six years before the date of the acceptance letter, and
(b) the premium is paid within six months from the date of the letter.

Relevant earnings

The net relevant earnings on which the maximum relief is calculated are defined in s 226(9) and s 227(4) and (5). Broadly speaking, the practical effect of these is that, for a self-employed person, his net relevant earnings will comprise his trading profits as computed for tax purposes, (or his share of a partnership assessment), less certain annual charges relating to the business, stock relief and capital allowances, plus balancing charges and any stock relief clawback. Non-business charges, such as mortgage interest on the taxpayer's home no longer have to be deducted. Annual interest is not deducted as a charge, though if it relates to the trade etc it would normally be deducted in calculating taxable profits. Loan interest allowed under FA 1972, s 75 and personal allowances are not deducted.

In the case of partnerships, the partner must be personally acting in the business, so that the income of limited or sleeping partners does not qualify.

For an employee, net relevant earnings will be his remuneration from a non-pensionable office or employment, including benefits in kind, less allowable expenses. Again, personal allowances and charges do not have to be deducted.

The relevant earnings of a married woman are not treated for this purpose as her husband's even though her income is aggregated with his for tax purposes. This means that she can pay her own retirement annuity premiums.

Loan back schemes

One of the problems with retirement annuity contracts can be that many individuals find it difficult to pay the premiums up to the maximum allowable limit. In these cases, loan schemes which are now available from many life offices may be the answer. The various schemes differ in detail, but the basic plan is that the individual can borrow back the greater part of the premiums he has paid.

An increasingly popular variant of this is to effect a loan with a life office or bank which will be repaid from the cash sum available on commutation of a retirement annuity contract. The amount of the loan is calculated by reference to the premiums already paid or payable under the contract. This is a very attractive proposition where loans are required to finance, for example, partnership capital or to purchase a house. The loan cannot be secured on the pension policy, so some other security may be required, although a number of unsecured loan schemes are available.

Planning points summarised

(1) Excess premiums cannot be carried forward, so the payment of premiums needs to be carefully planned to ensure that the permitted limits are not exceeded having regard to any unused relief brought forward and the carry back rules.
(2) Where the exact amount of net relevant earnings is not known until some time after the end of the year of assessment, it would be prudent to limit premium payments to an amount on which it is known relief can be obtained. Provided the net relevant earnings are determined by the end of the following year of assessment, an additional premium could then be paid and carried back one year to absorb the unused relief, or the unused relief could be carried forward and relief given in the following year.
(3) Although unused relief can be carried forward for six years this does not guarantee that the relief will be given. There must be sufficient relevant earnings from which the additional premiums can be deducted. If earnings have ceased altogether the relief will be lost, although premiums paid in the two years after cessation can be carried back to the year of cessation.
(4) The relief is maximised if premiums are paid in years when marginal rates of tax are high.
(5) If a married woman has earnings of her own, she can pay her own retirement annuity premiums.
(6) The ability to obtain death cover under s 226A policies and obtain full tax relief on the premiums should not be overlooked.
(7) Loan schemes should be seriously considered for house purchase, provision of partnership capital, etc.

31.2 COMPANY PENSION SCHEMES

Introduction

It is convenient to describe the provision of retirement benefits for the employees of a family business as a company pension scheme, but it should be understood at the outset that such schemes can be set up equally well for the employees of a partnership or even

31 Providing for retirement

(though less commonly) of a sole trader. However, although directors, even (since 1973) controlling directors, can be included in a company scheme, equity partners and sole traders cannot. The self-employed must look to retirement annuities for their retirement provision, and this subject has been covered in the previous section of this chapter.

Types of pension scheme

There are three main types of pension scheme.

(1) Insured schemes, where the funds are invested in insurance policies. These were the usual method of providing retirement benefits for the directors of family companies until the advent of self-administered schemes.
(2) Self-administered schemes (or 'in-house' or 'captive' schemes as they are sometimes called) which are controlled largely by the company itself.
(3) 'Hybrid' or 'mixed' schemes, which have more recently been introduced by insurance companies to meet the challenge of self-administered schemes, and which are partly insured and partly self-administered.

There are also group schemes, which are designed for a large number of employees, and executive pension plans (the modern name for 'top-hat' schemes) which are designed for one or two directors or executives. A 'one-man' scheme is simply an executive pension plan for one individual.

Matters which are applicable to all types of pension scheme will be considered in the remainder of this section. In the following section, the characteristics, advantages and special considerations applicable to small self-administered schemes will be examined.

Legislation and Inland Revenue practice

The relevant legislation is contained in FA 1970 Chap II Part II, as amended by FA 1971 and FA 1973, but references should also be made to the booklet IR12 and the various memoranda issued by the Inland Revenue from time to time. A complete list of the current memoranda is given in *Inland Revenue Practices and Concessions* (Oyez Longman) at FP2/IR12.

Tax benefits and advantages

Company pension schemes offer very substantial tax benefits and other advantages for the family business, and its directors or other employees. Provided the scheme is fully approved by the Inland Revenue, the following tax benefits are obtained.

(1) The pension fund is exempt from income tax (except on trading profits, if any) and capital gains tax.

(2) The employer's contributions are deductible in computing trading profits for tax purposes, and are not assessable on the employees.

(3) The employee's ordinary annual contributions, up to a maximum of 15% of his earnings, are tax deductible under Schedule E.

(4) There are substantial tax advantages on the benefits payable.
  (a) Pensions are taxable as earned income under Schedule E.
  (b) Lump sums
    (i) On retirement, part of the pension can be commuted for a tax-free lump sum not exceeding one and a half times the final salary.
    (ii) On death before retirement, a tax-free lump sum of up to four times final salary can be paid.

(5) There are several capital transfer tax advantages.
  (a) No CTT is payable on the death of a trustee (FA 1975 Sch 5 para 16).
  (b) The capital value of pensions is tax free (FA 1973 s 14).
  (c) Death in service benefits are usually exempt from CTT on the grounds that the payments are made at the trustee's discretion.

In addition to the above tax benefits, the following further advantages should be noted.

(1) Because the pension scheme is a tax exempt fund, its investments should grow at a faster rate than conventional investments.

(2) The timing and amount of the contributions can be varied to some extent to suit the needs of the company and reduce its tax liabilities.

(3) A pension fund can help to mitigate CTT and CGT, since the contributions to the fund will reduce both net assets and earnings of the company, and thus the value of the shares.

(4) A pension fund provides security for the employees. Because the assets of the fund are quite separate from the company's assets, pensions are not dependent on the continuing profitability of the company after retirement, and difficulties which might otherwise arise on the disposal of the company are avoided.

(5) A pension fund can be used to mitigate the personal tax liabilities of employees, eg by means of salary sacrifice. It can be particularly useful in mitigating the tax liability on ex gratia payments on

termination of employment by arranging for part of the payment to be used to provide additional pension benefits.

Inland Revenue approval

In order to enjoy all the tax benefits set out above, the pension scheme must be approved by the Inland Revenue through the Superannuation Funds Office (SFO). The conditions for approval are set out in FA 1970 s 19, but under s 20, the SFO is given wide discretionary powers to approve a scheme even though it does not meet all the prescribed conditions.

Bare approval will be sufficient to avoid the tax liability which would otherwise arise on the employee under FA 1970 s 23 in respect of the cost of funding the retirement benefits (FA 1970 s 24(1)). In this connection, it should not be overlooked that the mere promise of a pension could be treated by the Inland Revenue as a benefit assessable on the employee (FA 1970 s 23(2)).

Exempt approval must be obtained if the pension fund is to enjoy all the other tax benefits. To obtain exempt approval, the scheme must be established under irrevocable trusts (FA 1970 s 21(1)). In the case of large group schemes, there will usually be a formal trust deed, but for smaller individual schemes, a declaration of trust, or even a resolution of the directors, may be sufficient.

There are no special requirements as to who may act as trustees, except in the case of small self-administered schemes, when one of the trustees must be a 'pensioneer trustee' (see **31.3**). The employer himself can be a trustee.

An administrator will also be appointed to manage the scheme and to be responsible to the Inland Revenue for it.

Applications for approval must be submitted to the SFO within three months of the end of the tax year in which the scheme commenced. Approval, if given, will be backdated to the start of the scheme, but this does not mean that the employer's contributions can be backdated. The contributions must be paid before the end of the accounting period in which the scheme started if tax relief is to be obtained in that accounting period. The application must be accompanied by various documents and information. The detailed requirements are set out in SFO Memorandum No 65.

Who can qualify

Any employee of the company, including directors, whether controlling directors or not, can qualify for benefits under an approved pension scheme. Self-employed persons cannot qualify, nor can directors of an investment company.

Retirement ages

The scheme must specify a normal retirement age. The SFO will not usually approve a normal retirement age earlier than 60 for men and 55 for women. However, for certain occupations, eg professional sportsmen, an earlier retirement age may be approved. For 20% directors, the minimum retirement age is 60 for both men and women.

Maximum benefits

(1) A pension for the employee of two-thirds of his final remuneration after ten years service.
(2) Commutation of part of the pension for a tax-free lump sum of up to one and a half times final remuneration after twenty years service.
(3) If the employee dies after retirement, a pension for his widow or dependant of two-thirds of what the employee's pension would have been. No single pension can exceed this level, and where two or more pensions are paid, the total must not exceed the full amount of pension which the employee would have received.
(4) Benefits on death in service.
 (a) A tax-free lump sum not exceeding £5,000 or, if greater, four times final remuneration, and a refund of the employee's contributions, with or without interest. These sums would not normally be liable to CTT because they are payable at the trustees' discretion.
 (b) A pension for a widow or dependant of two-thirds of the maximum pension that could have been paid to the deceased employee had he lived and continued in employment to normal retirement age with the same final remuneration as at the date of death. This effectively means a maximum pension for a widow or dependant of four-ninths the employee's final remuneration.

Where an employee has deferred retirement and dies after normal retiring age, but still in service, benefits may be paid either on the assumption

(a) that he had died before normal retirement age, so that normal death in service benefits can be provided, or
(b) that he had retired the day before he died, so that death in retirement benefits can be paid.

The first of these two methods may clearly be more attractive in certain cases and, since the scheme rules must specify which basis is to apply, careful thought needs to be given to the personal circumstances of the employees concerned when planning the scheme.

31 Providing for retirement

Final remuneration

It will have been noted that maximum contributions and benefits are directly related to final remuneration and length of service, so what constitutes final remuneration is important. It means any income assessable under Schedule E, and therefore includes, as well as basic salary, bonuses, commission and benefits in kind. It can be calculated on either of the following bases.

(1) Remuneration for any of the five years preceding the normal retirement date; remuneration means basic pay for the year plus the annual average of any fluctuating earnings (eg bonuses or commission) over an appropriate period (usually three or more years).
(2) The annual average of total remuneration over a period of three or more consecutive years ending not earlier than ten years before the normal retirement date. This effectively means that the last thirteen years before the normal retirement date can be considered.

In either case, the actual remuneration can be increased in line with the increase in the Retail Price Index from the end of the relevant year to the normal retirement date. This is known as 'dynamised' final remuneration.

Length of service

It is length of service with the employer that counts, not the length of time the employee has been in the pension scheme.

Escalation of pensions

Pensions can be increased by 3% pa compound automatically, or the rise in the Retail Price Index, if this is greater.

20% Directors

For directors who control more than 20% of the voting rights in the company there are two main restrictions.

(1) Final remuneration must be based on an average of total remuneration over at least three years; it is not permitted to use one year only.
(2) The earliest normal retirement age is 60 for both men and women.

There are also restrictions on death in service benefits and on deferring retirement.

Contributions

To obtain approval of the scheme, the company must make contributions, usually at least 5% of the total contributions, but the actual amount will depend on the benefits to be provided. They are deductible in computing trading profits for tax purposes. It is necessary to distinguish between annual contributions and special contributions.

Annual contributions

Annual contributions are those which are normally made on a regular basis every year. They are tax deductible in the year of payment. If, due to adverse financial circumstances, the company is unable to continue making the same level of contributions, approval of the scheme will not normally be prejudiced, but the tax relief may be adjusted and spread forward.

Special contributions

It is possible for the company to pay special contributions from time to time in order to cover past service. Provided the special contributions do not exceed the annual contribution or £10,000, whichever is the greater, they will also be tax deductible in the year of payment. Where they exceed this limit, tax relief will be spread forward over a period of up to five years.

Contributions by employees

An employee may make annual contributions, which are tax deductible under Schedule E, of up to 15% of his total remuneration. There can, therefore, be some advantage in increasing an employee's salary by 17.65% in order to increase final remuneration, since, after deducting 15% on the increased salary, his net chargeable income will remain the same. Single lump sum contributions are not treated as annual contributions and are not tax deductible.

For PAYE purposes, tax is calculated on a net pay basis, ie on his salary after deducting annual contributions.

Refund of contributions

Where a refund of contributions is made to an employee, the pension fund is liable to income tax at 10% on the gross amount refunded, which will usually be deducted in calculating the net amount due to the employee. Any refund by the pension fund to the employer will be taxable in his hands.

31.3 SMALL SELF-ADMINISTERED PENSION SCHEMES

The characteristics of small self-administered schemes

A self-administered pension scheme is simply one that is largely under the control of the company itself. There is nothing new about this sort of scheme. Large companies have been operating them for more than sixty years. What is relatively new is the use of these schemes for the controlling directors of family companies, which became possible for the first time as a result of FA 1973. They are often referred to as 'in-house' or, more emotively, 'captive' schemes.

The essential characteristics of small self-administered schemes are that:

(a) they are designed mainly for the benefit of controlling directors of private companies;
(b) they usually have only two or three members, sometimes only one, and almost invariably less than twelve;
(c) they are not restricted to investment in insurance policies but can invest their funds in a variety of ways, often in the company itself;
(d) the directors of the company are usually trustees of the scheme, although, as will be seen, a 'pensioneer trustee' must also be appointed.

Advantages of small self-administered schemes

In addition to the tax benefits and advantages applicable to all pension schemes, self-administered schemes have the following additional advantages.

(1) The investments, benefits and funding are under the direct control of the directors, acting as trustees.
(2) They have almost complete freedom of investment (subject to one or two restrictions referred to later). In particular, they can purchase assets from, or make loans to, the company, which may help with liquidity problems. They can also acquire shares in the company, which may mitigate CGT and CTT liabilities, and prove a tax-efficient way of transferring control of the company to the next generation.
(3) Investments can usually be sold or switched easily as circum-

stances require, and without the penalties associated with the surrender of insurance policies.
(4) The rate of return on investments, taking expenses into account, should be better than from an insured scheme.
(5) They are probably cheaper to run than insured schemes, unless contributions are small.

On the other hand, it can be argued that insured funds provide greater security. They cannot, by their very nature, make risky investments, and they do have the strength of the insurance companies behind them, and they are probably cheaper where annual contributions are very small.

It is, however, becoming increasingly accepted that insured schemes are no longer adequate to meet the needs of controlling directors of private companies. The growing popularity of small self-administered schemes, and the development by insurance companies of executive pension plans which incorporate an element of self-administration, are evidence of this. It is dangerous to generalise, and circumstances alter cases, but it can safely be said that a small self-administered scheme should be seriously considered by the directors of most private companies which are in a position to establish one.

Inland Revenue treatment

In most respects, small self-administered schemes are treated by the Inland Revenue in the same way as any other pension scheme. However, because of the obvious possibilities for abuse, a number of special considerations are applicable to small self-administered schemes. These are outlined in SFO Memorandum No 58 published in February 1979, the main points of which will now be considered.

Meaning of 'small' scheme

The SFO will regard a scheme as 'small' if it has fewer than twelve members. However, even if the scheme has twelve or more members, it will still be regarded as 'small' if it is designed primarily for a few family directors, to whom are added some relatively low-paid employees entitled only to derisory benefits just to bring the total members up to twelve or slightly more (SFO Memorandum No 58 para 3).

Pensioneer trustee

One of the trustees of a small self-administered scheme must be a 'pensioneer trustee', ie somebody known to the SFO who specialises in occupational pensions. His primary function is to prevent the winding-up of the fund and distribution of the assets except in accordance with the normal winding-up rule. He is not there to act as a watchdog for the Inland Revenue in any other respect. A company can act as pensioneer trustee provided the directors are acceptable to the SFO (SFO Memorandum No 58 paras 4–8).

Investment of funds

Perhaps the biggest advantages of small self-administered schemes is that the trustees have almost complete freedom of investment. Of course, the trustees of the scheme, like all trustees, have a duty to invest prudently and to obtain the best return they can consistent with security. In general, however, the Inland Revenue will not interfere in the way the trustees invest trust monies, except where they suspect tax avoidance, or where the investment appears to be in conflict with the cash needs of the scheme for purchasing annuities. In order to monitor this, it will want to know when the application for approval is first considered, and periodically thereafter, how the funds are to be or have been invested.

However, the Inland Revenue have found it necessary to impose a few restrictions (SFO Memorandum No 58 paras 9–20) and these will now be considered.

(1) Loans to members

The trust deed must prohibit loans to members or any individual having a contingent interest under the scheme, ie who might conceivably benefit (eg relatives of members). This restriction is felt to be necessary because such loans might become, in reality, a charge on the retirement benefit, or might be made to avoid the tax liability arising on loans direct from close companies to their participators.

(2) Loans to the company

Loans to the company may be made provided that
(a) they are on commercial terms;
(b) they are not too frequent;
(c) the proportion of the total assets of the scheme lent to the company is not so great.
In connection with the last point, it would be inadvisable to lend more than 50% of the assets of the scheme.

(3) Purchase of assets from the company

The pension fund can buy assets from the company. This facility is one of the major advantages of self-administered schemes and, indeed, may very well enable a company to establish a scheme where problems of cash flow and liquidity would otherwise have prevented it from doing so. It may be especially useful where government grants are not available.

Where, however, assets are purchased from the company, the SFO will generally consult the local Inspector of Taxes to determine whether tax avoidance is involved, and particularly whether the acquisition is part and parcel of a 'transaction in securities' to which TA 1970 s 460 might apply. Needless to say that a scheme used in this way will not be approved, and any existing approval would be withdrawn.

(4) Purchase of shares in the company

The pension fund can, in principle, purchase shares in the company, and there could be occasions when it is desirable to do so, eg it may reduce the value per share for CTT purposes, or help solve family difficulties. However, the purchase of shares must be made at an independent valuation. It would also be desirable to obtain prior clearance from the Revenue to avoid the possibility of a charge to tax under TA 1970 s 460.

The potential CGT liability on the director disposing of his shares should also be considered, though this may be thought an acceptable price to pay for the potential saving in CTT. In this connection, it should be noted that contributions to the fund will reduce both the net assets and earnings of the company, thus reducing the value of the shares for CGT purposes. It would, therefore, be sensible to make contributions to the pension fund before any further transfer of shares by a controlling director, whether to the pension fund or anyone else.

Where the pension fund does purchase shares in the company, the SFO will, as in the case of buying assets from the company, consult with the local Inspector of Taxes, and the possibility of CTT avoidance may be grounds for withdrawing approval of the scheme.

(5) Investment in property

Investment in property may be quite acceptable where the members of the scheme are many years from retirement, but it may be more difficult to justify the purchase of the company's own business premises, which may be difficult to realise.

(6) Non-incoming producing assets

The investment of a significant amount of funds in works of art or other valuable chattels or non-income producing assets is unlikely to be approved by the SFO. As a matter of practice, an informal limit of 5% of the fund's assets appears to have been imposed. Even within that limit, the trustees would need to feel fairly confident that the capital growth in such investments will at least equal more orthodox investments. It should also be remembered that, if such an asset was kept at a director's home, or otherwise made available for his personal enjoyment, he would be taxed under Schedule E on an annual sum equal to 10% of the market value of the asset (FA 1976 s 63).

(7) Trading

Whilst there is nothing to prevent the trustees of the pension fund carrying on a trade, they will be liable to income tax on their trading profits. What constitutes trading or 'an adventure in the nature of trade' will be determined by the usual rules, but dealing in commodities and the leasing of plant and machinery are examples which have been regarded as trading.

(8) Purchase of annuities

The rules must provide for the purchase of an annuity within the first five years of a member's retirement. This will enable the trustees to choose a financially favourable time and avoid having to purchase at a time when annuity rates may be unfavourable or the market value of the scheme's investments depressed. However, cost of living increases to pensions do not have to be funded in this way, and the money to finance the increases can be kept in the fund.

The purchase of a widow's pension can be made at the same time as the member's pension or deferred until the husband dies.

Death benefits

All death in service benefits should be insured at the outset since the fund will not be in a position to meet these for some years. Furthermore, the scheme rules should provide that lump sum benefits payable on death in service and lump sum guarantee payments should be distributable at the trustees' discretion, except where SFO practice precludes discretionary distribution of a benefit payable on death on or after age 75 (SFO Memorandum No 58 para 21).

Full commutation of pension

The scheme rules must provide for full commutation on serious ill-health grounds to be subject to the agreement of the Inland

Revenue. The SFO will wish to confirm that proper medical evidence has been obtained and supports the conclusion that the member's life expectation is very short (SFO Memorandum No 58 para 22).

Funding, actuarial reports etc

Actuarial reports will have to be submitted to the SFO at least every three years, and the assumptions used as a basis for funding the scheme will be examined. Further, the SFO will require to know how the funds are to be or have been invested.

The payment of special contributions to the pension fund by the employer will not be acceptable unless justified by the actuary's recommendations and the requirements of the scheme (SFO Memorandum No 58 paras 23–24).

32 The use of trusts

32.1 HOW TRUSTS CAN HELP

There are a number of ways in which trusts can help tax and financial planning in the context of the family business and its proprietors. They can be used:

(1) To mitigate personal tax liabilities—by putting property into a trust the settlor can effectively remove it from his estate for CTT purposes, and the income from the property will no longer be treated as his income for income tax purposes.

(2) To make financial provision for the settlor's wife, children and other dependants by:
   (a) tying up property in succession by means of fixed interest trusts, or
   (b) making gifts now without deciding exactly who the donees will be or how much they will get, eg by means of a discretionary trust or an accumulation and maintenance settlement.

(3) To protect trust property from spendthrift or improvident children or relations, eg by means of a protective trust.

(4) To provide for employees and their dependants, eg with pension schemes, employees' trust and profit-sharing schemes.

(5) To carry on a trading business through a trading trust.

32.2 HOW TO ENSURE THAT INCOME IS ALIENATED

Generally, the income of a trust is treated for income tax purposes as the income of the trustees or the beneficiaries and not that of the settlor. However, there are a number of provisions in TA 1970 Part XVI under which the trust income can be taxed on the settlor. It is outside the scope of this book to examine these provisions in detail. It will be more useful to the reader to identify the practical planning rules which must be followed in order to ensure that the settlor does not come within any of them.

(1) It is essential to ensure that the settlement is irrevocable as defined in TA 1970 ss 439, 445 and 446.
(2) The settlor and his wife must be excluded from all possible benefit under the trust (see TA 1970 ss 447 and 448). The best way to do this is to insert a clause in the trust deed to this effect. It should be noted that it is not necessary to exclude a widow.
(3) Make certain that no income, or capital which could represent income, is paid to an unmarried infant child of the settlor (see TA 1970 s 437).
(4) Ensure that no loans or repayment of loans are made by the settlement to the settlor or his spouse (see TA 1970 s 451).
(5) If shares in a family company are settled great caution is required. Consider very carefully any loans between the settlor and the company and the possibility of any associated payments by the trustees to the company (see TA 1970 s 451(A)). If any loan repayments have to be made by the company they should be made before the beginning of the tax year in which the settlement is made. If there have been any associated payments the settlor should not borrow from the company.

32.3 FIXED INTEREST TRUSTS

A fixed interest trust is one where the trust property is held for the benefit of one or more beneficiaries who are entitled to a definite share of the trust income. Usually, but not necessarily, a beneficiary is entitled to the income for life, in which case he is known as a life tenant. The beneficiaries who will become entitled to the trust property or income from it on his death are the remaindermen or reversioners. Because of the life tenant's CTT liability on the entire trust fund although he receives only the income, fixed interest trusts will seldom be used purely for tax reasons. They are more likely to be used mainly where it is desired, for non-fiscal reasons, to keep property in trust for adults.

The revertor-to-settlor exemption, however, might be used to some advantage. A taxpayer who is unwilling for any reason to make an outright gift could settle the property on the donee, giving the trustees power to appoint the property back to him. Although the CTT paid on the gift to the trust cannot be reclaimed, there is no further charge on the reversion back to the settlor. The disadvantage of this is that all the trust income would be attributed to the settlor, so it would be better to use non-income producing assets if possible.

A fixed interest might also be useful in the case of non-income producing property. For example, a father might settle a house on his son for life. The son could occupy the house as his residence without any income tax consequences and it could be transferred to him absolutely during his lifetime free of CGT and CTT (CGTA 1979 s 104 and see *Sansom v Peay* [1976] STC 494).

So far as existing trusts are concerned, the old estate duty surviving spouse will trusts can still offer some opportunities for tax planning. As long as the property remains in the trust it will be exempt from CTT on the death of the surviving spouse. Lifetime gifts should, therefore, be made out of her free estate, leaving the exempt trust funds untouched. Similarly, unless absolutely necessary, the trustees should not advance property out of the trust to the widow, because it would then become chargeable to CTT as part of her estate. If the widow requires funds it might be better to make her a loan.

Apart from surviving spouse will trusts, any tax planning for fixed interest trusts must have regard to the beneficiary's free estate.

32.4 DISCRETIONARY TRUSTS

A discretionary trust is a trust in which there is no interest in possession, the trustees having power to accumulate or apply the trust income as they think fit. A beneficiary has, therefore, a mere spes or hope of receiving a benefit (*Gartside v IRC* [1968] 1 All ER 121, HL; *Leedale v Lewis* [1982] STC 835, HL). A discretionary beneficiary can, however, renounce his portion as a member of the discretionary class (*Re Gulbenkian's Settlement Trusts (No 2), Stephens v Maun* [1969] 2 All ER 1173.)

The original CTT provisions in FA 1975 were regarded as distinctly unfavourable to discretionary trusts and many existing trusts were unscrambled by creating an interest in possession therein or by appointing the trust funds absolutely. Often the trusts were converted into accumulation and maintenance trusts, which are favourably treated for CTT purposes. Provided this was done before 1 April 1983 (or 1 April 1984 where court proceedings were involved) the tax charge was only 20% rather than 30%, of the effective rate.

The old rules, however, were modified in FA 1982 and, although the CTT burden on discretionary trusts can still be heavy, especially for large settlements, it is now generally felt that discretionary trusts can once more have a useful role to play.

32.4 Discretionary trusts

The main reason for setting up a discretionary trust is to enable the settlor to reduce his estate for CTT purposes whilst retaining a considerable degree of control over both the capital and income of the trust. Where, for example, the intended donees are children or not financially mature, the settlor would not wish to hand over control of the property to them until later. Or he may wish to postpone a decision as to who will ultimately benefit and by how much having regard to changes in future circumstances. Or it could sometimes be the case that it would not be expedient to give a beneficiary property absolutely or an interest in possession in it as this would increase the donee's estate for CTT purposes. For example, there is no CTT charge on the death of a discretionary beneficiary so, if the potential beneficiaries are elderly or in poor health, a discretionary trust would be more advantageous than a fixed interest trust which would give them an interest in possession.

Similarly, the trust income can be distributed according to the beneficiaries' needs from time to time, or may be accumulated and added to the capital of the trust for future distribution.

In certain circumstances the settlor himself could be a beneficiary of the trust. For example, he may wish to make a substantial gift but feels he needs the whole of the income arising from his property. Of course, if he was a beneficiary, this would be fatal from an income tax point of view since the whole of the trust income would be taxed on him, but this would not matter if the intention was to pay the whole of the income to him in any case. The point is that the gift would still be effective for CTT purposes. It is even possible to provide in the settlement that the trustees might appoint the trust funds back to the settlor though a provision to do so would defeat the CTT effectiveness of the trust and should be resorted to only in extreme cases.

Enough has been said to underline the great advantage of a discretionary settlement—its flexibility. Maximum freedom of action is retained whilst obtaining the primary object of reducing the settlor's estate.

A discretionary trust can be a particularly appropriate vehicle for setting up a trading trust where it is desired to accumulate and capitalise the income (see **32.8** post).

Discretionary will trusts can also be very attractive where the testator is prepared to leave to the trustees the decision as to how his estate will devolve. The trustees have two years to make up their minds and they can plan their dispositions so as to obtain the maximum tax advantages.

Finally, it may be noted that the settlor can roll over any gain arising on the transfer of property to a settlement. On the death of a discretionary beneficiary, however, the gain would not crystallise as it would in the case of a fixed interest trust.

The CTT charge—planning points

It is outside the scope of this book to discuss in detail how CTT is charged on discretionary trusts. The broad idea is to maintain tax neutrality between property held in a discretionary settlement and property owned directly by an individual. On the basis that the latter is charged to CTT once every generation, there is a charge on property in a discretionary settlement once every ten years at 30% of lifetime rates, so that, roughly speaking, after thirty years, the tax suffered will be about the same as on a lifetime gift of the same amount.

This means that, following the effective reduction in rates by FA 1984, the highest rate at which the ten-year charge can be imposed is 9% as compared with the top rate on death of 60%. On this basis, an individual would have to live more than sixty years before the charge on the discretionary trust becomes less advantageous.

In calculating the rate of tax chargeable, one has to have regard not only to the value of the property in the trust but also the chargeable transfers made by the settlor in the ten years before making the settlement. If, therefore, the settlor has made substantial transfers during that period, the settlement will have higher rates of tax subsequently throughout its life. Therefore, the advice must be to make, if possible, chargeable transfers after, rather than before, making a discretionary settlement.

If substantial lifetime gifts have already been made, it may be worth postponing the settlement until the ten years have elapsed. Alternatively, the settlor could make a gift to his wife to enable her to make the settlement, but there must be no condition that she does so as the settlor might then be caught by the associated operations rules. There is, too, the danger that the husband might still be regarded as the settlor in view of the very wide definition of the term in FA 1975 Sch 5 para 1(6).

Particular care is needed where it is proposed to add funds to an existing settlement. If, prior to that occasion, the settlor has made chargeable transfers which are greater than the transfers made in the ten years immediately before making the settlement, the former will be used for the purposes of calculating the rate of tax charged on the trust.

In addition to the ten-year charge, there will be interim charges whenever property is taken out of the settlement. The rate of tax will depend on whether the charge arises before the first ten-year charge, or subsequently. The rate of tax on an interim charge before the first ten-year anniversary is calculated by reference to the value of the settled property when it was first put into the settlement. This is very advantageous because it means that, although the value of property may have increased very considerably, a relatively low rate of tax will apply if it is taken out of the trust before the first ten-year charge.

For charges between ten-year anniversaries the rate at which tax is charged is the appropriate fraction of the rate charged at the last ten-year anniversary. Where, therefore, property is increasing in value, it will usually be advantageous to appoint funds out of the trust before the next ten-year charge. The opposite will apply, if property is decreasing in value.

Distribution and accumulation of income

The reader is referred to **32.8** below where a number of important planning points in connection with the distribution and accumulation of income in accumulation trusts are considered.

32.5 ACCUMULATION AND MAINTENANCE TRUSTS

An accumulation and maintenance trust is a form of discretionary trust which meets the requirements of FA 1982 s 114. As will be seen later, such a trust has very considerable tax advantages.

The conditions

The conditions which must be satisfied before a trust qualifies as an accumulation and maintenance settlement are as follows:

(1) One or more of the beneficiaries will, on or before reaching the age of 25, become entitled to the trust property absolutely or to an interest in possession in it. The important word is 'will', so there must be no possibility under the settlement of the beneficiary's interest being defeated. In *Lord Inglewood v IRC* [1981] STC 318 a power of revocation was fatal. A special power of appointment would also offend the requirement unless it could only be exercised in favour of a beneficiary before he was 25.

It is irrelevant that a beneficiary's interest might be defeated by events outside the settlement, eg a beneficiary might assign his interest or the trusts might be varied under the Variation of Trusts Act 1958. The possible exercise of the statutory power of advancement, even though incorporated in a settlement under Trustee Act 1925 s 69(2), is also ignored (see Inland Revenue SP21/1975).

(2) Before a beneficiary becomes entitled to the trust property absolutely or an interest in possession in it, the income must be accumulated so far as not applied for the maintenance, education or benefit of the beneficiaries. Strictly, there must be a trust to accumulate; a mere power to accumulate would not be sufficient to meet the requirements. Where it is proposed to postpone the vesting of the property or interest in possession until after the beneficiary has attained the age of 18, the requirements of the Perpetuities and Accumulations Act 1964 s 13 must be carefully considered because in certain circumstances it may not then be possible to accumulate. In that case the income will pass to whoever is entitled to it and this may disqualify the settlement.

(3) All the beneficiaries must be grandchildren of a common grandparent, but a grandchild's share can be taken by his widow and children in the event of his death. The grandparent need not be the settlor, so a settlement by a settlor on his own children is possible.

Where the common grandparent condition is not satisfied, and after twenty-five years no beneficiary has become entitled to the property absolutely or an interest in possession in it, the settlement will cease to qualify.

Tax advantages

An accumulation and maintenance settlement has considerable CTT advantages. It is not subject to the ten-year charge nor the interim charge (FA 1982 ss 107, 108) and when a beneficiary becomes absolutely entitled to trust property or obtains an interest in possession in it there will be no CTT charge (s 114(4)).

If property ceases to be held on accumulation and maintenance trusts in any other circumstances CTT may be charged. This will be a very rare occurrence but could happen, for instance, if one of the beneficiaries has assigned his reversionary interest to a person who will be over 25 when his interest falls in. Another example would be where the common grandparent condition has not been satisfied and twenty-five years have passed from the making of the settlement without any beneficiary becoming entitled to an absolute interest or interest in possession. Where a charge does not arise in these circumstances, it will be at an increasing rate depending on how long the property has been in the fund (s 113).

There are also the income tax advantages, common to all discretionary settlements, eg income distributions can be made to meet the personal tax circumstances of the beneficiaries, or income can be capitalised and paid out to beneficiaries without any further income tax charge. The reader is referred to **32.8** below where these and a number of other planning points in connection with the distribution and accumulation of income on accumulation settlements are dealt with.

32.6 TRADING TRUSTS

A trading trust is simply a trust in which the trustees carry on a trade. Given that the top rate of tax on accumulated income is 45%, a trading trust is at some disadvantage compared with, say, a small company, where the top rate of tax is now 30%. It is also true that profits would have to be fairly substantial before a sole trader or partner paid tax at an effective rate of 45%. But there can be advantages. The trust income can be capitalised and paid out to beneficiaries free of further income tax (see **32.8** below). Also interests in trusts, unlike shares in a company, can be sold free of CGT.

Assuming a suitable type of trust is used, a trading trust might be worth considering. An individual might set up an accumulation and maintenance settlement for his children and the income could be accumulated until they reach the age of 25. If there are no children, a small discretionary trust might be used.

32.7 EMPLOYEES' TRUSTS

Employees' trusts can be very useful in several ways. First, they can be useful as a means of mitigating tax. The payments made by the company to the trust will be tax deductible for corporation tax purposes (see *Heather v P E Consulting Group Ltd* (1972) 48 TC 293—the leading case on employees' trusts). It is essential that several payments are made since a single lump sum payment set aside for invalid employees has been held to be not allowable (*Rowntree & Co Ltd v Curtis* (1924) 8 TC 678, CA). See also *Atherton v British Insulated and Helsby Cables* (1925) 10 TC 155, HL where a

32 The use of trusts

lump sum paid to set up an approved pension fund was not allowable.

For CTT purposes, provided the trust satisfies the requirements of FA 1975 Sch 5 para 17, there will be no ten-year charge or interim charge. There is also relief from CTT where property is put into the trust, subject to certain conditions (FA 1976 s 90 as amended by FA 1978 s 67 and Sch 11).

There is a special CGT relief where an individual or company disposes of an asset to an employees' trust, subject to satisfying certain conditions (CGTA 1979 s 141). The broad effect of this is that the disposal is treated as being made on a no gain/no loss basis unless the consideration is more than cost. Where the consideration exceeds cost the chargeable gain is to be based on the actual consideration even if this is not market value.

Secondly, employees' trusts can be used to purchase shares in the company on the death of a shareholder or during his lifetime.

Thirdly, employees' trusts can be used to provide for employees and their dependants, particularly during times of hardship, and can help to improve their morale, and encourage them to work harder.

32.8 DEALING WITH INCOME IN ACCUMULATION TRUSTS

Capitalising income by accumulation

Income which is accumulated by the trustees becomes part of the capital of the trust fund and if it is later paid out to a beneficiary he normally receives it as capital and cannot be taxed on it (*IRC v Blackwell Minor's Trustees* (1925) 10 TC 235, CA; *Stanley v IRC* (1944) 26 TC 12, CA; *IRC v Countess of Longford* (1928) 13 TC 573, HL; *Reid's Trustees v IRC* (1929) 14 TC 512). Accordingly, if a trust has power to accumulate income, that income can be converted into capital by accumulating it. This could apply to discretionary and accumulation and maintenance settlements, but not to fixed interest trusts since in such trusts the income cannot be accumulated.

In order to achieve this result the trustees must positively exercise their power of accumulation. It is not sufficient merely to leave the income in suspense, for in that case if it is paid out to a beneficiary it may be taxed in his hands as income. The trustees should make a decision as to whether to accumulate or not within a reasonable time and record it in the minutes.

Capital payments treated as income

There are circumstances where the above rule does not hold good. A payment out of capital and accumulated income will be taxable on the beneficiary if it has the quality of income in his hands. For example, in the leading case of *Brodie's Will Trustees v IRC* (1933) 17 TC 432, payments made out of capital to a widow to make up a shortfall of income were taxable as income in her hands. It does not matter that the payments may be made only at the trustees' discretion (*Lindus and Hortin v IRC* (1933) 17 TC 442; *Cunard's Trustees v IRC* and *McPheeters v IRC* (1945) 27 TC 122, CA). Nor does it matter how the payment is described by the trustees (*Jackson's Trustees v IRC* (1942) 25 TC 13).

The main criterion by which the nature of the payment will be judged is the frequency of recurrence and, therefore, if the trustees wish to avoid the risk of having capital payments treated as income, they would be well advised to make irregular payments and of irregular amounts.

The payment of school fees out of capital could be at risk. In a letter to the Law Society Gazette of 2 June 1982, the Revenue expressed the view that such payments are for an income purpose and have the quality of income in the hands of the beneficiary. The Revenue accept that the payment of a lump sum under certain schemes is not an income payment, but are considering the question of liability to tax when the fees are paid. Also, they would not seek to contend that a capital payment was income where it would be covered by the single personal allowance and the beneficiary had no other income.

There may be occasions when it would be beneficial to have capital payments treated as income, eg where the beneficiary has unused personal allowances or a marginal rate of tax lower than that suffered by the trust.

It should, however, be remembered that, if the payment is made out of pure capital (not accumulated income), the trustees will be liable to tax at 45% of the gross payment under FA 1973 s 17 and, since the capital will not have borne any tax, there will be no amount to set off against this assessment. Where the payment is made out of accumulated income, any tax suffered on it when it was received can be set off against the s 17 assessment. Where the income was received before 6 April 1973 an amount of tax equal to two-thirds of the net income available for distribution at the end of 1972–73 can be set off under s 17.

Another occasion when it may be desirable to convert pure capital (not accumulated income) into income arises when the rate of interim charge on a transfer for CTT purposes is higher than the rate of income tax chargeable on a payment of income to a beneficiary.

Distributing income

Where there are beneficiaries whose marginal rate of tax is lower than 45% it would be advantageous to pay income out to them so that the excess tax can be reclaimed. This would be especially appropriate in the case of infant beneficiaries with no other income since tax on their personal allowances could be reclaimed.

Following the abolition of investment income surcharge (but not the additional rate charge on discretionary trusts) with effect from 6 April 1984, a beneficiary will in many cases, have to pay less tax than previously on distributions received after 5 April 1984, while retaining an entitlement to a 45% tax credit thereon.

Non-resident beneficiaries may be able to take advantage of Extra-Statutory Concession B8, which allows beneficiaries:

(a) to claim the personal allowances available to non-residents under TA 1970 s 27;
(b) to receive interest on government securities free of tax under TA 1970 s 99;
(c) to claim tax exemption for income from overseas securities under TA 1970 ss 100 and 159; and
(d) to claim the protection available under double taxation treaties on the same basis as if the income in question had been received directly by them rather than as a distribution out of a trust.

Section 228 claims

It should not be overlooked that where income which has been contingently accumulated before 6 April 1969 is paid to a beneficiary he may be able to claim repayment of tax by reference to the personal allowances which were available to him over the period during which the income was accumulating (TA 1952 s 228 as kept alive by TA 1970 Sch 14 para 1).

33 Sheltering income

33.1 DEEDS OF COVENANT

This chapter is concerned with ways in which a person receiving taxable income from a family business can shelter that income by using means which are external to the business. In most cases this will be the second part of a two stage process. The first step is to try to plan the affairs of the business to reduce to a minimum the taxable profits it produces; the second step is to try to mitigate the tax suffered by the recipients of those profits. One form of income sheltering available to many taxpayers is the use of deeds of covenant to transfer income to members of their families who have little or no taxable income.

Unmarried children under 18

There are no tax advantages in parents making deeds of covenant in favour of their own infant (ie under 18) unmarried children because the income of the child under such a covenant is treated as the income of the parent (TA 1970 s 437). However, grandparents, uncles and aunts, etc can make covenants in favour of a child without it affecting the income tax position of the parents. Provided that the gross amount of the covenanted payment plus any other taxable income the child may have (eg investment income, casual earnings) does not exceed the amount of the single personal allowance (£2,005 for 1984–85) he will not be liable to income tax and can reclaim all the tax deducted from the covenanted payment.

Children over eighteen

A taxpayer with a son or daughter over 18 who is at school or university may find a deed of covenant a useful means of contributing to the student's maintenance. The parent would save basic rate tax on the gross contribution and provided the student's normal taxable income, including the gross amount of the covenant, does not exceed the single person's allowance, the student can reclaim the tax deducted from the gross covenant and so effectively receive the full parental contribution.

The Inland Revenue Claims Branch have indicated that a deed of covenant to a single student providing for payment to him of an amount equal to the single person's allowance in any year of assessment would be effective for tax purposes.

Provided that the parent is expected to make a contribution to the student's maintenance, the amount received under the deed of covenant will not be treated as part of the student's income for the purpose of assessing his grant, event though the amount of the covenanted payment exceeds the required parental contribution. However, where the parents are divorced or separated and the student receives sums under a deed of covenant from the parent with whom he is not resident, then such sums will normally be treated as the student's income for grant purposes. Where the covenant is made by the parent with whom the student is resident, the amount of the covenant will not affect the grant.

Covenants by relatives other than the parents are taken into account in assessing the grant. Even so, they could well be useful in certain circumstances. The first slice of the student's income (£375 for 1984–85) is disregarded, so that provided the covenanted amount does not bring the student's income above this limit, the grant would not be affected. A covenant above this figure would still be worthwhile if the student is on the minimum maintenance grant since the grant would not be affected.

It would normally be advisable to make the covenant for a period determined on the child ceasing to be in full-time education. This would still be a covenant for a period which could exceed six years, although not expected to do so.

The Inland Revenue have made available a form IR47 which can be used by a parent to make a deed of covenant in favour of his student son or daughter who is 18 or over. This does not prevent the parents from making a deed of covenant in any other form.

Other relatives

Covenants in favour of other members of the family may be useful in certain circumstances, for example, elderly or poor relatives. A retired single person would receive a retirement pension of 1,804 for 1984–85 and be entitled to an age allowance of £2,490, so, if he had no other income, a covenant of £686 gross would enable him to reclaim the tax deducted of £205.80. The margin for a married couple, assuming the wife was not a contributor, would be £1,068 (the age allowance of £3,955 less the joint pension of £2,887), so a gross covenant of £1,068 would enable tax of £320.40 to be recovered. These savings are not spectacular but they could make a welcome difference to a pensioner on this level of income.

Charities

Since 1980–81 covenants in favour of charities have been effective for tax purposes as long as they are capable of lasting more than three years instead of more than six years (TA 1970 s 434(1A)). In practice the minimum period is four years since the period is counted from the first to the last payment.

Furthermore, since 1983–84, covenanted payments to charities up to a maximum of £5,000 (£3,000 in 1981–82 and 1982–83) per year gross are allowable for the purposes of higher and additional rates of tax (TA 1970 s 457(1A)).

Payments under deeds of covenant

In certain cases the Inland Revenue will request evidence that covenanted payments have in fact been made after the deduction of tax. They will also call for declarations by covenantors that they have entered into their covenants with no counter-stipulations for the return of any part of the benefit to the covenantor. They will not accept that any document constitutes a valid deed of covenant for the purposes of the Taxes Acts unless the word 'sealed' occurs in the attestation clause.

Index-linked deeds of covenant

The Inland Revenue Claims Branch has indicated that a deed of covenant to a charity made for a period of seven years (being pre FA 1980), for an amount which increases by predetermined steps each year, would not be effective. Under TA 1970 s 434 a disposition for a period which cannot exceed six years is treated as income of the settlor. Under the covenant envisaged, for the payment of varying sums, only the first payment would be capable of being made for a period in excess of six years. The increases in the years after the first would therefore be treated as the income of the covenantor, and no repayment would be due to the charity.

However, the inspector pointed out that a 'fixed formula' to determine the payment, rather than a fixed amount, is acceptable for the purposes of s 434, provided that the formula can continue for more than six years. An example is given of such a formula where it is desired to update payments for the effect of inflation.

$$£x \times \frac{\text{Current retail price index}}{\text{Retail price index in first year of deed}}$$

It is also understood that a well known national charity is using deeds of covenant expressed as being for £x × A/B where A is the retail price index for the month of January preceding each annual payment, and B is the retail price index for the month of January preceding the execution of the deed. No objection has been raised to this by the Inland Revenue.

33.2 INDUSTRIAL BUILDINGS

Before the FA 1984, the 75% initial allowance available on the cost of construction of a qualifying industrial building and the 100% allowances available for 'small' and 'very small' workshops made the acquisition of such buildings a tax-effective exercise for the high income earner. The reduction in the general rate of initial allowance to 50% for expenditure incurred between 13 March 1984 and 31 March 1985 and to 25% for expenditure incurred during the year to 31 March 1986 and its abolition after 1 April 1986 have, however, considerably reduced the attractiveness of this means of sheltering income.

100% initial allowances remain available for

(a) qualifying hotels (as defined in FA 1978 s 38) and commercial buildings or structures within a designated enterprise zone (FA 1980 s 74 Sch 13); and

(b) workshops of 1,250 square feet or less where the expenditure is incurred between 26 March 1981 and 27 March 1985 (FA 1982 s 73).

Because of their location it is unlikely that individual proprietors of a family business will find the acquisition of buildings in an enterprise zone commercially attractive. However, the availability until 27 March 1985 of the 100% allowance for expenditure on very small workshops remains an effective way of sheltering high levels of income whilst providing the investor with a relatively safe investment. Allowances in excess of the rental income received can be set against general income of the year in which the expenditure is incurred by election under CAA 1968 s 71(1) (proviso).

Taxpayers wishing to use qualifying buildings as a tax shelter will normally deal with an estate agent specialising in such transactions,

33.2 Industrial buildings

and should ensure that they acquire the building unused from the person constructing it. The whole of the cost of construction will then qualify for relief in his hands under CAA 1968 s 5(1).

It is necessary for the purchaser to establish that the building is to be an industrial building or structure as defined in CAA 1968 s 7. In SP 4/80 the Inland Revenue have indicated that they will normally be prepared to deal with industrial buildings allowance claims for estates consisting of small industrial workshops on a global instead of an individual basis. Where individual workshop units of 2,500 sq ft or less intended for separate letting as industrial buildings to small businesses are constructed as an estate, the inspector will normally be satisfied with a general description of the uses to which the units will be put and, unless the circumstances suggest the need for further enquiry, he will not ask for particulars of the trades carried on by the individual tenants or the uses to which the premises are put. This practice will not, however, apply where several units in one estate are let to the same tenant or connected tenants, where the estate is to a significant extend used for trades which do not attract industrial buildings allowance, and in any other circumstances where the relief available would be significantly lower on strict interpretation of the industrial buildings allowance rules.

The legislation limits 100% allowances to factories of less than 1,250 sq ft and the most popular units are currently about 1,000 sq ft each. They are usually built in estates of between twenty and a hundred units and they appeal to people starting up in business for the first time or transferring from cramped accommodation elsewhere. It is conventional to let these units for terms of nine or fifteen years on full repairing and insuring leases with rent reviews every two-and-a half or three years.

In choosing a unit to buy an investor should concentrate on the following criteria:

(1) The factory must be in an area where there is constant demand from small businesses for accommodation. Areas of low economic activity or where most of the demand comes from larger businesses should be avoided. The key indicator of a good location is the presence of other small factories fully occupied.

(2) The factory will be held by the investor for a long term and must be capable of producing a good rent for many decades. It must be built of permanent materials which will not be damaged by heavy use and it must be capable of meeting the rising expectations of work people for good working conditions. The key indicators here are traditional building materials, a high quality of finishes and central heating.

(3) The factory must appeal to a wide range of trades and must provide sufficient room for expansion. It should therefore be regular

in shape, have the largest possible loading door and room for expansion. If any of these features is missing the factory will only appeal to a small sector of the market and this will have a depressing effect on rental values.

(4) The terms of the agreement with any company managing the property on behalf of the investor should be considered carefully.

Good quality factories which meet the above standards for location, specification and flexibility provide the owner with a secure, trouble-free income and there is every prospect for good rental growth.

The use of these capital allowances as a tax shelter will generally be limited to reducing the impact of taxation on income expected to be exceptionally high in a period forming the basis period for 1984–85 assessments, because of the time limit on expenditure of 27 March 1985. Situations in which the investment may be useful include

(a) the expected receipt of a terminal payment substantially in excess of the £25,000 exemption limit; or
(b) unusually high trading or professional profits, perhaps on the completion of a one-off 'adventure in the nature of trade'.

33.3 BUSINESS EXPANSION SCHEME

The Finance Act 1981 ss 53–67 and Sch 12 introduced relief against the total income of an individual for the amount subscribed for shares in new corporate trades. The legislation is voluminous and complex and was little used by individuals wishing to invest in specific businesses, largely because relief was denied where the investor was a paid director or held more than 30% of the company's share capital (which ruled out most potential investors considering risk investment for commercial reasons) and where the investor is 'associated' with paid directors or persons holding more than a 30% interest (which effectively excluded investments by relatives of the entrepreneur controlling the company). Investment opportunities were severely restricted by the requirement that the company in which the investment was being made should not have been trading for more than five years.

Many of the short-comings of the original legislation were corrected in the business expansion scheme legislation in FA 1983 s 26 and Sch 5 and F(No 2) 1983 s 5 and Sch 1. The key changes in the new rules are that

33.3 Business expansion scheme

(a) the relief is no longer limited to 'new' companies or 'new' trades;
(b) the maximum amount of the relief available in any year is increased from £20,000 to £40,000; and
(c) relief may be claimed earlier than previously and may be given through the PAYE system.

Relief under the business expansion scheme will be given in respect of shares issued between 6 April 1983 and 5 April 1987.

Relief is given to an individual by allowing him to deduct from his total income the money applied by him in subscribing for 'eligible shares' in a qualifying company which are issued to finance that company's, or its subsidiary's, qualifying trade. 'Eligible shares' comprise only ordinary shares which, for five years from the date of issue, carry no present or future preferential rights to dividends, to assets available for the distribution in a winding up, or to redemption.

A variety of conditions relating primarily to the individual, the company and its trade must be satisfied throughout the 'relevant period' of two, three or five years. Detailed consideration of the qualifying rules is outside the scope of this book, but they may be summarised briefly as follows:

(1) Relief is available only for money subscribed for shares; the purchase of shares already in issue does not qualify.
(2) The individual claiming relief must subscribe for shares on his own behalf, be resident and oridinarily resident in the UK at the time when the shares are issued and not be 'connected' with the company at any time in the relevant period. A person is 'connected' with a company if he controls it, is its employee or paid director or controls more than 30% of the company's voting power or capital. In determining whether these conditions apply, the person's 'associates' (spouse, parent, grandparent, child etc but not brother, sister, uncle or aunt) are taken into account.
(3) The company in which the investment is made must be unquoted, resident in the UK and carrying on a qualifying trade in the UK or acting as the holding company of one or more subsidiaries carrying on such trades. Most trades are qualifying trades. Excluded activities include farming, finanial and leasing trades, trades comprising dealing in shares, commodities or land, and those dealing in goods other than ordinary wholesale or retail distribution trades. The trade must be conducted on a commercial basis and with a view to realising profits.

The foregoing summary of the rules is necessarily brief and readers should refer to the full text of the legislation before committing themselves to an investment under the scheme. The intention of this section is to draw attention to the possibility of sheltering the income of high rate taxpayers by making invesments which qualify for relief under the scheme. It is likely that such investments will be made in one of two ways:

(1) Individuals may invest in specific companies of which they or their investors have particular knowledge. Because of the restrictive rules prohibiting relief where the investor is 'connected' with the company this is likely to be relatively uncommon. However, readers may be interested to know that the Industrial and Commercial Finance Corporation Limited (ICFC) operate a clearing house scheme to bring together potential investors with businesses requiring equity funds.
(2) The investment may be through an investment fund approved by the Inland Revenue under FA 1983 Sch 5 para 19, the fund being treated as the individual's nominee in relation to the amount he puts into it. The fund managers take upon themselves the task of identifying suitable investments. Once identified the qualifying status of the company and its trade will be established with the Revenue, leaving the individual investor only to establish with his Inspector of Taxes that he is a qualifying individual in relation to that company. The individual will still become entitled to relief only when the managers invest his money rather than on his placing the money in the managers' hands.

The business expansion scheme offers significant advantages to the high rate taxpayer. However, it is not a licence to acquire risk free equity investments at the treasury's expense. The following caveats should be borne in mind by potential investors:

(1) The company in which the investment is made may not be successful in which case the value of the investment will diminish or it may be lost altogether.
(2) The conditions of the scheme may not be satisfied for the required period after the issue of the shares (between three and five years, depending on the condition in question). In that case relief may be lost in whole or in part, so altering the financial basis upon which the subscription was originally made. Investors should normally seek an indemnity from the company against loss of relief, eg as a result of the company seeking a quotation or ceasing to carry on a qualifying trade. Similarly, the investor is locked in to the shareholding for five years. Once the time limit is up, if he wishes to realise his investment he will have to find a willing purchaser and this may not always be easy. Unless the company has grown

33.3 Business expansion scheme

sufficiently to qualify for a quotation on the Unlisted Securities Market the well known difficulty in marketing minority shareholdings in unquoted companies may prove to be a major problem.

(3) The amounts charged to investors by the fund managers vary significantly. Investors should also be aware that most fund managers retain interest earned on money deposited with the fund until it is used to subscribe for shares.

Despite the foregoing, investment in business expansion scheme funds is becoming very popular. If the investor is able to acquire more than 5% of the shares in a company in which he is investing he may obtain an added advantage by borrowing the money used to subscribe for the shares and claiming relief for the interest on the borrowings under FA 1974 Sch 1 para 9. An individual paying tax at 60% who borrows money to make a business expansion scheme investment, uses the immediate repayment of tax to repay part of the borrowings, and claims interest relief on the balance for the five year qualifying period will find that more than 80% of the cost of his investment has been funded by the tax relief obtained.

The relief is not given automatically; it must be claimed. A claim must be accompanied by a certificate from the company stating that the conditions relating to the company and its trade are satisfied. Before issuing any certificate the company must deliver to the Inland Revenue a statement in writing that the conditions are fulfilled and obtain the inspector's consent to the issue of a certificate.

The claim cannot be made in any event before 1 January 1984 and not until the company has traded for *four* months. The claim must be made within two years of the end of the year of assessment in which the shares were issued or, if later, within twenty-eight months from the commencement of trading. For the claim to be allowed, the trade must have been carried on by the company either at, or within two years after, the date of the share issue.

The use of moneys invested under the Business Expansion Scheme for financing a family company is discussed at **19.4** above.

34 Handing on the business

The impact of capital taxes on the handing on of a business to the following generation is not so serious a problem as it used to be. So far as capital gains tax is concerned, the general relief for gifts introduced by FA 1980 s 79, and further extended by FA 1981 s 78 and FA 1982 s 82 (see **30.1** above), means that any CGT can be deferred, perhaps indefinitely, or even eliminated altogether. If the taxpayer has reached the age of 60, he will be eligible for the much increased retirement relief, which may exempt part or all of his gains (see **29** above). Furthermore, the new indexation allowance introduced by FA 1982 may reduce the gains quite considerably as time goes by. The result of all this is that CGT need no longer be much of a problem.

On the CTT front, we have seen the introduction of business property relief by FA 1976, the ten year cumulation rule by FA 1981 and a progressive reduction in lifetime rates of tax. Finally, under FA 1982 it has become possible for a company to purchase its own shares to provide money to pay CTT arising on death.

Even so, CTT can still pose serious problems for the family business. Unless action is taken in good time, the death of the owner may yet lead to a forced sale of the shares or break-up of the business, and this could happen at a most unfavourable time. The purpose of this chapter is to suggest ways in which this can be prevented. It is assumed that the reader will be familiar with CTT and CGT and how the various reliefs, particularly business and agricultural property reliefs, operate.

34.1 SOLE TRADER

Probably the best way for the sole trader to hand on his business is to form a partnership. The partners would normally be his wife and children or other members of the family. Where the children are very young, the other partners could include the trustees of an accumulation and maintenance trust for the benefit of his children. In this case, the trustees' share of profits should be withdrawn each year and not left in the business, so as to avoid TA 1970 s 451.

There are several advantages in an arrangement of this sort. Because it is possible to give small fractional shares in a partnership, it is easy to make regular gifts, and indeed this is a very convenient and common way of using the annual CTT exemption. By the use of *Boden* type accruer clauses or cross-options it is possible to pass on a share in the goodwill of the business in a CTT effective way. It is also possible to carry out value freezing exercises which will enable all or part of the future growth in value of the business to pass to the younger partners. This would be particularly appropriate in the case of farming businesses, where land is a major part of the value of the business. These, and other, ideas will be discussed more fully in the next section.

Transferring the business to a company would not be nearly so attractive, unless limited liability was an essential requirement, and even then, the usual requirement for the directors of a company to give personal guarantees for bank borrowings often makes limited liability more theoretical than real. In the first place, the full 50% business or agricultural relief is not available unless the transferor controls the company, although the lower value of a non-control holding may compensate for the lower rate of business relief. There is, too, the potential double charge to tax on capital gains on land held in a company, so where a company is formed it is generally considered desirable to keep land out.

If profits are substantial, the marginal rate of tax paid in a partnership may be higher than in a company, but at least there is normally no problem in withdrawing profits from a partnership (liquidity permitting!). Extracting profits from a company except by way of remuneration or dividend is fraught with difficulties. The lower rates of corporation tax envisaged over the next three years under FA 1984 s 18 may begin to tilt the balance in favour of companies again, but, for the present, a partnership is, in most cases, likely to be the better structure.

Business relief

The full 50% relief is available on the transfer of a business or an interest in a business (FA 1976 Sch 10 paras 2 and 3(1)). The important point to watch here is that relief is not available on the transfer of mere assets. The point is similar to that discussed earlier in connection with retirement relief (see Chapter **29** above).

It should not be overlooked that investment and property holding or dealing businesses do not qualify for business relief at all (FA 1976 Sch 10 para 3(2) and (3)).

It should be noted, too, that relief will not be available if a binding obligation to sell the business has been entered into (in effect the transferor will be giving cash). There is an exception to this rule where the sale is either to a company in consideration for shares (ie on incorporation) or the sale is for the purposes of a reconstruction (FA 1976 Sch 10 para 3(4)).

The business must have been owned for a minimum period of two years before it qualifies for relief, although the rule is relaxed for replacement and inherited property in certain cases (FA 1976 Sch 10 paras 4 and 5). The timing of the gift is therefore important.

Relief will be restricted where assets are either not used wholly or mainly for business purposes throughout the two years preceding the transfer, or not required at the time of transfer for present or future use for business purposes. An asset is not treated as being used wholly or mainly for business purposes if it is used wholly or mainly for the personal benefit of the transferor or a person connected with him, eg living accommodation with a shop (FA 1976 Sch 10 para 8).

There are provisions to avoid double relief on agricultural property and woodlands. As regards agriculture, it should be remembered that business relief will be available on the value of land in excess of the agricultural value, and also on other assets such as farm animals, plant and machinery and stock (FA 1976 Sch 10 paras 10–12).

34.2 PARTNERSHIPS

Setting up the partnership

There will normally be no transfer of value by any of the partners when a partnership is first set up provided that it is determinable at will. If, however, the partnership is for a fixed period of time, or for a period determinable only by the death of one or all of the partners, there could be a transfer of value if the terms are unduly favourable to one of the partners. In particular, the amount of capital contributed by each partner, the profit sharing ratios and the amount of time the partners are required to devote to the partnership business would all need to be considered.

Gifting a share in partnership assets

One of the advantages of forming a partnership is that it is relatively easy to give away a share in the partnership. This might be desirable in order to use up the annual exemption or the nil rate band, or to take advantage of the lower lifetime rates, or of the ten year cumulation rule. The assignment of a share of a partnership must be in writing and signed by the donor (Law of Property Act 1925 s 136). It is important to remember that a gift of a share in partnership assets may be worth considerably more than the book value of the assets as shown by the accounts. The Revenue accept that a partner's capital account represents an interest in a business and that, accordingly, a transfer from one partner's capital account to another will qualify for business relief. In that case, a partner could transfer £6,000 per annum within the exemption.

It is important to study the partnership agreement carefully to see precisely what effect the transfer of capital will have. There might be circumstances where the value transferred is more than the book value of the transfer, eg where a share in goodwill attaches to a partner's share in capital.

Accruer clauses

A common method of passing on a share of goodwill in a family business to the younger generation is the inclusion in the partnership agreement of an accruer clause under which, on the death or retirement of the senior partner, his share in goodwill accrues to the younger continuing partners without any cash payment. The consideration given by the younger partners is that they are required to devote their whole time to running the business, whilst the senior partner is at liberty to do as much work as he pleases. By entering into such an agreement, the senior partner will no doubt have made a disposition for CTT purposes but, provided the undertakings given by the younger partners are full consideration, there should be no transfer of value either at the time the agreement is entered into or later when, on the death or retirement of the senior partner, his share in goodwill passes to them (FA 1975 s 20(4)).

This sort of arrangement is founded on the principle established in *A-G v Boden* [1912] 1 KB 539 that the undertakings in a partnership agreement can be full consideration for the acquisition of a share in a partnership. The *Boden* case was concerned with estate duty, but it is understood that the Inland Revenue accept the principle as valid for CTT purposes. It is important that the undertakings given by the younger partners are such as will constitute full consideration. If they do not, there will be a transfer of value not only at the time when the partnership agreement is entered into, but also when the share of goodwill passes to the younger partners on the retirement or death of the senior partner. This follows from FA 1975 Sch 10 para 5, which provides that where, by a contract (eg a partnership agreement), the right to dispose of any property has been excluded or restricted then, in determining the value of the property for the purpose of the first relevant event happening after that time, the exclusion or restriction will be taken into account only to the extent (if any) that consideration in money or money's worth was given for it.

It is extremely doubtful that a *Boden* type clause could be relied upon to pass a share in partnership assets other than goodwill. It is one thing to say that the extra work of the younger partners is full consideration for goodwill, the value of which is directly related to their efforts; it is quite another to argue that it could be consideration for a share in tangible assets. It would be prudent to confine a *Boden* type arrangement to goodwill only.

Immediate gift of share in goodwill

The problems associated with FA 1975 Sch 10 para 5 might be avoided if, instead of using a *Boden* clause, the senior partner made an immediate gift of a large share in goodwill to the younger partner, but retained a lion's share of the profits for a substantial period of time, say ten or fifteen years. It seems probable that, in these circumstances, the goodwill given away would have little value.

Freezing the value of a partnership share

It seems that the assignment of only a small part of a partnership share could be a relevant event for the purposes of FA 1975 Sch 10 para 5. If that is right, it might be possible to freeze the value of a partner's share in the partnership. For example, a father in partnership with his son, sharing profits 90% and 10% respectively, might transfer land to the partnership on the basis that the son has the right to purchase his father's share, on the father's death or retirement, at the value placed on the land when it was transferred to the partnership. If the father were to make an immediate transfer of a further 5% of his partnership share, it seems that this would be the first relevant event to which para 5 would apply. On a subsequent transfer of the father's remaining 85% share, the restriction on his right to dispose of his interest would have to be taken into account.

It should not be overlooked that, where a partnership was entered into before 27 March 1975, FA 1975 Sch 10 para 5(1) will apply only if the first relevant event is a transfer on death (para 5(2)). Thus, for example, where a partnership between father and son commenced before that date on the basis that the father's share will pass to the son without payment on the father's death or retirement, there will be no transfer of value if the share passes to the son during the father's lifetime. Where there is such a partnership, it would be advisable not to tamper with the terms of the partnership agreement if the benefit conferred by para 5(2) is to be preserved.

Another, and perhaps more reliable, way of freezing a partner's share might be for, say, a father to transfer land to be held on trust for sale for the benefit of a partnership comprising himself and his son. The value of the land at the time of transfer is credited to the father's capital account, but any future increase in the value of the land is to be credited to the son's capital account. As long as the partnership is terminable at will there will be no transfer of value by these arrangements since the father can recover his capital at any time. He would have given away the possibility of future growth but this would not reduce the value of his estate. It might be contended that by failing to terminate the partnership the father has omitted to exercise a right and would therefore have made a disposition within FA 1975 s 20(7), but such a disposition would not be a transfer of value because it does not decrease the value of his estate.

The position with regard to CGT where a partner makes a disposal of an asset to the partnership is far from clear. The matter is not specifically referred to in the Inland Revenue Press Statement of 17 January 1975. On a practical level, the partner disposing of the property is treated as making a part disposal to the extent to which other partners acquire a fractional share in it. It appears to follow, therefore, that if in the example given above, the son does not have any share in the value of the land transferred, no disposal will be treated as having been made. If that view is not correct and there is a part disposal, any gain would presumably be rolled over. It is arguable that, as the land increases in value, the father will make a part disposal of the land to the son for CGT purposes. However, if this is correct, any gain could be rolled over.

Partnership annuities

The payment of an annuity to a retired partner has become an increasingly common way of paying for his share in goodwill. For income tax purposes, the annuity is treated as earned income provided it does not exceed the limits specified in FA 1974 s 16, and is deductible for both basic rate and higher rate tax purposes from the income of the continuing partners. For CGT purposes, the capitalised value of the annuity is disregarded. As far as CTT is concerned, there will be no transfer of value on the retirement of the partner provided the capitalised value of the annuity equates with his loss of goodwill, and the value of the annuity, provided it ends on death, will not be included in his estate (FA 1975 Sch 10 para 9(1)(a)).

Business relief

There are two rates of business property relief in relation to an unincorporated business. A business or an interest in a business attracts 50% relief, whilst business assets owned by a partner and used by a partnership of which he is a member qualify for 30% relief.

It is, therefore, necessary to consider carefully how property should be held. The considerations are similar to those discussed in connection with family companies (see **34.3**). However, the problem of the double charge to tax on capital gains does not arise where property is held in a partnership. We have also seen earlier in this section how the transfer of property to a partnership can be used to freeze the value of a partner's share, hopefully without any CGT or CTT liability, whilst obtaining the benefit of 50% business relief.

Business relief may be lost where there is an agreement between partners whereby, in the event of the death of one of them before retirement, the personal representatives of the deceased partners are obliged to sell and the continuing partners are obliged to purchase the deceased partner's interest in the business. The Revenue view is that such an agreement constitutes a binding obligation to sell and therefore business relief is not available (FA 1976 Sch 10 para 3(4)).

It should be noted that it is only where the partnership agreement imposes an obligation on the executors to sell and the surviving partners to buy that business relief will be lost. Where the executors have only an option to sell and the surviving partners an option to buy, business relief will still be available.

Companies or trustees as partners

A company owned by the younger members of the family could be introduced as a partner in a business. The idea would be to accumulate any share of profits within the company, which might be used later to purchase a further interest in the business and provide cash to pay CTT. It should not be forgotten though that an election cannot be made for the continuation basis under TA 1970 s 154(2) on the introduction of a company partner and there can be problems in extracting funds from a company.

A similar arrangement might be made by giving an interest in a business to trustees of an accumulation and maintenance settlement established for the benefit of the children. The profits would be accumulated within the trust and possibly used to purchase a further interest in the business later. The profits would have to be fairly substantial to justify this approach given that the trustees will be paying tax at 45%. It would be almost essential that the trustees' share of profits is withdrawn and not left in the business since otherwise the settlor, as one of the partners, could be said to be deriving a benefit (see TA 1970 s 451).

Land held outside partnerships

One way to reduce the value of land, including agricultural land, for CTT purposes might be for the landowner to give the freehold reversion subject to the retention of a long lease at a low rent. The amount of the transfer of value will be the difference between the value of the freehold with vacant possession and the value of the long lease retained. The value of the long lease, which will be quite substantial at first, will gradually waste away to nothing, whilst the value of the freehold reversion given away will increase. If the landowner survives for ten years, the gift of the freehold reversion will drop out of account altogether and, on his death, the value of the lease will be much reduced. Instead of giving away the reversion, the landowner could sell it at its market value, in which case there would be no transfer of value.

There are a number of disadvantages with this scheme. In the first place, the donee or purchaser of the reversion will have a fairly low base cost for CGT purposes should he one day come to dispose of the freehold. However, if the disposal is by way of gift, the gain may be rolled over, and in any case, the saving in CTT may outweigh any CGT which may become payable.

Another difficulty may arise if, during the currency of the lease, it is decided to sell the land. If the tenant joins in the sale by assigning his tenancy to the purchaser, there is a danger of the assignment being caught by TA 1970 s 81. It would be safer if the tenant surrendered his tenancy to the reversioner, who would now be able to sell the unencumbered freehold.

CGTA 1979 s 26 referred to earlier may also pose a problem. It is arguable that, on the gift or sale of the reversion, the Revenue could seek to substitute a higher market value on the grounds that the value of the freehold was materially reduced. This would not be so serious a problem in the case of a gift since the gain could be rolled over.

34.3 FAMILY COMPANIES

Relief for controlling shareholdings

50% relief is available where the shares transferred (either by themselves or together with other shares owned by the transferor) give the transferor control of the company immediately before the transfer (FA 1976 Sch 10 paras 2(1A) and 3(1)(b)). A number of points call for comment.

(1) Control means voting control (a bare majority will suffice) on all questions affecting the company as a whole, except that control on a question of winding up the company or on any question primarily affecting the rights of a class of shares is not necessary. Related property (eg shares owned by a wife) and shares in a settlement in which the shareholder has an interest in possession must be taken into account (FA 1976 Sch 10 para 13(2) and FA 1975 Sch 4 para 13(7)).

(2) It is not necessary that the shares actually gifted confer control; it is sufficient that the holding out of which the gift is made gives control.

(3) It is the shares themselves which must give control, so control by virtue of a chairman's casting vote given to him as chairman under the company's Articles of Association is not relevant.

(4) Non-voting shares cannot give control and would not normally qualify, though it might be different in the unusual circumstance that, under the Articles, a holder of a voting share had also to hold a non-voting share and could not vote unless he did.

(5) The shares must give control immediately before the transfer, so the fact that they may cease to do so afterwards is immaterial. This suggests that the rights attaching to a minority holding of shares, which would not otherwise qualify for 50% relief, might be altered so as to give control for a limited period of just over two years. After two years, but shortly before the rights expire, the shares could be given away. It seems that the 50% relief would be available, although control would have little value if it was about to expire. A charge under CGTA 1979 s 25 could be avoided by balancing the acquisition of control with decreased rights to dividends or surplus assets on a winding up.

It is advisable that the rights of control should be held for a minimum period of two years to be on the safe side, because it is understood that the Inland Revenue take the view that the shares must give control throughout the minimum two year period of ownership prescribed by FA 1976 Sch 10 para 4(1)(a). However, there is nothing in that paragraph about control, and it can be strongly argued that it is enough that control is held immediately before the transfer.

Relief for non-controlling shareholdings

Relief at 30% is given on shares which are not quoted on a recognised stock exchange and which do not give control. The Unlisted Securities Market is not considered to be a recognised stock exchange for this purpose.

Although the relief for minority shareholdings is lower than for controlling shareholdings, the lower valuation of a minority shareholding is usually more advantageous. A reduction in a minority valuation of about 29% will make up for the difference in the rates of relief.

Giving up control

Whether it is desirable to give up control depends on a number of factors, not all of them fiscal ones. It is understandable that a man may be reluctant, whatever the CTT consequences, to give up control of a business which he has built up by hard endeavour over a long period. Sometimes it is the case that the younger members of the family are not yet ready to assume their father's mantle and he is therefore unwilling that they should yet have absolute ownership of the shares. One possible solution here is the establishment of a trust, of which the father could be a trustee. Still, in general, it will usually make sense from a CTT point of view to give up control, there will be able and responsible sons (and, increasingly often in these enlightened times, daughters!) ready to take the reins, and father is more than ready to take a back seat.

Amongst the fiscal factors which will lead to the decision to give up control are, first, that the gift of the shares will be taxed, if at all, at the lower lifetime rates. Secondly, if the donor survives for ten years, it will drop out of account altogether, and thirdly, the future growth in value of the company will not be reflected, to anything like the same extent, in a minority holding as in a control holding.

One disadvantage of giving up control is that the rate of relief on the retained minority holding is only 30%. Once, therefore, a controlling shareholder has decided to give up control, it would usually make sense for him to reduce his shareholding substantially in order to get the maximum benefit overall from the 50% relief. He should do this by one single gift, if possible, rather than a series of separate gifts where he ends up making gifts out of a minority holding.

Where both husband and wife hold shares in a company, the effect of the related property rules needs to be watched carefully. If neither have control individually, but together they have control, the principle is that the smaller shareholder should make the gift which reduces the combined shareholding to less than a controlling shareholding.

Business assets owned by shareholders

Any land or buildings, or machinery or plant, owned by a controlling shareholder and used by the company for the purposes of its business qualifies for 30% business property relief. A question often asked is whether or not it is desirable to have property inside or outside a company. The major tax disadvantage of keeping property inside a company is the double charge to tax on liquidation of the company—once on disposal of the asset by the company and again on the disposal of shares by the shareholder, the value of which would reflect the value of the land.

On the other hand, it could be argued that there is some CTT advantage in having land in the company because, in as much as its value is reflected in the value of the shares, it qualifies in effect for 50% relief as compared with 30% relief for property held outside the company. The astute reader will see that this comparison is not quite right because a control holding below 90% will usually be valued at a discount on net assets. There may, however, be other non-tax factors. Property outside the company may be useful in raising funds to pay CCT, and it might provide an income for the owner after he has retired. It used to be the case that a wealthy shareholder could make better use of the industrial buildings allowances, but with the phasing out of capital allowances under FA 1984 s 58 this can no longer be said. It is difficult to generalise. On balance it will probably usually be better to keep property outside the company.

Wills and business relief

Care should be taken not to waste business property relief where a substantial part of a testator's estate qualifies for business relief. A considerable CTT advantage can be obtained by leaving the surviving spouse a pecuniary legacy rather than a share in residue. Suppose, for example, that the husband's estate comprises a controlling holding of shares in a family company worth £400,000 and by his will he leaves the residue of his estate to his wife and children in equal shares. The chargeable transfer will then be as follows:

Value of estate	£400,000
Less 50% relief	200,000
	200,000
Less half residue to widow —exempt	100,000
Chargeable transfer	£100,000

If, however, he leaves his wife a pecuniary legacy of £200,000 to be satisfied by shares, if she consents, and the residue to his children, the chargeable transfer will be nil as follows:

Value of estate	400,000
Less 50% relief	200,000
	200,000
Less exempt legacy to widow	200,000
Chargeable transfer	Nil

But there is still £200,000 worth of shares in the estate, which will pass, tax-free, to the children. The reason for this somewhat anomalous result is to be found in FA 1975 Sch 6 paras 19 and 20. Under para 19(1), such part of the value transferred must be attributed to specific gifts as corresponds to the value of the gifts. Only to the extent that the value transferred is not attributable to specific gifts under para 19 can it be attributed to gifts of residue or shares in residue (para 20). 'Specific gifts' means any gift other than a gift of residue or a share of residue (para 23(1)). So, in the above example, the whole of the value transferred is attributable to the pecuniary legacy and there is no value left to attribute to the residuary gift to the children.

It seems that the widow's consent is necessary, notwithstanding that stamp duty will be payable, since otherwise there would have been simply a legacy of shares.

A similar arrangement can be made where the estate comprises agricultural property which qualifies for agricultural relief.

Loans on family company shares

Loans charged on family company shares will restrict business relief (FA 1975 Sch 10 para 2). Where possible, loans should be charged on property which does not qualify for relief.

Timing of transfers

The timing of transfers can be of considerable significance in valuing the shares of a company. Their value will depend very largely on the profits of the company, so that, other things being equal, it would be beneficial to make a transfer when profits are relatively low. The general level of prices on The Stock Exchange could also have an effect on the share value, since the yields which are being obtained on comparable quoted companies are frequently used in valuing private company shares.

Use of exemptions

The transfer of shares in a family company is a convenient and relatively painless way of using the annual exemption. The annual exemption applies to the transfer of value after deducting business relief, so a controlling shareholder could transfer shares worth £6,000 each year within the exemption.

The valuation thresholds need to be watched carefully. The main one is, of course, at 50%, because of the control factor, but 75% and 25% are also considered to be significant.

Transfers within the nil rate band will not attract any tax liability and, after ten years, will drop out of account altogether.

Sales instead of gifts

One of the difficulties confronting the shareholder in a family company who wishes to give up control is that the value per share of a controlling shareholding is very much greater than that of a minority holding, so that the consequential loss to his estate is that much greater when he crosses the 50% threshold. The problem can be particularly acute where shares are held by both husband and wife, so that the related property rules apply.

One way of overcoming these problems is to substitute a sale for a gift, thus hopefully avoiding CTT altogether. For this to work, there must be no intention to confer any gratuitous benefit on any one and the sale must be at arm's length or on such terms as might be expected to be made in a transaction at arm's length between persons not connected with each other (FA 1975 s 20(4)). In considering the value of the shares for the purposes of a sale, one would be concerned only with the value of the shares being sold, not with the consequential loss to the transferor's estate as would apply for CTT.

In considering the possibilities of a sale rather than a gift, it should be borne in mind that, on a sale, no business or agricultural property

34.3 Family companies

relief is available. Furthermore, CGT may be payable on a sale, whereas the gain on a gift could be rolled over.

If necessary the transferor could make cash gifts to the purchasers to put them in funds to buy the shares, though the associated operations rules under FA 1975 s 44 should be watched carefully.

Reorganisation of share capital to freeze or reduce the value of shares

Various schemes involving the reorganisation of share capital can be used to freeze or reduce the value of shares. At the outset, however, the complex anti-avoidance legislation for CGT and CTT should be borne in mind, particularly the value shifting provisions of CGTA 1979 ss 25 and 26 and the associated operations provisions of FA 1975 s 44.

It should also be remembered that these schemes depend on the passage of time, usually a considerable number of years, to achieve their objective, and the rules of the game may well be changed or the shareholder may not live to see their fruition.

Another problem is that the success of these schemes does depend to a large extent on the values placed on the various classes of shares and these will have to be agreed with the Shares Valuation Division. This does introduce an element of uncertainty, since it would be impractical to agree values before the scheme is implemented.

Finally, the possible implications of the *Ramsay* doctrine will have to be considered carefully before any scheme is embarked upon. With those important caveats in mind, some possibilities will be outlined.

Freezing the value of shares

One possibility might be to create a new class of 'A' ordinary shares, by way of a bonus issue, which would carry votes and be entitled to dividends and a share of surplus assets on a winding-up, only when profits or surplus assets exceeded certain limits. The existing ordinary shares would continue to receive dividends and to share in surplus assets on a winding-up, but only up to the prescribed levels. The effect of this would be to freeze the value of the existing ordinary shares and to channel future growth in value of the company into the new 'A' ordinary shares. The controlling shareholder would give the new shares away to the next generation.

The issue of the new shares would not involve any CGT as it would be a reorganisation under CGTA 1979 s 77. There would be little, if any, gain on the gift of the shares, and such as there was could be rolled over under FA 1980 s 79.

For CTT purposes, although the scheme would be caught by FA 1975 s 39(5), the value of the existing ordinary shares ought not to reduce in value by very much, so the transfer in value would be small. Similarly, the gift of the new shares would have little CTT consequence. The existing ordinary shares would still carry control and therefore be entitled to 50% business assets relief.

Deferred share scheme

An alternative to the above would be a bonus issue of deferred shares which would have only minimal rights for a period of years, at the end of which they would rank *pari passu* with the ordinary shares. As in the previous scheme, the value of the existing shares should be little changed at first. The value of the new shares would be very low, so that they could be given away without any adverse CGT or CTT consequences.

Although the deferred shares would become valuable at the end of the prescribed period, it is thought that there should not at that time be any alteration of rights attaching to the shares within FA 1975 s 39(5) because the rights have always been embodied in the shares and simply accrue through the passage of time. CGTA 1979 s 25 should not apply as there will be no exercise of control at that time.

The effect of CGTA 1979 s 26 on any disposal of the existing ordinary shares should not be overlooked, but it is thought that, even if the section did apply, the effect would be fairly small and any gain could be rolled over.

The deferred ordinary shareholder should be given the right to vote on any question of winding up the company or reorganisation of the share capital, so as to avoid the application of FA 1975 s 20(7). Otherwise, it could be argued that the ordinary shareholders had omitted to exercise their rights to wind up the company or restrict the rights of the deferred shares so as to deprive them of the value of future growth. For the same reason, it would be advisable to limit the amount of dividends which could be declared so that the ordinary shareholders could not distribute all the undistributed profits just before the deferred shares ranked *pari passu* with the ordinary shares.

As a variant to this scheme, it could be arranged that the existing ordinary shares would lose all their value at the end of the prescribed period when the deferred shares obtain their full rights. It would be advisable to keep the shares after they have become valueless to avoid the risk of a possible charge under CGTA 1979 s 26.

Parallel trading

The basic idea here is that a new company is formed to carry on trading alongside the existing company. The business of the old company is gradually run down as its contracts and connections are taken up by the new company. In particular, new developments would be channelled through the new company. The new business would be owned and carried on by the younger members of the family, who would acquire their shares at the start before they had grown in value.

This sort of arrangement is intended to prevent the shares of the old company from growing in value, so it is a sort of freezing operation. In due course, the new company might purchase the shares of the old company for cash, although it would first be advisable to obtain clearance under TA 1970 s 460.

Waiver of dividends

There is no transfer of value for CTT purposes on waiving a dividend on shares in a company provided the waiver is made within twelve months before the dividend becomes due (FA 1976 s 92). A final dividend becomes due when it is declared in general meeting, and an interim dividend becomes due when it is paid. The waiver should be under seal.

Waiver of remuneration

Similarly, a waiver or repayment of remuneration is exempt from CTT provided

(a) the remuneration would have been assessed to tax under Schedule E if it had not been waived, and
(b) the remuneration is not deductible as a trading expense of the employer (FA 1976 s 91).

Purchase of own shares by a company

The difficulty of finding the money to pay CTT on family company shares may be overcome if the shares can be sold to the company. The subject is dealt with at **19.5** above.

34.4 AGRICULTURAL RELIEF

There are a number of interesting planning opportunities in connection with agricultural relief, which will now be considered.

Obtaining 50% relief on tenanted value

In order to obtain 50% agricultural relief, the transferor must have the right to vacant possession or the right to obtain it within twelve months (FA 1981 Sch 14 para 2(2)(a)). Thus, where 50% relief is available, the land will usually be valued on a vacant possession basis. It may, however, be possible to obtain 50% relief on the tenanted value.

For example, a farmer who is due to retire, might grant a reversionary lease to his son to take effect in a year's time. Before the lease takes effect, he could give the reversion to another member of his family or, possibly, the trustees of a settlement for the benefit of his grandchildren. At the time of the gift he would have vacant possession and would be entitled to 50% relief, but because the lease was shortly to come into effect, the value of the land would be reduced to tenanted value.

If he wanted to give the reversion to his son, he would have to grant the reversionary lease to take effect sometime after a period of three years has elapsed from the date of the grant. Then, after the three years has elapsed but before the lease takes effect, he could make the gift of the reversion. In this way, the associated operations rules are avoided, since the grant of the lease cannot be associated with the gift of the reversion (FA 1975 s 44(2)).

Another opportunity to obtain 50% relief on tenanted value is available where a farming partnership farms land which is owned by one of the partners. The land owning partner might grant an option to his partners enabling them to take a tenancy of the land should he die or retire from the partnership. On his death, the value of the land would be much reduced because of the option, but 50% relief would still be available.

A variant to this would be for the landowner to put the land into the farming partnership as part of his capital on condition that, on his death, the land was to revert to him, but the continuing partners would have an option to take a tenancy of the land on arm's length terms—at a full market rent and so on. On his death, the land would form part of his estate at tenanted value but with full 50% relief.

How land should be held

Agricultural relief is available only on the agricultural value of land (FA 1981 Sch 14 para 2(1)). Where the value of land is greater than the agricultural value (eg because of development or mineral value) business relief may be available on the excess provided the relevant conditions are satisfied. In such cases it is necessary to consider carefully how the land is held. For example, if the land is owned by a partnership, the development value will be reflected in the value of the interest in the business and will qualify for 50% business relief. However, if the land is owned personally by a partner and occupied by the partnership, the rate of business relief will be only 30%.

Loans secured on land

As in the case of business relief, loans secured on land are deducted from the value of the property (FA 1975 Sch 10 para 2). It is important, therefore, to ensure that, so far as possible, loans are secured on property which does not qualify for agricultural relief.

Contracts for sale

As in the case of business relief, agricultural relief will be lost if there is a binding contract for sale at the time of the transfer, except where the sale is to a company wholly or mainly in consideration for shares which will give the transferor control (FA 1981 Sch 14 para 14). Where, therefore, it is intended to sell land and give the proceeds, it would be better to make the gift before entering into the contract of sale. This would have the added advantage of enabling the gain to be rolled over for capital gains tax under FA 1980 s 79.

Accruer arrangements in partnerships

Accruer arrangements and their effect on business relief have been discussed at **34.2** above. The effect is similar for agricultural relief and the advice is the same—where the proposed arrangements would constitute a binding obligation to sell, use cross-options instead.

Where there is an agreement between partners that, on the death of one of them a lease of agricultural land will be granted to the surviving partners, it is important to ensure that the lease does not take effect until after the partner's death, since otherwise the land will not carry the right to vacant possession. In this connection it should be noted that an agreement to grant a lease can constitute a lease if it is specifically enforceable.

Timing of gifts

The timing of gifts when a sole trader is about to retire is extremely important. It would be advisable to make any gifts before he retires as it will then be necessary to show only that he has farmed the land for the previous two years. If he waits until after he has retired, agricultural relief will depend on the seven years owner and occupation test (FA 1981 Sch 14 para 3).

35 Selling the family company

35.1 BUSINESS OR SHARES?

General principles

There are two basic methods of selling a corporate business or trade—selling the shares of the company which carries on the business or selling the underlying assets which the company uses to carry on the business. The two methods are fundamentally different in both their company law and tax law aspects. In general, it is likely that the purchaser will wish to acquire assets and the vendor to sell shares, but the abolition of stock relief in FA 1984 s 48 has removed one of the main stumbling blocks in the way of an asset sale from the vendor's point of view, that is the clawback of stock relief on the cessation of trading. Where significant amounts of plant or machinery are involved, however, the principle remains, at least until 1 April 1986, that the vendor will wish to avoid a balancing charge by selling shares and the purchaser will wish to obtain first year allowances by buying assets. Once first year allowances are phased out, it is likely that asset sales will be more common than hitherto; any tax advantages inherent in a share sale will be outweighed by the elimination of the need for the complex warranties and indemnities which almost invariably feature in any agreement for the sale of shares. The main circumstances in which the share sale route is likely to be used is where the company owns valuable assets which have appreciated in value during the period of ownership by the company and the proprietors would face a double charge to CGT (see **2.3** above) if they were to arrange for the company to sell the assets and then liquidate the company in order to get at the cash.

Retirement relief

It is likely that a family company will be sold outside the proprietors' families only if the current owner/managers wish to retire and there is no one else in the family who wishes to take on the running of the business. Shareholders in such a position are likely to want cash in their hands (rather than in the company); they will be entitled to retirement relief if they sell the shares in their family company (CGTA 1979 s 124(1)(b)) or cause the company to sell the assets and then, within a period of three years from the sale liquidate the company and distribute the cash (by concession—see Extra-Statutory Concession D13). Accordingly, the availability of retirement relief will not normally be a factor in the decision whether to sell shares or sell assets. For a full discussion of planning to maximise retirement relief, see Chapter 29 above.

Allocation of the purchase price

Following the changes in the capital allowances regime and the rates of corporation tax introduced in FA 1984, it has become less important to either vendor or purchaser how the purchase price is allocated. In principle the vendor will want to see relatively high values attributed to freehold buildings and goodwill (which attract tax at the rate applicable to chargeable gains) and low values attributed to stocks and plant and machinery (which attract tax at income rates). Where, however, a company is paying tax at the 30% small companies rate and the choice is between a balancing charge or a capital gain, it makes no difference to the vendor's tax bill where the charge falls and he can afford to accommodate the purchaser's wishes.

35.2 PAYMENTS TO 'FAMILY' DIRECTORS

The purchasers of a family company will often not be unduly concerned about how the payments to the vendors are structured and will welcome means whereby part of the purchase consideration can be met by the company itself. Terminal payments within TA 1970 s 187 can often be very useful in this respect.

TA 1970 s 187 applies to any payment not otherwise chargeable to tax which is made to the holder or past holder of an office or employment, either under a legal obligation or as an *ex gratia* payment, directly or indirectly in connection with the termination of the holding of the office or employment or any change in its functions or emoluments. Under s 188, the first £25,000 of any payment within s 187 is tax-free, and under TA 1970 Sch 8 there is a sliding scale of relief for payments of between £25,000 and £75,000. The inclusion of payments of up to £25,000 in arrangements for the sale of a family company (with an appropriate reduction in the price asked for the shares) can be very tax-effective. The payments put tax-free cash in the hands of the outgoing director/proprietors. The purchasers of the company are unlikely to get any tax deduction for the payments (see below) but they would not in any event obtain a deduction for any amount paid for the shares until the shares are sold at some time in the future.

As stated above, it is necessary that the payment should not be otherwise chargeable to tax if it is to be within s 187. Accordingly, it must not be an emolument of the recipient's employment in that it is received for services already rendered or under the terms of a service agreement (see, for instance, *Henry v Foster* (1931) 16 TC 605, CA and *Dale v de Soissons* (1950) 32 TC 118, CA). For examples of payments falling outside the general rules of Schedule E, see *Hunter v Dewhurst* (1932) 16 TC 605, HL and *Duff v Barlow* (1941) 23 TC 633.

The scheme would be doubly attractive if the company could obtain a tax deduction for the payments it makes. In the context of the sale of shares in a family company, such a deduction is unlikely. To qualify for a deduction, the payment would have to satisfy two tests:

(a) the expenditure must be incurred wholly and exclusively for the purposes of the company's trade; this will normally be difficult to establish unless the company can show material benefits arising from the introduction of new management; and

(b) the transaction must not be part of a larger transaction affecting the capital structure of the company.

The leading cases on this point are *James Snook & Co Ltd v Blasdale* (1952) 33 TC 244, CA and *George J Smith & Co Ltd v Furlong* (1968) 45 TC 384. In the *James Snook* case the Commissioners found as facts that the business of the appellant company was on the market, that the compensation paid to the retiring directors was an integral part of the sale agreement, and that the payment was therefore not made wholly and exclusively for the purposes of the trade. Donovan J took the view that the decision that the payment was not made wholly and exclusively for the purposes of the trade was one of fact, and that there was evidence to support the commissioners' findings. On p 251 the learned judge set out the key principle governing compensation payments to directors/shareholders, which was quoted with approval by the Court of Appeal and in later cases:

'The mere circumstances that compensation to retiring directors is paid on a change of shareholding control does not of itself involve the consequence that such compensation can never be a deductible trading expense. So much is common ground. But it is essential in such cases that the company should prove to the Commissioners satisfaction that it considered the question of payment wholly untrammelled by the terms of the bargain its shareholders had struck with those who were to buy their shares and came to a decision to pay solely in the interest of the trade.'

The *George J Smith & Co Ltd* case involved compensation payments to directors at the same time as those directors sold 2,005 out of the 3,000 issued shares in the company. The commissioners again found as a fact that the payment of the compensation was an integral part of the share deal and that the compensation was not paid wholly and exclusively for the purposes of the trade. Cross J held that there was evidence to support this view. Before quoting with approval the passage from the judgment of Donovan J referred to above, Cross J said:

'There is, of course, no doubt that compensation paid to a retiring director for loss of office may in certain circumstances be an expense deductible for tax purposes. If, for instance, his colleagues on the board have formed the view that the continuance in office of a certain director is most prejudicial to the prosperity of the company, that in the interests of the company he must be induced to resign and that the sum to be paid to secure his resignation is no more than has to be paid, then clearly the expense would be deductible—and it would not cease to be deductible because contemporaneously, so as to get rid of him altogether, the retiring director sold his shareholding to his colleagues.'

However, the chances of proving that there is no connection between the payment of compensation and the sale of shares in a family company are very slim: it is likely to be impossible to prove that the company 'considered the question of payment wholly untrammelled by the terms of the bargain with its shareholders'.

35.3 STAMP DUTY SAVING

The 'pref trick'

Stamp duty is payable on a share transfer document when shares are transferred by way of sale or gift. The duty is at 1% on the value of the shares transferred. It used to be possible to reduce this stamp duty bill to negligible proportions by use of a device known as the 'pref trick'. When a company proposes to issue shares it may indicate to the applicant that shares have been allotted to him. This 'letter of allotment' may be expressed to be renounceable by the allottee and, so long as the rights under the letter are renounceable not later than six months after the date of its issue, such a letter, even though renounced is not charegable to stamp duty. It was on this fact that the 'pref trick' depended.

There were two main steps involved in the scheme:
(a) the issue of new shares on renounceable letters of allotment; and
(b) the diversion of the value of the company out of the existing shares and into the new shares.

In the normal course of events, the following transactions were required:

(1) New ordinary shares carrying normal rights to vote, to dividends and to capital participation were issued on renounceable letters of allotment. If sufficient reserves were available these could be capitalised in a bonus issue; otherwise a rights issue was required and a small amount of capital duty was payable.
(2) The entire original equity of the company was converted into shares with negligible rights and of little value, such as 3% non-cumulative non-voting preference shares (hence the name 'pref trick').
(3) The purchaser acquired the whole of the share capital. A negligible amount of the consideration was allocated to the now valueless original shares and stamp duty was paid on this amount. The balance of the consideration was allocated to the new ordinary shares which, being on renounceable letters of allotment, did not attract stamp duty.
(4) After a suitable interval the purchaser could tidy up the capital structure if he wished.

On 27 July 1984 the Financial Secretary to the Treasury announced in reply to a parliamentary question that the Board of Inland Revenue have been advised that the decisions in the *Ramsay* and *Furniss v Dawson* cases (see **1.3** above) apply to the 'pref trick', with the result that the planned stamp duty saving is not achieved. The text of the Financial Secretary's statement is as follows:

'The Board of Inland Revenue are advised that the House of Lords' decisions in *Ramsay* and *Furniss v Dawson* are likely to apply in a stamp duty context to the arrangements, commonly known as the 'pref trick', for the transfer of shares on the occasion of a take-over by one company of another. Where those decisions do apply the effect would be as follows. If on a take-over the offer for shares of the company being taken over is conditional on a reorganisation of its capital so that the shares to be acquired are reduced in value by the creation of new shares for the purpose of achieving a stamp duty saving the chargeable consideration for the transfer of the old shares will include the value of the shares issued in exchange for the newly created shares.

These arrangements have been standard commercial practice for

35.3 Stamp duty saving

many years and the Board will not seek to challenge the use of the 'pref trick' on the basis of the decisions in *Ramsay* and *Furniss v Dawson* where on or before today as a result of having purchased shares or having obtained the necessary number of commitments the acquiring company has obtained effective control of more than 50% of the votes in the company being taken over.

It is proposed to provide an exemption from stamp duties in next year's Finance Bill for transfers of shares in a company being taken over in exchange for shares or other marketable securities in the acquiring company resulting in a general offer made by the acquiring company to the members of the company being taken over, or any class of them, in consequence of which the one company has obtained control of the other. [*Authors' note—this is unlikely to be of much use to most family companies.*] It is intended that this legislation shall apply to instruments giving effect to transfers of shares which are executed on or after 28 July 1984. The proposed exemption will not apply where the shareholders of the company being taken over get cash for their shares. The Board of Inland Revenue have been authorised to treat as exempt any qualifying transfer until this change can be given legislative effect'.

The authors take the view that the new approach of the Inland Revenue to tax avoidance is not applicable to stamp duty. Stamp duty is a tax on documents, not on transactions. Even if the Inland Revenue are now entitled to disregard elements of a stamp duty saving scheme, they must still be able to produce a stampable document which they can show ought to be stampable by reference to the full consideration given for the assets acquired under the scheme as a whole and not only by reference to the actual transaction which the document covers. Nonetheless it must now be recognised that at the moment it is only worth doing the pref trick if the purchaser is prepared to pursue his case to the House of Lords. However, in view of the Revenue's attempts to apply *Furniss v Dawson* etc to other stamp duty saving schemes, it may not be long before the application of the 'new approach' to stamp duty is tested in the courts.

Other points to be borne in mind in the context of the 'pref trick' are:

(1) If the company were inadvertently to obtain some tax advantage other than the stamp duty saving out of the transactions involved, it might fall foul of the anti-avoidance provisions at TA 1970 ss 460 to 468 (see **35.4** below).

(2) TA 1970 s 234 and F(No 2)A 1975 s 34 tax as distributions any repayment of share capital following a bonus issue and certain stock options. These provisions should be kept in mind once the company has made the bonus as part of the scheme.

Reconstructions and amalgamations

Where consideration for the sale of a family company is shares in another company, or where a group of companies is reorganised (eg under the sort of arrangements described at **24.6** above) it will usually be possible to avoid stamp duty and capital duty by relying on the reliefs available under FA 1927 s 55 (stamp duty), FA 1973 Sch 19 para 10 (capital duty) and FA 1930 s 42 (intra-group transfers of assets). The operation of these reliefs is extremely complex and is outside the scope of this book. Readers should be aware that the provisions exist and consult the relevant legislation and reference books when the occasion arises.

35.4 TA 1970 ss 460 to 468

TA 1970 ss 460 to 468 is one of the major anti-avoidance provisions in the Taxes Acts, but many otherwise tax-aware businessmen are unaware of its existence. The provisions are complex and the legislation is difficult to read because much of it is brought in by reference to other sections. In outline, s 460 allows the Inland Revenue to make assessments under Case VI of Schedule D to counteract any tax advantage which a person obtains or is in a position to obtain as a result of a transaction in securities when the tax advantage arises in one of the five circumstances headed A to E in s 461. Circumstances A to C are concerned with dividend stripping and will not normally concern the proprietors of a family company. The provisions do not apply where the taxpayer can show that the transactions under consideration were entered into

(a) for bona fide commercial reasons; or
(b) in the ordinary course of making or managing investments; and

that none of them had as their main object or one of their main objects the obtaining of a tax advantage.

The term 'transaction in securities' is very wide and includes a liquidation (*IRC v Joiner* [1975] STC 657, HL) and the payment of a dividend (*Greenberg v IRC* (1971) 47 TC 240, HL).

Section 461D is the provision most likely to apply to a family company. Rewritten to bring in matters dealt with by reference to other sections, it brings within s 460 a situation where

'in connection with the distribution of profits of a company which is unquoted or under the control of five or fewer persons, the person who obtains the tax advantage receives consideration in money or money's worth so that he does not pay or bear tax on it as income and which is assets or represents the value of assets which are available for distribution by way of dividend or would have been so available apart from anything done by the company, or is received in respect of future receipts of the company or is trading stock of the company or represents the value of trading stock of the company.'

It is clear that the sale of a family company which has distributable reserves at the time of the sale is within this provision: the vendor shareholders have, in consequence of a transaction in securities (the sale) received consideration (the sale proceeds) in a form not taxed as income (any gain on the shares will be charged to CGT) which, to the extent that reserves were available to make a distribution, represents the value of assets available for distribution. In practice the Inland Revenue do not appear to take this point except in cases with an obvious tax avoidance motive such as *IRC v Cleary* (1967) 44 TC 399, HL. In that case two taxpayers owned the whole share capital of two companies, one of which had substantial reserves. They sold the shares in one company to the other company, as a result of which they continued to control the assets of both companies but had received cash in a way not attracting liability to income tax. The House of Lords upheld the Inland Revenue counter-action under s 460. By way of contrast, in a similar situation in *Clark v IRC* [1978] STC 614 the Revenue's action failed because the taxpayers could show bona fide commercial reasons and a main motive which was not tax-avoidance. Section 461D could also apply where shares are sold for a price which includes an element of deferred consideration which depends on the company's future results.

Section 461E applies where in connection with any transaction in securities in which two or more s 461D companies are concerned, a person receives consideration in a form not chargeable to income tax which is or represents the value of assets available for distribution by a s 461D company and which consists of shares or other securities issued by such a company. In *Williams v IRC* [1980] STC 535 the House of Lords held that where a transaction falls within s 461E it cannot also be taxed under s 461D. This is important because the charge under s 461E arises only when the shares or securities in question are disposed of. In a family company context, s 461E could apply where a company with distributable reserves is sold for shares in another unquoted or closely controlled company, and the shares then acquired are subsequently sold.

It would be unwise for the vendors of a family company to rely on the 'bona fide commercial reasons' exclusion where the transactions involve anything other than a straightforward outright sale of the company's shares. Section 464 provides a clearance procedure and persons considering anything other than an outright sale should make use of it. If clearance is refused the Inland Revenue are not obliged to give reasons for the refusal, although they will normally do so (SP 3/1980).

PART IV

Other planning points

36 Farming
37 Pitfalls to avoid

36 Farming

36.1 AVERAGING OF PROFITS

FA 1978 s 28 provides a measure of relief where farming profits of an unincorporated business fluctuate significantly from year to year. The relief is available where the profits of two consecutive years show a difference of at least 30% of the higher figure; the detailed rules for computation of the relief are at s 28(2) and (3). Stock relief and capital allowances are not directly affected by a claim under s 28, although their availability will be relevant in deciding whether to make the claim. Averaged profits are effective for all tax purposes except the application of TA 1970 s 118 on a discontinuance (s 28(5)). The relief may be claimed by a partnership and is applied to the profits of the firm as a whole, not to be individual profit shares (s 28(6)).

Averaging must be claimed within two years of the end of the second year of assessment entering into the calculations (s 28(8)). The time limit for any claims affected by the averaging is extended to the end of the year of assessment following the year in which the adjustment is made. This extension does not, however, apply to an election for separate taxation of wife's earnings which is an election and not a claim.

A claim under s 28 is useful in minimising the impact of high rates of tax on the profit of exceptionally good years by transferring some of those profits to less profitable years. Whether a claim will be beneficial will depend on the actual figures involved and on the capital allowances and stock relief available. It is likely that averaging claims will become more common following the abolition of stock relief and the reduction in first year allowances introduced in FA 1984. Voluminous calculations will often be necessary to determine which years should be averaged.

36.2 HERD BASIS ELECTION

As a general rule animals other than working animals kept by a farmer for farming purposes are treated as trading stock. Increases and decreases in the value of animals on the farm will thus be reflected in taxable profits of the farming trade, although the effects of inflation have hitherto been mitigated by stock relief.

TA 1970 s 139 and Sch 6 provides for an irrevocable election for the application of the 'herd basis' as an alternative to the treatment of production animals as stock in trade. The effect of such an election is that

(a) the initial cost of the herd and the cost of additions is not a charge on profits;
(b) the net cost of replacing animals in the herd is charged to profits;
(c) home reared animals transferred to the herd are transferred at their cost of rearing (conventionally 75% of market value);
(d) on the sale of the whole or substantial part of the herd (20% or more), any profit or loss is not taxable;
(e) less substantial sales result in taxable profits or losses.

The election must be made within two years of the end of the tax year in which the herd is first kept. The time limit is extended to two years after the end of the first period of account of the person making the election commencing on or after 13 March 1984. This extension is contained in FA 1984 s 48 (which abolished stock relief) provisions abolishing stock relief, and opens up the possibility that farmers who have in the past opted not to claim herd basis may review their decision. Where an election is made and is valid only because of the extensions of the time limit, it will have effect only from the first year of assessment or accounting period for which the profits or losses are computed by reference to the first period of account beginning on or after 13 March 1984.

In the present state of uncertainty which surrounds farming in general and livestock farming in particular, the decision whether to elect for herd basis is a difficult one. Prima facie the abolition of stock relief suggests that herd basis elections ought to be more popular as the effect of an election is to take inflationary gains out of charge to tax, a function previously performed by stock relief. However, whilst it seems likely that input costs will continue to rise, there is a very real possibility that the market value of production animals will fall as measures to reduce meat and milk surpluses begin to bite. A farmer forced to sell in such conditions would, if he had elected for the herd basis, be unable to obtain any relief for the loss suffered. It remains true that in principle the greater the difference between the cost of the animals in a herd and their ultimate market value, the greater is the potential advantage of the herd basis through the realisation of a tax-free profit, and the less is the risk of having to sell below cost and realise a loss which cannot be tax relieved. The difference is likely to be greatest with home bred pedigree animals. Where, on the other hand, animals are bought in at full market prices the difference between cost and market value is likely to be small and the farmer who elects for the herd basis will have little margin in the way of falling market prices before he finds himself with a potential loss for which no tax relief is available.

36.3 LOSSES

TA 1970 s 180(1) denies relief under s 168 for losses of a trade of farming or market gardening if in each of the prior five years a loss was incurred in carrying on that trade; relief for related capital allowances is also excluded. A number of points of practice arise in connection with this provision:

(1) The Inland Revenue take the view where a trade commences part way through a tax year, this part year will be counted as a full year for the purpose of determining the first year to which s 180(1) applies.
(2) For a new farming trade s 180(8) has the effect of extending by one year the cover against s 180(1) being applied; losses in the first six years and not the first five years will be available for relief under s 168, subject to the usual 'commercial basis' restrictions in TA 1970 s 170.
(3) Section 180(1) will not prevent a claim for relief under s 168(2) for a loss incurred in a previous year, unless that previous year's loss was in itself debarred by s 180(1). Section 168 grants relief for losses against years of assessment whereas s 180(1) is concerned with the number of years in which a loss arises.
(4) The existence of s 180(3) is often overlooked. This section is not a test of the competence of the farmer, and what the Revenue is concerned with is the intrinsic nature of the farming activity itself. Section 180(3) is meant to take account of those types of farming such as breeding racehorses or pedigree cattle which by their very nature require many year's investment before a profit is realised. Each year therefore after the fifth year, or sixth year for a new trade, of losses it is necessary to consider whether the particular type of farming is such that it would take a further year to turn round into a profit making situation.

36 Farming

FA 1978 s 30 provides relief for losses arising in the early years of an unincorporated trade. The Inland Revenue take the view that where a person with an existing trade of farming begins another farming activity, TA 1970 s 110(2) (which provides that all farming carried on by any particular person or partnership or body of persons shall be treated as one trade) precludes relief under FA 1978 s 30 for any losses arising out of the new activity.

37 Pitfalls to avoid

37.1 CAPITAL SUMS PAID TO SETTLOR TA 1970 s 451

Section 451 is a very formidable tax avoidance section which must be considered very carefully in connection with settlements.

The section is designed to catch capital sums paid directly or indirectly to a settlor or his wife by the trustees of a settlement, to the extent of the net income accumulated under the settlement in the year of payment or in any earlier year. Where it applies the effect can be very serious because the capital sum is taxed as income of the settlor in the year of payment. If the capital sum is greater than the net accumulated income, the balance can be carried forward for the following ten years and any income accumulated during those years is treated as the settlor's income until the capital sum is wiped out (s 451(1)).

The purpose of the section is clearly to prevent the settlor from putting funds into an accumulation settlement and avoiding higher rates of tax, while the trustees return to him an equivalent amount in a non-taxable capital form. A capital sum is widely defined to include:

(a) a loan or a repayment of a loan, and
(b) any other capital sum which is not paid for full consideration in money or money's worth (s 451(8)).

It should be noted that a loan or repayment of a loan is a capital sum whether or not there is full consideration for it, and the period for which it has been outstanding is irrelevant (see *IRC v De Vigier* (1964) 42 TC 24, HL).

In the case of a loan to the settlor, if the whole loan is repaid no part of it can be treated as his income for any year of assessment after that in which repayment occurs (s 451(3A)).

Where the capital sum paid to the settlor is a complete repayment of a loan then, if an amount not less than that sum is thereafter lent

271

by the settlor to the trustees, no part of the original repayment will continue to be treated as his income for any year of assessment after that in which the further loan is made (s 451(3B)). The effect of this is that repeated loans of the same amount will not be cumulatively taxed when repaid.

Capital sums paid to a third party, eg a creditor or bank, used to escape as a result of the decision in *Potts' Executors v IRC* (1950) 32 TC 211, HL, but this loophole has been closed and all sums paid to third parties are caught (s 451(9)).

Section 451 can be particularly dangerous where the shares in a family company are settled because in certain circumstances a capital sum paid to a settlor by a company connected with the settlement can be treated as having been paid by the trustees (s 451A(1)). A company is connected with the settlement if it is a close company (or would be a close company if it were resident in the UK) of which the trustees or a beneficiary are participators. This connection commonly arises where shares in a family company are settled and it is therefore very important that the section is carefully considered before any loans are made to the settlor or his wife by the company or the company repays any loans previously made to it by the settlor.

The section will apply only where a capital sum is paid by the company to the settlor and an associated payment is made directly or indirectly from the settlement to the company (s 451A(2)). The effect of this is to restrict the application of the section to payments made out of funds provided by the trustees. An associated payment is:

(a) any capital sum (as defined above) paid to the company by the trustees, and
(b) any other sum paid, or asset transferred, to the company by the trustees which is not paid or transferred for full consideration in money or money's worth in the five years beginning or ending on the date the capital payment is made to the settlor (s 451A(3)).

In the case of loans, the section does not apply if the whole of the loan is repaid within twelve months and the period during which loans to the settlor or by him are outstanding in any period of five years does not exceed twelve months (s 451A(6)). This applies to all companies connected with the settlement, so the section cannot be avoided by borrowing and repaying loans from a series of connected companies.

Finally, it should be noted that a capital sum paid by a company to a settlor (eg to repay a loan) before the settlement is made may be caught if the settlement is made and the company becomes connected with it subsequently but in the same year of assessment. So s 451 is a pitfall which must be watched right at the beginning when the settlement is being considered.

37.2 TRANSACTIONS IN SECURITIES TA 1970 ss 460–468

Reference should be made to **35.4** above where these provisions are discussed.

37.3 TRANSFER OF ASSETS ABROAD TA 1970 s 478 AND FA 1981 s 45

Section 478 needs to be carefully considered where it is proposed to set up an overseas company or trust. The section is designed to prevent the avoidance of tax by individuals ordinarily resident in the UK making a transfer of assets as a result of which income becomes payable to non-residents. The section deems the income to be the income of the UK resident if he or his spouse has 'power to enjoy' it. 'Power to enjoy' is widely defined in s 478(5).

Following *Congreve v IRC* (1948) 30 TC 163, HL it was thought that anybody who could, or did, benefit from the transfer of assets abroad could be assessed under s 478. However, in 1979 the House of Lords decided in *Vestey v IRC* [1980] STC 10 that *Congreve* was wrongly decided and held that only the transferor or his spouse could be assessed.

The loopholes created by the *Vestey* decision were closed by FA 1981 s 45 which applies to persons not liable to tax under s 478. Like s 478, there must have been a transfer of assets as a result of which income becomes payable to a resident abroad. It applies only where an individual ordinarily resident in the UK receives a benefit out of the assets transferred. Where the benefit is a capital sum there are rules for identifying it with past and future income of the non-resident.

Neither s 478 nor s 45 will apply if it can be shown that the transfer was a bona fide transaction not designed for the purpose of avoiding tax.

37.4 COMPANY MIGRATION TA 1970 s 482

Under TA 1970 s 482, it is illegal, without consent of the Treasury:

(a) for a UK resident company to cease to be resident;

(b) for the trade or business (or any part of it) of a UK resident company to be transferred to a non-UK resident;
(c) for a UK resident company to allow a non-UK resident subsidiary to create or issue any shares or debentures;
(d) for a UK resident company to transfer (or allow to be transferred) any shares or debentures in a non-UK resident subsidiary to any person (including another UK resident).

Thus, if a business is being started abroad, it is necessary to ensure that no part of the business already being carried on here by a UK company is transferred abroad without consent.

The holding of investments is specifically stated to be a business for the purposes of the section.

Anyone who is party to any act which to his knowledge results in an offence under the section is liable to heavy penalties, including imprisonment. The directors of the company are presumed guilty of complicity unless they are proved innocent.

37.5 CHANGE IN OWNERSHIP OF A COMPANY: LOSSES TA 1970 s 483

TA 1970 s 483(1) imposes two restrictions on the right to carry forward trading losses under TA 1970 s 177. No relief can be given in the following circumstances:

(a) if within a period of three years there is both a change in ownership of the company and a major change in the nature or conduct of the trade, or
(b) if, after the scale of the activities of the trade carried on by a company becomes small or negligible, and before any considerable revival of the trade, there is a change in the ownership.

A 'major change in the nature or conduct of the trade' includes

(a) a major change in the type of property dealt in, or
(b) a major change in customers, outlets, or markets, and the section applies even if the change is a gradual process which began outside the period of three years (s 483(3)).

Section 484 contains rules for ascertaining a change in ownership.

The section has been largely successful in stopping the sale of tax loss companies. It is difficult to see what steps could be taken to turn a loss making company into a profitable one without making the sort of changes caught by the section. Where, nevertheless, a tax loss company is bought it should be on a contingency basis, ie that the losses will be paid for only when the Revenue have agreed that they can be carried forward or, better still, only when the losses have actually been utilised.

37.6 SALE OF INCOME FROM PERSONAL ACTIVITIES TA 1970 s 487

TA 1970 s 487 is concerned with transactions or arrangements which are made to exploit the earning capacity of an individual in any occupation by putting some other person in a position to enjoy his earnings. If the main object, or one of the main objects, of the transactions or arrangements is the avoidance of tax, any capital sum received by the individual as a result of the arrangements is taxable as income under Schedule D Case VI.

The section was originally aimed at entertainers and is usually restricted to them, but it can be applied to any occupation.

37.7 ARTIFICIAL TRANSACTIONS IN LAND TA 1970 s 488

Anyone involved in property transactions should be aware of the dangers of TA 1970 s 488. A tax charge can arise under the section where a capital gain is made from the disposal of land and one of the following conditions is met;

(a) the land (or any property deriving its value from land) was acquired with the sole or main object of realising a gain from disposing of it; or
(b) the land was held as trading stock; or
(c) the land was developed with the sole or main object of realising a gain from it.

The tax charge can be made on

(i) the person acquiring, holding or developing the land, or
(ii) any person who is a party to, or concerned in, any arrangement or scheme which enables a gain to be realised by any indirect method or by any series of transactions.

Such a person may be assessed even though he has obtained the gain for some other person and not for himself (s 488(2)).

Furthermore, under s 488(8) a person may be charged even though he has not himself realised the gain but has provided value or an opportunity of realising the gain, whether or not the value or opportunity has been put at the disposal of the person to whom the gain arises (see *Yuill v Wilson* [1980] STC 460, HL).

Property deriving its value from land may include shares in a company, a partnership share or an interest in a trust (s 488(12)). However, a gain arising from the disposal of shares in a company which holds land as trading stock is exempt unless there has been a scheme or arrangement within (ii) above (s 488(10)).

Where land is developed, any gain arising before the intention to develop was formed cannot be charged under the section unless it is within (a) or (b) above (s 488(7)). Where a gain is chargeable under s 488 it is assessed under Schedule D Case VI (s 488(3)).

There is an advance clearance procedure under s 488(11) which is dealt with by the local inspector of taxes, but it is understood that refusals (for which the Revenue are not obliged to give any reason) are more common than clearances.

It should be noted that the section is aimed at capital gains not income profits. If the purchase and sale of land is a trading transaction or an adventure in the nature of trade (as it is likely to be if the land was acquired with the sole or main object of realising a gain from disposing of it) any gain will be taxable as income and will not be a capital gain within s 488.

Furthermore, capital gains can be caught only if one or more of the conditions referred to above are satisfied. It is not the case that all large gains from property which cannot be taxed as income are automatically within s 488. Moreover, the section is aimed at the avoidance of tax, which is defined in TA 1970 s 526 as income tax and corporation tax, so if no tax is being avoided (eg because the gain is already taxable as a trading profit) or the tax being avoided is, say, DLT, the section cannot apply.

Since the section was introduced in 1969 there have been three cases on it. It is outside the scope of this book to discuss these but readers who may be involved with the section may like to refer to them. They are *Yuill v Wilson* [1980] STC 460, HL; *Winterton v Edwards* [1980] STC 206 and *Chilcott v IRC* [1982] STC 1.

37.8 VALUE SHIFTING CGTA 1979 ss 25 AND 26

CGTA 1979 s 25

CGTA 1979 s 25(2) applies where a shareholder exercises control in such a way that value passes out of shares owned by him or a connected person and into other shares in the company. In that event, the person whose shares have lost value is treated as having

37.8 Value shifting CGTA 1979 ss 25 and 26 CGTA 1979 s 25

disposed of his shares and the consideration for the disposal is the price which would have been paid in a bargain at arm's length. It was held in *Floor v Davis* [1979] STC 379, HL, that the section applies where persons are able jointly to exercise control, and also where a person able to exercise control allows value to pass out of his shares by failing to act. Where there is such a deemed disposal there cannot be an allowable loss (s 25(3)).

CGTA 1979 s 25(4) applies where there is a transaction which results in the owner of land becoming the lessee (eg on a sale and leaseback) and there then follows an adjustment of rights under the lease in favour of the lessor. The adjustment is treated as a disposal by the lessee for an arm's length consideration.

CGTA 1979 s 25(5) is concerned with the cancellation of a right or restriction over an asset by the person entitled to enforce it. The cancellation is deemed to be a disposal of the right or restriction for the consideration which a person at arm's length would have paid for its release.

CGTA 1979 s 26

CGTA 1979 s 26 was introduced in 1977 to combat schemes such as those considered in *W T Ramsay Ltd v IRC* [1981] STC 174, HL and *Eilbeck v Rawling* [1981] STC 174, HL. The section applies to any disposal of an asset if a scheme has been effected or arrangements made (whether before or after the disposal) whereby—
(a) the value of the asset has been materially reduced, and
(b) a tax-free benefit has been or will be conferred either on the person making the disposal or someone connected with him, or, sometimes, any other person (s 26(1)).

A tax-free benefit is widely defined in s 26(2) to include money or money's worth, any increase in the value of an asset or relief from liability.

Where these conditions are present, the Revenue are entitled to increase the consideration for the disposal by such amount as appears to them to be just and reasonable having regard to the scheme or arrangement and the tax-free benefit (s 26(4)).

Where the consideration is increased under s 26(4) and the tax-free benefit under s 26(1)(b) above was an increase in the value of another asset then, for the purposes of calculating the gain or loss on a subsequent disposal of that other asset, the consideration may be reduced by such an amount as appears to the Revenue to be just and reasonable (s 26(5)).

Certain disposals which give rise to neither gain nor loss are excluded, ie

(a) disposals between husband and wife;
(b) disposals by personal representatives to legatees;
(c) intra-group disposals (s 26(6)).

There is also an exception where the disposal is by a company of shares in another company in the same 75% group, and the reduction in value is effected by the payment of a dividend or the transfer of an asset (s 26(7)). The effect of this is to allow dividend or asset stripping in order to reduce the value of a company's shares prior to sale or liquidation, though the creation of allowable losses in this way is prevented by TA 1970 s 280.

As is often the case, although this section was intended to combat specific value shifting devices, it is drafted in such wide terms that it can catch transactions not originally contemplated. An example is the use of reserved leases discussed in 34.2 above, although the Revenue have indicated that they would not seek to invoke s 26 where the reversion is sold at market value and the lease is at a rack rent.

The sale of shares by a controlling director/shareholder on retirement after receiving a golden handshake (tax-free up to £25,000) and/or additional pension benefits might also come within the section. The *ex gratia* payment and/or contribution to the pension fund would reduce the value of the shares by extracting cash from the company.

37.9 TRANSACTIONS BETWEEN CONNECTED PERSONS CGTA 1979 s 62

A disposal of an asset by a person to another person connected with him is treated as being made otherwise than by way of a bargain at arm's length (s 62(2)). It follows that, in accordance with CGTA 1979 s 29A(1), the consideration for the disposal is deemed to be equal to the market value of the asset.

If a loss arises on such a disposal it may be deducted only from a chargeable gain arising on another disposal to the same person, provided they are still connected persons (s 62(3)). However, this restriction does not apply to losses arising on gifts in settlement for certain educational, cultural or recreational purposes (s 62(3) proviso).

Where the asset is an option granted by the person making the disposal, the person acquiring the asset cannot realise an allowable

37.9 Transactions between connected persons CGTA 1979 s 62

loss unless he disposes of the option at arm's length to a person not connected with him (s 62(4)).

Where the asset is subject to some right or restriction in favour of the transferor or a person connected with him, the market value of the asset is taken to be:

(1) the market value of the asset without the right or restriction, minus
(2) the smaller of:
    (a) the market value of the right or restriction, or
    (b) the amount by which its extinction would enhance the value of the asset to its owner (s 62(5)).

This provision is to ensure that the amount by which the market value is depressed is the commercial value of the right or restriction.

For the purposes of s 62(5) certain rights or restrictions are to be ignored altogether, namely;

(1) if the enforcement of the right or restriction would or might effectively destroy or substantially impair the value of the asset with no advantage to the transferor or the transferee;
(2) if the right is an option to acquire the asset;
(3) in the case of intangible property (eg a lease), if the right would enable the transferor to extinguish the asset in the hands of the transferee (s 62(5) proviso).

This proviso will prevent the value of an asset being depressed by artifical restrictions which it is never intended to enforce.

Section s 62(5) does not apply to:

(a) a right of forfeiture or other right exercisable on breach of a covenant under a lease of land or other property, or
(b) a mortgage or other charge (s 62(6)).

Index

Accomodation, living. *See* LIVING ACCOMMODATION
Accounting date
corporation tax, change of, 152–154
income tax. *See* INCOME TAX
Accounts
commencement of trading. *See* COMMENCEMENT OF TRADING
cost-effective solutions, 23–24
input of data from client's records, 23–24
interiom, 23
management, 23–24
monthly figures, 23–24
need to forecast results, 23–24
Accumulation and maintenance trusts. *See* TRUSTS
Advance corporation tax. *See* CORPORATION TAX
Agent
partner as, 12
Agreement
partnership, 12
Agricultural relief
50% relief on tenanted value, 254
accruer arrangements, 255
agricultural value of land, 254
contracts for sale, 255
how land should be held, 254–255
loans secured on land, 255
planning opportunities, 253–255
timing of gifts, 255
Agriculture, *See* FARMING
Aircraft
roll-over relief, 167

Annuities
partnership, 243–244
purchase by small self-administered pension scheme, 216
retirement. *See* RETIREMENT
Anti-avoidance. *See* TAX AVOIDANCE
Apportionment. *See also* DISTRIBUTIONS
cessation, on, 122–123
choice between distribution or, 123
clearance, 123
liquidation, on, 122–123
reducing distributable income, 120–121
relevant income, meaning, 120
requirements of business, 121–122
roll-over relief, 168
Articles of association
purchase by company of own shares, 139
Assets
appreciating, retention outside company, 18–19
business, gifts of, 198–199
double charge on disposal, 14–15, 18
financing acquisition of. *See* CAPITAL EXPENDITURE
floating charge over, 14
gifts of, 198–199
hold-over relief for gifts of, 93–94
intra-group transfers, 164–165
partnership, 172–173

281

Assets—*contd*
purchase by small self-administered pension scheme, 214–215
retirement relief. *See* RETIREMENT
roll-over relief. *See* ROLL-OVER RELIEF
transfer of
  abroad, 273
  distributions, as, 115–116
Associates
meaning, 136–137
vendor's associate owning shares in company, 136–137
Bad debt
credit note issued to obtain relief on, 52
Bank
interest paid to, 144
Benefits in kind
advantage of incorporation, as, 19
car. *See* CAR
distributions, 115
family company, 109
general principles, 108–109
living accommodation. *See* LIVING ACCOMMODATION
receipt does not confer tax benefit on recipient, 109
rule for assessment, 109
Schedule E, 109
valuation for tax purposes, 109
Buildings
industrial. *See* INDUSTRIAL BUILDINGS
occupied only for purposes of trade, roll-over relief, 167, 170
Business
assets. *See* ASSETS
disposal of, retirement relief, 188
expansion scheme. *See* BUSINESS EXPANSION SCHEME
gift of, 196
Business expansion scheme
caveats to be borne in mind by potential investors, 236–237
claim
  certificate to accompany, 237
  time for making, 237

Business expansion scheme—*contd*
conditions on relief, 131–133
eligible shares, 235
equity investment in companies, 14
external equity finance, 132
individual investments, 132
key changes in new rules, 234–235
lower limit of investments by fund, 132
methods of making investments, 236
person connected with company, 131
qualifying rules, 235
qualifying trade, meaning, 132
short comings of original legislation corrected in, 234
Business property relief
family company, 248
shareholding in unquoted trading company, 139
Business relief
agriculture, 240
transfer of business, 239–240
unincorporated business, 244
Business structure
company. *See* COMPANY
factors in choice
  long-term planning, 10
  non-tax objectives, 10
  tax liabilities, 10
  whether or not business should be incorporated, 10
unincorporated business. *See* UNINCORPORATED BUSINESS
Capital allowances
changes to system, 25
claiming best relief, 34–36
disclaimer
  companies, 37–38
  partnerships, 36–37
  sole traders, 36–37
first year allowance, 25–28
importance of detailed records, 36
industrial buildings. *See* INDUSTRIAL BUILDINGS
inherited by new company after reconstruction, 161

Capital allowances—*contd*
initial allowance, 25–26
loss relief augmented or created by, 84
order of claim, 34
prevention of double allowances for same expenditure, 34
wirting-down allowance, 25
Capital expenditure
capital allowances. *See* CAPITAL ALLOWANCES
commencement of trading, 61
financing
  hire purchase, 30
  leasing, 31–34
  methods of, 28
  purchase for cash, 28–30
  purchase on deferred terms, 30–31
pre-trading expenditure, 42
reducing taxable profits, 98–100
timing of, 25–28
Capital gains tax
connected persons, transactions between, 174–175, 278–279
deemed consideration, 171
deemed disposals, 171
disposal, time of, 6
employees' trusts, 226
gifts. *See* GIFTS
handing on business, 238 *et seq.*
loss relief for loan, 126
partnership
  assets
    disposal to outside party, 172
    division of acquisition costs and disposal consideration, 172–173
    expenditure on acquisition, 172
    part disposal, 172
    Inland Revenue Statement of Practice, 172, 173
  transactions between partners
    adjustments through accounts, 175, 177
    assets divided in kind among partners, 176

Capital gains tax—*contd*
transactions between partners–*contd*
    changes in partners, 173–174, 176–177
    connected persons, transfers between, 174–175
    downward revaluation of chargeable assets, 175
    errors of principle, 173
    gain deferred by using general relief for gifts, 177
    market value of partner's share, 173
    partnership sharing ratios, changes in, 173–174, 176–177
    payments outside accounts, 175–176
    upward revaluation of chargeable assets, 175
retirement relief. *See* RETIREMENT
roll-over relief. *See* ROLL-OVER RELIEF
service company shares, 76
tax avoidance scheme, 6
transfer of business to company
  capital gains on assets rolled over against base cost, 94–95
  chargeable gains rolled over against cost of shares, 91–92
  hold-over relief for gifts of business assets, 93–94
  legislative provision to facilitate, 91
  transfer of land with development value, 92
  value of stocks of trade at discontinuance, 93
  whole of assets must be transferred to obtain relief, 92
value shifting, 276–278
Capital transfer tax
accumulation and maintenance trusts, 224–225
discretionary trust. *See* TRUSTS
dividend waiver, 119
employees' trusts, 226
fixed interest trust, 219
gifts, impact on, 195 *et seq.*

Capital transfer tax—*contd*
handing on business, 238 *et seq.*
purchase by company of own shares to discharge liability, 138
Car
business mileage, 110
cylinder capacity, 110
fuel benefit, 111
leasing, 33–34
original market value, 110
provision as tax-efficient measure, 110–111
scale benefit, 111
secondhand, 110
unavailable throughout year of assessment, 110–111
outright purchase of assets for, 28–30
Cessation of trading
apportionment, 122–123
change in persons carrying on trade, 62
factors relevant to determine, 61–62
incorporation, on, 90
loss relief, 85
timing of, 62–63
Chargeable gains. *See* CORPORATION TAX
Charges
acceleration of payment, 144
deferral of payment, 144
income tax, effect of date of payment on, 145
interest. *See* INTEREST
meaning, 142
timing of payment, 144–145
Charities
deeds of covenant in favour of, 231
Child. *See also* PROPRIETOR'S FAMILY
deed of covenant, 229
legal restrictions on employment of, 105
payment of wages as means of spreading income, 82
remuneration. *See* PROPRIETOR'S FAMILY
school fees, payment out of capital, 227

Cleaning
living accommodation, 112
Commencement of trading
basis periods
choice of, 59
overlapping, 61
capital expenditure, 61
choice of accounting date, 58–61
election under s 117, 59, 61
entry in company's minute book, 58
factors on which dependent, 58
first year accounts
family members brought into business, 60
interest, 60
leasing, 60
profits expected to show rising trend, 60
relevant expenses included in, 59
rent on premises used by partnership, 60
repairs to assets acquired in dilapidated state, 59–60
loss relief, 85
measures to achieve low first year profits, 59–60
pre-trading expenditure relieved against profits earned after, 59
Commission
selling on, 56
Company
accummulation of value, 14
amalgamations, stamp duty saving, 261
associated, small companies rate relief, 100–101
benefits in kind. *See* BENEFITS IN KIND
change in ownership, carry forward of losses, 274–275
chargeable gains. *See* CORPORATION TAX
choice between unincorporated business and, 10–11
close
basic strategy, 96
distributions. *See* DISTRIBUTIONS

Index

Company—*contd*
close—*contd*
  loan to acquire interest in, 129–130
  loans to participators, 123–124
  corporation tax. *See* CORPORATION TAX
  disclaimer of capital allowances, 37–38
  disincorporation, expense in tax of, 16
  double charge on disposal of assets, 14–15, 18
family. *See* FAMILY COMPANY
groups of. *See* GROUPS OF COMPANIES
incorporation
  cessation of trade, 90
  deferral, 90
  election for separate taxation of wife's earnings, 90
  envisaged from start, 90
  retirement relief, effect on, 189
  stamp duty, 95
  timing of, 90–91
  transfer of business to company
    capital gains tax provisions, 91–94
    company as legal person separate from owners, 91
  legal distinction between employer and employee, 14
  legal person separate from shareholders, as, 14
  level of wages challenged by Inland Revenue, 15
limited liability
  availability of sources of finance, 14
  compliance to statutory provisions, 13
  effectiveness, 13
  family company, 13
  shareholders in limited company, 13
liquidation. *See* LIQUIDATION
losses cannot be relieved against personal income, 15
meaning, 14

Company—*contd*
migration, 273–274
minority shareholders, 14
National Insurance contribution and benefit, 12, 15
non-tax factors, 13–14
parallel structure, 19–20
partner, as, 244
pension schemes. *See* PENSIONS
point at which incorporation becomes tax efficient, 17–18
pre-trading expenditure, 41, 43
profits, rates of tax, 14
purchase of own shares. *See* SHARES
receivership. *See* RECEIVERSHIP
reconstructions, stamp duty saving, 261
retention of appreciating assets outside, 18–19
Schedule E/PAYE liability, 15
small companies rate relief. *See* SMALL COMPANIES RATE RELIEF
tax advantages, 14
tax advantages and disadvantages compared with partnership, 12–13, 16–20
tax disadvantages, 14–15
trading losses. *See* CORPORATION TAX
transfer of business by sole trader before handing on, 239
transfer of shares in small parcels, 14
value added tax. *See* VALUE ADDED TAX

Compensation payments
family directors, to, 257–259

Connected persons
gifts to, 197
transactions between, 174–175, 278–279

Contract
retirement annuities. *See* RETIREMENT
sale of land, 255

Contributions
company pension schemes. *See* PENSIONS

Contributions—*contd*
National Insurance. *See* NATIONAL INSURANCE
Conventional basis. *See* PROFITS
Corporation tax
  accounting date, change of, 152–154
  advance
    claim for carry-bank of, 150
    distributions, 117
    liquidation, effect of, 156
    loans to participators, 123, 124
    surrender of, 159–160
    timing of dividend payments, 119
  basic strategy for proprietary company, 96
  benefits in kind. *See* BENEFITS IN KIND
  capital losses, use of, 147
  chargeable gains
    capital losses, use of, 147
    computation, 146
    general principles, 146
    groups of companies, 164–166
    intra-group transfers of assets, 164–165
    reduction in amount of, 146
    roll-over relief, 165–166
    timing of realisation, 146
    trading losses, relief for, 147
  deferred payment of, 163
  higher limits, 97–98
  interest. *See* INTEREST
  limits, 97–98
  liquidation, 156
  lower limits, 97–98
  marginal relief, 97
  payment of, 162–163
  purchase by company of own shares. *See* SHARES
  rates, 98
  receivership, 155–156
  reconstructions. *See* RECONSTRUCTIONS
  remuneration of proprietors. *See* PROPRIETOR
  roll-over relief, 165–166
  small companies rate relief. *See* SMALL COMPANIES RATE RELIEF

Corporation tax—*contd*
  timing of dividend payments, 119
  trading losses
    accounting date, change of, 152–154
    carry forward to future periods, 148
    carry forward to trade charges, 148
    chargeable gains, set against, 147
    claim displaces non-trade charges, 149
    company suffering temporary set-back in trade, 149
    double taxation relief, 151
    effect on other reliefs, 150–151
    franked investment income, relief against, 148, 151–152
    group relief, 148, 149, 157–159
    offset against capital gains, 14
    repayment supplement, 149–150
    statutory provisions, 148–149
    strategy, 149–152
    terminal losses, 148
    time limits for relief, 148–149
    total profits of current and past periods, relief against, 148
  unlimited company, 13
  waiver of director's remuneration, 107
Court
  application of new approach to tax avoidance schemes by, 9
Credit note
  issued to obtain relief on bad debt, 52
  need for care when issuing, 52
Death benefits
  company pension schemes, 209
  small self-administered pension schemes, 216
Debt
  joint liability of partners, 11
Deeds of covenant
  charities, in favour of, 231
  children over 18, 229–230
  index-linked, 231–232
  other relatives, 230–231

Deeds of covenant—*contd*
payments under, 231
pensioner, to, 230–231
sheltering income by, 229
student, to, 230
unmarried children under 18, 229
Development areas
first year allowance, 25
Development land tax
£50,000 exemption, 180
£75,000 exemption, 180–181
actual disposal, 178
basis of planning, 180
deemed disposal, 178
deferral, 182–183
industrial purposes, meaning, 182
intention of legislation, 178
land
   bought with planning permission, 181–182
   developed for person's own use, 182
   used for industrial purposes of trade, 182
limit on carry forward of liability, 183
occasions when proprietors of family business may encounter, 178
part deferral, 182
project of material development
   deferral of tax, 183
   exemption, 181
   meaning, 179
rate, 178
realised development value, meaning, 178
specified operations, meaning, 179–180
transfer of land with development value, 92–93, 94
Director. *See also* PROPRIETOR
20%, restrictions on company pension scheme, 210
family. *See* PROPRIETOR'S FAMILY
remuneration at tax-effective level, 99, 102–103
Discount house
interest paid to, 144
Discretionary trusts. *See* TRUSTS

Distributions. *See also* APPORTIONMENT
benefits in kind, 115
choice between apportionment or, 23
close company, 115
definition, 114–115
dividends
   family company, waiver of, 253
   group, 159
   income, as, 117–118
   remuneration compared with payment of, 118
   timing of payments, 119–120
   waiver, 118–119
general principles, 114–118
meaning, 106
tax planning, 116–117
transactions amounting to, 115–116
transfers of assets, 115–116
Dividends. *See* DISTRIBUTIONS
Dividing a business
avoiding single VAT registration by, 47–48
Double taxation
relief, trading losses, 151
tax avoidance schemes, 8
Earnings basis. *See* PROFITS
Employee
net relevant earnings, 204
pension contributions, 211
trusts. *See* TRUSTS
Employment
child, legal restrictions on, 105
Enterprise zone
acquisition of industrial buildings in, 232
Expenditure
capital. *See* CAPITAL EXPENDITURE
pre-trading. *See* PRE-TRADING EXPENDITURE
Family
proprietor's. *See* PROPRIETOR'S FAMILY
Family business. *See also* FAMILY COMPANY
company, not generally carried on by, 16

Family business—*contd*
financing
  business expansion scheme. *See* BUSINESS EXPANSION SCHEME
  loans. *See* LOANS
  purchase of own shares. *See* SHARES
  shares. *See* SHARES
form. *See* BUSINESS STRUCTURE
handing on. *See* HANDING ON BUSINESS
importance in national economy, 3
meaning, 3
partnership as recommended structure, 11
persons carrying on, 3
size, 3
Family company. *See also* FAMILY BUSINESS
business assets owned by shareholders, 248
control
  giving up, 247–248
  meaning, 246
handing on business
  business assets owned by shareholders, 248
  controlling shareholdings, relief for, 246–247
  dividends, waiver of, 253
  giving up control, 247–248
  loans on family company shares, 249
  non-controlling shareholdings, relief for, 247
  parallel trading, 253
  remuneration, waiver of, 253
  reorganisation of share capital, 251–252
  sales instead of gifts, 250
  timing of transfers, 250
  use of exemptions, 250
  wills and business relief, 248–249
relief
  controlling shareholdings, 246–247
  non-controlling shareholdings, 247

Family company—*contd*
sale of
  allocation of purchase price, 257
  business or shares as basic methods, 256
  retirement relief, 256–257
  stamp duty saving
    'pref trick', 259–261
    reconstructions, 261
  tax avoidance, 261–263
shares
  loans on, 249
  reorganisation of share capital
    deferred share scheme, 252
    freezing value of shares, 251–252
    generally, 251
  sales instead of gifts, 250–251
  transfers
    timing of, 250
    use of exemptions, 250
wills and business relief, 248–249
Farmer
retirement relief, 188
Farming
agricultural relief. *See* AGRICULTURAL RELIEF
averaging of profits, 267
business relief, 240
herd basis election, 40, 268–269
provisions to avoid double relief, 240
Fixed interest trusts. *See* TRUSTS
Forecasting
results, 23–24
Fuel
car fuel benefit, 111
living accommodation, 112
Furniture
provided for living accommodation, 112
Gifts
asset acquired before 6 April 1965 and sold at under value, 196
asset retained until death, 195–196
business, of, 196
business assets, 198–199
capital transfer tax, impact of, 195 *et seq.*

Gifts—*contd*
cash, 196
connected person, to, 197
donee becoming non-resident within six years, 198
general relief, 195–198
immediate gift of share in goodwill, 242
land, timing of, 255
mutual, 196
partnership gain deferred by using general relief for, 177
planning points, 195 *et seq.*
retirement relief, 188, 192, 196
roll-over relief, 195
second home given by taxpayer to son, 196
share in partnership assets, 240–241
specific, meaning, 249
trustees, to, 197
Going concern
new activity started with view to sale as, 16
Good faith
partnership as relationship of, 12
Goods
time of supply, 50
Goodwill
partnership
 accruer clauses, 241–242
 immediate gift of share in, 242
 payments outside accounts, 175
 purchased on reconstruction, 162
 retirement relief, 190
 roll-over relief, 167
Group relief
75% group, 157
change of accounting date to maximise, 152, 153
corresponding accounting periods, in respect of, 158
group maintained through whole of relevant accounting periods, 158
more than one company to benefit from surrender of losses, 158–159
residence of companies, 157

Group relief—*contd*
subsidiaries held by single parent company, 158
trading losses, 148, 149, 157–159
Groups of companies
chargeable gains. *See* CORPORATION TAX
corporation tax. *See* CORPORATION TAX
disadvantages, 15–16
dividends, 159
family company, 16
general principles, 157
group relief. *See* GROUP RELIEF
holding company, relationship established under, 16
interest, 159
intra-group transfers of assets, 164–165
new activity started with view to sale as going concern, 16
purchase of own shares, 137
purpose of, 15
reconstructions. *See* RECONSTRUCTIONS
restriction of certain reliefs, 15–16
single commercial entity, as, 157
surrender of ACT, 159–160
Taxes Acts, provisions in, 15
trading losses, relief for, 148, 149
VAT registration, 45
Handing on business
agricultural relief. *See* AGRICULTURAL RELIEF
family company. *See* FAMILY COMPANY
input of capital taxes, 238
partnership. *See* PARTNERSHIP
sole trader. *See* SOLE TRADER
Hire-purchase agreement
acquisition of assets, 30
first year allowance, 26
machinery and plant, 26, 27–28
Holding company
group relationship established under, 16
Hovercraft
roll-over relief, 167

Husband and wife
election for separate taxation of wife's earnings, 90
giving up control in family company, 248
net relevant earnings, 204
purchase of company's own shares, 140
retirement annuities, 200
retirement relief, 193

Income
personal activities, from, sale of, 275
sheltering
  business expansion scheme. See BUSINESS EXPANSION SCHEME
  deeds of covenant. See DEEDS OF COVENANT
  industrial buildings. See INDUSTRIAL BUILDINGS
  trusts. See TRUSTS

Income tax
accounting date
  change of, 63-64
  choice of. See choice of accounting date *post*
  partnership change involving merger, 68
accumulation and maintenance trusts, 225
charges, effect of date of payment, 145
choice of accounting date
  30 April, reasons for choice of, 57-58
  cessation of trading. See CESSATION OF TRADING
  commencement of trading. See COMMENCEMENT OF TRADING
  general tax factors, 57-58
  non-tax factors, 64
loss relief. See LOSS RELIEF
partnership changes. See PARTNERSHIP
partnership service companies. See SERVICE COMPANY
profits
  general principles, 69-70
  post-cessation receipts, 70-72

Income tax—*contd*
saving scheme, application of new approach, 9
Schedule E
  accounts basis, 108
  benefits in kind. See BENEFITS IN KIND
  waiver of director's remuneration, 107
sharing profits with proprietor's family. See PROFITS
trusts, 218

Incorporation of business. See COMPANY

Index-linking
deeds of covenant, 231-232

Industrial buildings
75% initial allowance, 232
100% initial allowances, 232, 233
bringing forward legal acquisition, 25-26
certain expenditure treated as though plant, 34
criteria when choosing unit to buy, 233-234
enterprise zone, in, 232
good quality factories as source of secure trouble-free income, 234
initial allowance, 25
items within, whether parts of building or plant, 34
leasing, 31
reduction in general rate of initial allowances, 232
sheltering income, 232-234
situations in which investment useful, 234
small workshops, 232
very small workshops, 232

Inland Revenue
level of wages paid to family employees challenged by, 15

Interest. See also LOAN
acceleration or deferment of payment, 29
bank, 30, 144
charge on profits, as, 142-144

Index 291

Interest—contd
close company, in, loan to acquire, 129–130
corporation tax, 142–144
debited to borrower's account with lender, 29
discount house, paid to, 144
groups of companies, 159
member of Stock Exchange, paid to, 144
paid at commencement of trading, 60
paid on borrowings to acquire assets, 29
paid on securities, 115
relief for interest paid, 128–131
trading expense, as, 142–144
when deductible, 142–144
when paid, 29–30
Investment
small self-administered pension schemes. See PENSIONS
Investment income
deferral of receipt of investment income, 100
franked, company losses relieved against, 148, 151–152
Invoice
time of supply fixed by issue of, 51
Land. See also DEVELOPMENT LAND TAX
agricultural relief. See AGRICULTURAL RELIEF
artificial transactions, 275–276
bought with benefit of planning permission, 181–182
contracts for sale, 255
held outside partnerships, 245
let at commercial rent, loan to purchase, 130–131
loans secured on, 255
occupied only for purposes of trade, roll-over relief, 167, 170
transfer of land with development value, 92–93
Leasing
acquisition of assets, 31–34
attractions of, 32
commencement of trading, 60

Leasing—contd
creation of subsidiary interest in property, 31
finance lease, 31–32
industrial buildings, 31
land, loan to purchase or improve, 130–131
machinery and plant, 31
motor cars, 33–34
operating lease, 31
Limited liability. See COMPANY
Liquidation
appointment of liquidator, effect of, 156
apportionment, 122–123
rate of tax, 156
service company, 76–77
surrendered ACT received from parent company, 156
Living accommodation
annual value, 112
cost includes improvement expenditure, 113
costing more than £75,000, 113
fuel, repairs, cleaning and furniture costs met by company, 112
provision by reason of employment, 111–113
value to him, meaning, 111–112
Loan
acquisition of assets, tax relief for interest paid, 29
acquisition of interest in close company, 129–130
family company shares, on, 249
financing family company by, 125 et seq.
land
let at commercial rent, loan to purchase to improve, 130–131
secured on, 255
loan back schemes, 204–205
loss relief for CGT, 126
machinery or plant, for purchase of, 130
participator, to, 123–124
relative advantages of shares and loans, 126–128

Loan—*contd*
relief for interest paid, 128–131
small self-administered pension schemes. *See* PENSIONS
written agreement, 126

Loss relief
anti-avoidance legislation, 86
augmented or created by capital allowances, 84
carry forward of losses not otherwise relieved, 84
cessation of trading, 85
commencement of trade, 85
interaction with other claims and elections, 88
loss sustained in year of assessment or preceding year, 84
order of set off, 86–87
personal allowances, 87
pre-trading expenditure, 85
retirement annuity premiums, 87–88
statutory provisions, 84–86
strategy, 86–89
time limits for claims, 84–86
timing, 88–89
trade transferred to company, 85
trading losses. *See* CORPORATION TAX

Losses
cannot be relieved against personal income, 15
capital, use of, 147
change in ownership of company, 274–275
farming, 269–270
group, intra-group transfers to utilise, 9
partnership, relieved against partners' total income, 13
relief. *See* LOSS RELIEF
trading. *See* CORPORATION TAX

Machinery and plant
acquired on deferred terms, 26
bringing forward legal acquisition, 25–26
certain expenditure on buildings treated as plant, 34

Machinery and plant—*contd*
definition of plant, 34–35
first year allowance, 25
fixed, meaning, 169–170
functional test, 35–36
hire purchase agreement, 26, 27–28
leasing, 31
loans to purchase, 130
reducing taxable profits by expenditure on, 98–100
roll-over relief, 167
partnership change involving, 68

Motor car. *See* CAR

National Insurance
company, 12, 15
liability to account for, 79
partnership, 12
proprietor, contributions of, 103–104

Objectives
non-tax, choice of business structure to achieve, 10

Owner of business. *See* PROPRIETOR

PAYE
directors's remuneration, 106–107

Partial exemption. *See* VALUE ADDED TAX

Participator
loans to, 123–124

Partnership
accruer arrangements, 255
agent, partner as, 12
agreement
  allocation of assessable profits according to, 81
  cannot override facts, 80–81
  desirability of, 12
  transfer of capital, effect of, 241
  written, 80
annuities, 243–244
business relief, 244
capital gains tax. *See* CAPITAL GAINS TAX
changes
  assessment to income tax, 65 *et seq.*

Partnership—*contd*
changes—*contd*
  continuation basis election, 65, 66–67
  engineered partnership change, 67–68
  excluded from continuation basis election, 66
  general rule, 65
  inevitable change of partners, 66–67
  merger, involving, 68
  planning opportunities, 66–68
  tax consequences, 65 *et seq.*
commencement of business as, 17
commercial risks, 80
company as partner, 244
conducting of business, 12
debt, liability of partners, 11
disclaimer of capital allowances, 36–37
evidence necessary to establish relationship, 11
flexible and tax-effective business form, as, 11
flexible way of spreading income, as, 12
formation by sole trader before handing on business, 238–239
fundamental non-tax disadvantage, 11
handing on share
  accruer clauses, 241–242
  business relief, 244
  companies or trustees as partners, 244–245
  freezing value of share, 242–243
  gifting share in partnership assets, 240–241
  immediate gift of share in goodwill, 242
  land held outside partnerships, 245
  partnership annuities, 243–244
joint liability of partners, 11–12
land held outside, 245

Partnership—*contd*
losses or low levels of profits expected in early years of trading, 17
losses relieved against partners' total income, 13
meaning, 11, 80
National Insurance contribution and benefit, 12
net relevant earnings, 204
non-tax consequences of taking member of family into, 80
not legal person for tax purposes, 13
parallel structure, 19–20
post-cessation receipts. *See* POST-CESSATION RECEIPTS
pre-trading expenditure, 41
profits
  assessed on preceding year basis, 12
  liable to progressive rates of income tax, 13
  tax charged as profits arise, 13
recommended structure for family business, as, 11
relationship of extreme good faith, as, 12
retirement provision, 13
service company. *See* SERVICE COMPANY
setting up, 240
sharing profits with family group
  agreement, 80–81
  alleged partner's participation in decision making, 81–82
  criteria to test existence of partnership, 82–83
  establishing whether partnership exists, 80–83
  generally, 80
  immaturity of alleged partner, 82
tax advantages and disadvantages compared with company, 12–13, 16–20
tort, liability of partners, 11–12
trading from premises not owned by partners, 60

294 Index

Partnership—*contd*
transfer of interests, 13
trustee as partner, 245
uberrima fide, 12
unanimous decision required for major decisions, 12
VAT registration, 46
deed of covenant to, 230–231
Pensions
company, tax advantages, 14
company schemes
  20% directors, 210
  administrator, 208
  advantages, 206, 207–208
  approval
    applications for, 208
    bare, 208
    exempt, 208
    Inland Revenue, 208
  benefits
    commutation of part of pension, 209
    death in service, on, 209
    employee dies after retirement, 209
    final remuneration, 210
    maximum, 209–210
  contributions
    amount of, 211
    annual, 211
    employees, by, 211
    refund of, 211–212
    special, 211
  escalation of pensions, 210
  executive pension plans, 206
  group schemes, 206
  hybrid schemes, 206
  Inland Revenue practice, 206
  insured schemes, 206
  legislation, 206
  length of service, 210
  mixed schemes, 206
  one-man scheme, 206
  provision of, 205–206
  retirement ages, 209
  self-administered schemes, 206
  tax benefits, 206–207

Pensions—*contd*
company schemes—*contd*
  top-hat schemes, 206
  trustees, 208
  types of, 206
  who can qualify, 208
contribution to company scheme to reduce taxable profits, 99–100
partnership, 13
small self-administered schemes
  actuarial reports, 217
  advantages, 212–213
  captive schemes, 212
  characteristics, 212
  death benefits, 216
  full commutation of pension, 216–217
  funding, 217
  in-house schemes, 212
  Inland Revenue treatment, 213
  investment of funds
    freedom of investment, 214
    loans to company, 214
    loans to members, 214
    property, in, 215
  non-income producing assets, 215–216
  payment of special contributions, 217
  pensioneer trustee, 213–214
  purchase of annuities, 216
  purchase of assets from company, 214–215
  purchase of shares in company, 215
  small, meaning, 213
  trading, 216
Personal allowances
loss relief, 87
Planning
long-term, choice of business structure to facilitate, 10
permission, land bought with, 181–182
Plant. *See* MACHINERY AND PLANT
Post-cessation receipts
deemed discontinuance, 71, 72

Post-cessation receipt—*contd*
liabilities imposed by legislation, 70–72
trading stock, 71
work-in-progress, 71, 72
Pre-trading expenditure
capital expenditure, 42
company, 41, 43
loss relief, 85
partnership, 41
relieved against profits earned after commencement of trading, 59
revenue expenses, 41–42
sole trader, 41
unincorporated trader, 43
value added tax, 42–43
Premiums
retirement annuities. *See* RETIREMENT
Professional fees
awareness of, 23
barristers, 70
Profits
apportionment. *See* APPORTIONMENT
company, meaning, 146
conventional basis
  advantages arising from adoption of, 69
  change to, 70
  examples, 69
  judicial approval, 69
  meaning, 69
distributions. *See* DISTRIBUTIONS
earnings basis
  alternatives to, 69
  meaning, 69
farming, averaging of, 267
meaning, 69
partnership. *See* PARTNERSHIP
post-cessation receipts, 70–72
service company, 74–75
sharing with proprietor's family
  example, 78–79
  partnership. *See* PARTNERSHIP
  payment of wages, 79, 82
  reasons for, 78

Profits—*contd*
sharing—*contd*
  savings achieved, 78
small companies rate relief. *See* SMALL COMPANIES RATE RELIEF
taxable, reduction of, 98–100
Property
investment by small self-administered pension scheme, 215
Proprietor. *See also* DIRECTOR
basic strategy for proprietary company, 96
family. *See* PROPRIETOR'S FAMILY
gifts. *See* GIFTS
providing for retirement. *See* RETIREMENT
remuneration
  accounts basis, 108
  benefits in kind. *See* BENEFITS IN KIND
  commercial constraints, 106–107
  disallowance, 106
  general principles, 102–104
  National Insurance contributions, 103–104
  PAYE, 106–107
  tax-effective level of, 102–103
  waiver of, 107
retirement. *See* RETIREMENT
selling family company. *See* FAMILY COMPANY
sharing profits with family. *See* PROFITS
sheltering income. *See* INCOME
use of trusts. *See* TRUSTS
Proprietor's family
payments to, 257–259
remuneration
  benefits in kind. *See* BENEFITS IN KIND
  challenging excessive levels, 104–106
  legal restrictions on employment of children, 105
  obtaining tax deduction for, 104–105

296 Index

Proprietor's family—*contd*
remuneration—*contd*
  paid in proportion to members' shareholdings, 106
  single person's allowance, up to, 105
  substantial, justification of payment of, 105
Receivership
appointment of receiver, 155
benefits of continuing to trade, 155
company reconstructions, 155–156
corporate tax planning devices, 155
Reconstructions
capital allowances inherited by new company, 161
goodwill, purchase of, 162
groups of companies, 160–162
provisions, 160
receivership, on, 155–156
reorganising affairs of group by, 161
transferring trade distinguished from transferring assets, 161–162
Registration for VAT. *See* VALUE ADDED TAX
Relief
agricultural. *See* AGRICULTURAL RELIEF
family company. *See* FAMILY COMPANY
interest paid, for, 128–131
retirement. *See* RETIREMENT
retirement annuities. *See* RETIREMENT
roll-over. *See* ROLL-OVER RELIEF
small companies rate. *See* SMALL COMPANIES RATE RELIEF
trading losses. *See* CORPORATION TAX
Remuneration
directors', tax-effective level to reduce taxable profits, 99, 102–103
family company, waiver of, 253
minor, of, 82
paid to family employees challenged by Inland Revenue, 15

Remuneration—*contd*
payment of dividends compared with, 118
payment of wages as way of transferring profits, 79, 82
personal activities, from, sale of, 275
proprietor. *See* PROPRIETOR
proprietor's family. *See* PROPRIETOR'S FAMILY
tax-effective levels of, liability for National Insurance contributions, 79
Repairs
living accommodation, 112
Repayment supplement
company losses, 149–150
Results
need to forecast, 23–24
Retail schemes. *See* VALUE ADDED TAX
Retirement. *See also* PENSION
Retirement
annuities
  loan back schemes, 204–205
  premiums
    carry back of, 201–202
    excess, 205
    payment into policy, 200
  relief
    amount of, 201
    late assessments, 203–204
    nature of, 201
    relevant earnings, 204, 205
    strategy, 87–88
    unused, carry forward of, 202–203
  summary of planning points, 205
  types of contract, 200
relief
  asset owned by partner personally, 192
  asset owned by shareholder personally, 192–193
  chargeable business assets, 190–191
  extra-statutory concessions, 188 *et seq.*

Retirement—*contd*
relief—*contd*
family company
requirements, 188
sale of, 256–257
farmer, 188
gifts, 188, 192, 196
husband and wife, 193
incorporation, effect of, 189
Inland Revenue consultative document, 194
interaction with roll-over relief, 192
maximum, 187
minimum age, 187
not confined only to retirement, 192
opportunity to obtain forgone to achieve greater benefit, 187
ownership conditions, 187
preservation of, 189–190
qualifying period, 187
sales, 188
take-over, 190
voting rights exercisable by taxpayer, 188–189
Roll-over relief
acquisition within specified period, 169
apportionment, 168
asset owned by individual and used by family company, 169
deemed consideration, 171
deemed disposals, 171
depreciating asset, 168, 170–171
effect of claiming, 168
general principles, 167–169
gifts, 195
groups of companies, 165–166
interaction with retirement relief, 192
qualifying assets
aircraft, 167
fixed plant or machinery, 167, 169–170
goodwill, 167
hovercraft, 167

Roll-over relief—*contd*
qualifying assets—*contd*
land or building occupied only for purposes of trade, 167, 170
ships, 167
strategy, 169–171
taxpayer carrying on two trades, 168
School fees
payment out of capital, 227
Second-hand schemes
value added tax, 55–56
Securities
interest paid on, 115
transactions in, 273
Self-administered pension schemes. *See* PENSIONS.
Self-employed person
net relevant earnings, 204
Selling the family company. *See* FAMILY COMPANY
Service company
accumulation of working capital by, 73
advantages, 73
apportionment of income, 76
cessation, 76–77
liquidation, 76–77
partnership activities not strictly of professional nature, 73
profit uplift
excessive, 75
limit on amount of, 75
method of achieving, 74
reasonable, establishment of principle of, 75
setting up, 73–74
shares, holding of, 75–76
uses, 73
Services
time of supply, 50
Settlements. *See* TRUSTS
Shareholders
limited company, 13
minority, rights of, 14
owning asset personally, retirement relief, 192–193
Shares. *See also* DISTRIBUTIONS
controlling shareholder, 128

Shares—*contd*
disposal, capital loss arising on, 125–126
family company. *See* FAMILY COMPANY
financing family company by, 125 *et seq.*
issue
  capital value on nominal value, 125
  legal costs involved in, 125
partnership. *See* PARTNERSHIP
permanent capital of company, as, 125
purchase by company of own
  advantages, 133
  articles of association, 139
  associates, 136–137
  avoidance of undue hardship, 138
  business property relief, 139
  clearance procedure, 138–139
  conditions, 133 *et seq.*
  connected with company, meaning, 138
  economic advantages, 133
  groups of companies, 137
  holding company of trading group, 135, 138
  husband and wife, 140
  increase in percentage shareholdings, 139–140
  intention of change, 133
  market value of shares, 140–141
  no continuing connections, 137–138
  not part of scheme or arrangement, 140
  payment applied to discharge CTT liability, 138
  period of ownership, 136
  purchase not part of scheme or arrangement, 135
  purpose of benefiting trade, 135
  residence of vendor, 136
  retention of family control, 133
  section 53(1) purchases, 134–138
  section 53(2) purchases, 138
  small shareholdings, 133

Shares—*contd*
purchase by company of own—*contd*
  substantial reduction of shares, 136
  tax consequences, 133–134
  trading company, 134–135, 138
  unquoted company, 134, 138
  valuation of minority holding, 139
purchase by small self-administered pension
relative advantages of shares and loans, 126–128
retirement relief. *See* RETIREMENT
roll-over relief exemption, 166
service company, 75–76
time to make family dispositions, 128
transfer in small parcels, 14
use of different classes of, 128
who should hold, 128
Sheltering income. *See* INCOME
Ships
roll-over relief, 167
Small companies rate relief
associated companies, 100–101
background, 97–98
chargeable gain, deferring or accelerating realisation of, 100
reducing taxable profits
  acceleration of payment of charges, 99
  capital expenditure, 98–100
  contribution to company pension scheme, 99–100
  deferral of receipt of investment income, 100
  foreseeable losses or write-offs fully reserved, 100
  tax-effective level of directors' remuneration, 99, 102–103
Sole trader
disclaimer of capital allowances, 36–37
handing on business
  business relief, 239–240
  formation of partnership as best method, 238–239

Sole trader—*contd*
handling on business—*contd*
  transfer to company, 239
pre-trading expenditure, 41
tax factors, 11
Special development areas
first year allowance, 25
Stamp duty
amalgamations, 261
application of new approach to tax avoidance schemes, 9
reconstructions, 261
sale of family company. *See* FAMILY COMPANY
transfer of business to company, 95
Stock Exchange
interest paid to member of, 144
Stock relief
abolition, 39
calculation, 39–40
carry-forward of unused relief, 150
commenced of trade before 13 March 1984, 39–40
herd basis election by farmers, extension of time limit, 40
period straddling 12 March 1984, 39
tax planning, 39–40
trading losses, effect of, 150
unused, 40
Student
deed of covenant to, 230
Take-over
retirement relief, effect on, 190
Tax avoidance. *See also* TAX PLANNING
capital sums paid to settlor, 271–273
importance of planning, 9
loss relief, 86
sale of family company, 261–263
schemes
  ability of Inland Revenue to disregard statutory provision, 7
  agreement having particular legal nature not to be ignored, 7
  application of new approach by courts, 9
  capital gains tax, 6

Tax avoidance—*contd*
schemes—*contd*
  change in judicial attitude, 4–5
  consequences determined by substance of transaction, 7
  end result proposed must not give rise to double tax liability, 8
  future tax treatment of new assets, rights or liabilities, 8
  inter-connected transactions between artificial persons, 7
  intra-group transfers to utilise group losses, 9
  new approach, 4–9
  postponement of payment of tax, 5
  pre-planned series of transactions, 5–9
  self-cancelling, 5
  tax consequence inherent in scheme itself, 8
  transaction giving rise to tax liability in own right, 8
Tax liability
choice of business structure to minimise, 10
Tax planning. *See also* TAX AVOIDANCE
acceptability of, 4
agricultural relief. *See* AGRICULTURAL RELIEF
basic strategy for proprietary company, 96
benefits in kind. *See* BENEFITS IN KIND
capital expenditure. *See* CAPITAL EXPENDITURE
choice of business structure, 10
distributions. *See* DISTRIBUTIONS
flexibility, 4
gifts, 195 *et seq.*
group chargeable gains, 164–165
implications of *Ramsay* etc., 4–9
liquidation. *See* LIQUIDATION
loss relief, 86–89
meaning, 4
need to forecast results, 23–24

300 Index

Tax planning—*contd*
partnership changes. *See* PARTNERSHIP
pre-trading expenditure. *See* PRE-TRADING EXPENDITURE
protection of innocent taxpayer, 4
purchase by company of own shares, 139–141
receivership. *See* RECEIVERSHIP
retirement annuities. *See* RETIREMENT
roll-over relief, 165–166
stock relief, 39–40
trading losses. *See* CORPORATION TAX
trusts. *See* TRUSTS
unincorporated business. *See* UNINCORPORATED BUSINESS
value added tax. *See* VALUE ADDED TAX
Terminal payments. *See* COMPENSATION PAYMENTS
Time of supply. *See* VALUE ADDED TAX
Tort
joint liability of partners, 11–12
Trading
cessation. *See* CESSATION OF TRADING
commencement. *See* COMMENCEMENT OF TRADING
trustees of pension fund, by, 216
Trading stock
post-cessation receipts, 71
value at time of discontinuance, 93
Trading trusts. *See* TRUSTS
Transfer of assets. *See* ASSETS
Transfer of business
retaining seller's VAT number, 49
VAT liability, 48–49
Trustee
company pension schemes, 208
gifts to, general relief, 197
partner, as, 245
small self-administered pension scheme, 213–214

Trusts
accumulation and maintenance
capital transfer tax, 224–225
conditions, 223–224
income tax, 225
meaning, 223
tax advantages, 224–225
capital sums paid to settlor, 271–273
discretionary
accumulation of income, 223
advantages, 221
beneficiary, 220
capital transfer tax
charge, 222–223
distribution of income, 221
modification of old rules, 220
original provisions, 220
reduction of estate for purposes of, 221
settlor as beneficiary, 221
distribution of income, 223
meaning, 220
roll over of gains, 222
employees'
capital gains tax, 226
capital transfer tax, 226
uses, 225–226
ensuring income not alienated, 218–219
fixed interest
beneficiary entitled to income for life, 219
capital transfer tax liability, 219, 220
meaning, 219
surviving spouse will trusts, 220
uses, 219–220
income
accumulation trusts, 226 *et seq.*
capital payments treated as, 227–228
capitalising by accumulation, 226
contingently accumulated, claim for repayment of tax, 228
distributing, 228
school fees, payment of, 227
methods of helping tax and financial planning, 218

Trusts—*contd*
partnership arrangement treated as settlement, 83
trading
  advantages and disadvantages, 225
  meaning, 225
  use of, 218 *et seq.*
Unincorporated business. *See also* PARTNERSHIP
business tax regime, efect of changes in, 10–11
choice between company and, 10–11
incorporation. *See* COMPANY
sole trader, 11
Unincorporated trader
pre-trading expenditure, 43
value added tax, 43
Value added tax
acquisition of company, 49
application of new approach to tax avoidance schemes, 9
companies, 43
credit notes, 51–52
deregistration, 46–47
dividing a business
  criteria to be met, 47–48
  practical limitations, 48
  purposes, 47
exempt supplies, 53
number, taking over another's, 49
partial exemption
  apportionment, 53–54
  de minimis rules
    generally, 52
    inputs rules, 53
    outputs rules, 52–53
  exempt supplies, 53
  planning, 54
  rules, 52
  partial exemption, 54
  retail schemes, 55
  time of supply, 51

Value added tax—*contd*
pre-trading expenditure, 42–43
registration
  dividing a business, effect of, 47
  divisional, 45–46
  group
    advantages, 45
    disadvantages, 45
    one company partially exempt, 45
  importance of, 44
  partnerships, 46
  quarterly turnover, 44
  requirements, 44
  taxable supplies intended to exceed limits, 44–45
  trader making only zero-rated supplies, 45
  trader making taxable supplies below limits, 45
  voluntary, 45
retail schemes
  choice of, 54–55
  planning, 55
  secondhand schemes, 55–56
  selling on commission, 56
  taking over another's VAT number, 49
time of supply
  basic rules, 50
  goods, of, 50
  issue of invoice, 51
  planning, 51
  services, of, 50
transferring a business, 48–49
unincorporated traders, 43
Wages. *See* REMUNERATION
Wills
business relief and, 248–249
Woodlands
provisions to avoid double relief, 240
Work-in-progress
post-cessation receipts, 71, 72